ON THE ROAD TO HIGH-QUALITY EARLY LEARNING

ON THE ROAD TO HIGH-QUALITY EARLY LEARNING

Changing Children's Lives

MARJORIE E. WECHSLER, DAVID L. KIRP,

TITILAYO TINUBU ALI, MADELYN GARDNER,

ANNA MAIER, HANNA MELNICK, PATRICK M. SHIELDS

TEACHERS COLLEGE PRESS

TEACHERS COLLEGE | COLUMBIA UNIVERSITY

NEW YORK AND LONDON

Published by Teachers College Press, 1234 Amsterdam Avenue, New York, NY 10027

Copyright © 2018 by Teachers College, Columbia University

Cover design by adam b. bohannon. Cover composite: car photo by maglara, Adobe Stock Images; star by Carlos Caetano, Shutterstock.

Library of Congress Cataloging-in-Publication Data is available at loc.gov

ISBN 978-0-8077-5938-7 (paper)
ISBN 978-0-8077-7718-3 (ebook)

Printed on acid-free paper
Manufactured in the United States of America

25   24   23   22   21   20   19   18   7   6   5   4   3   2   1

Contents

Preface

Since you've started reading this book, you already know that good pre-school can work wonders—that, as countless studies show, it has the potential to change the arc of children's lives. It can prepare children for kindergarten, reduce the chances they will be placed in special education or retained in a grade, increase the likelihood they will graduate from high school, and boost their incomes. "Potential" is the key—only if early education is of high quality can these long-term benefits be realized. The research has generated a consensus, among professionals in the field, about the meaning of quality. What's needed are small classes with well-trained teachers, as well as an engaging curriculum that reaches well beyond the Three Rs to encompass the physical, social, and emotional dimensions of a child's life. In a good preschool, parents play a pivotal role, since they are children's first and most important educators. Ideally, the system of early education should reach from birth through third grade, with age-appropriate strategies at each stage of children's development.

In short, a good preschool is a place to which you'd happily send a child you love.

Yet even as states are enrolling more and more children in publicly funded preschools, those working in the field report a pronounced lack of understanding of how to get from here to there—how to convert our well-defined understanding of what effective early education requires into a system that delivers, on a statewide scale, what children need in order to thrive.

This book is designed to fill that gap. It does so by closely examining how four states—North Carolina, Michigan, Washington, and West Virginia—have succeeded in creating this kind of system. Teams of researchers from the Learning Policy Institute waded through piles of reports and evaluations, met with experts, and fanned out across the country, spending time in statehouses, state agencies, school districts, and schoolhouses. They interviewed state senators, state administrators, state and county super-intendents, the heads of nonprofits and advocacy groups, and reporters. And they interviewed those most engaged with the children—preschool directors, teachers, and parents. These case studies are the result of that research. The four states are not the only ones that are doing a good job— Oklahoma and Georgia have come in for deserved praise, for instance— but the four reflect the variety of strategies that states have adopted.

This kind of system-building is a hard, complicated business. It requires, at the outset, the mobilization of advocates, inside and outside government, to get early education on the political agenda, and a champion to lead the charge. The coalition's work isn't done once the initial legislation is on the books. Often, a program starts small, and, because the coalition keeps pushing, it expands to reach more and more students. A funding stream must be established and maintained. An evaluation can give the coalition ammunition with which to persuade the skeptics that the program is working, and can also show where improvements are needed.

Good state administration is equally important, and so agencies must be formed, inside or outside of existing bureaucracies, to distribute funds, provide technical support, and turn legislative language into standards that can be used at the local level. That agency must collaborate with other child-serving bureaus, on the one hand, and with the K–12 system, on the other.

These state agencies face in two directions—to the politicians, for broad guidance, and to the local authorities, for supervision and support. Those school district and county authorities are responsible for putting the statewide standards into practice, adapting them to meet local needs, and—vitally—assuring that the high-quality education that state officials envision is actually being delivered in every classroom.

Across the country, politicians, advocates, and administrators have been looking for guidance as they build, and expand, state early education systems. Principals, supervisors, and teachers also need to understand where the levers of power are located. Because they are the people who are doing the work, they know, at first hand, where the needs are greatest, and they make the best advocates for quality. This book offers something of value to all of them.

CHAPTER 1

Introduction

Turning Smart Ideas Into On-the-Ground Reality

A bookshelf's-worth of well-conducted studies conclusively establishes that high-quality early childhood education can change the arc of children's lives.[1] But what does it take to convert good ideas into sound practice? That is the issue we address.

We know a lot about early education. Research on preschool programs demonstrating positive results, as well as the professional standards for early education, have identified important elements of quality.[2] There is a plethora of in-depth descriptions of programs, from the iconic Perry Preschool and Abecedarian Project, to privately developed models such as the Chicago Child-Parent Centers and EduCare, to publicly funded programs such as New Jersey's Abbott Preschool Program and Boston's preschool program. And after years of program evaluations and academic research, there is a substantial body of literature showing the many short- and long-term benefits of preschool.[3]

Yet, despite all we do know, there is a paucity of material that those interested in implementing a quality program—to convert their vision of good early education into on-the-ground reality—can turn to. How do policymakers and advocates build and sustain the political will required to ensure that adequate public dollars will be invested in early education? What is the most efficient way to pay for these programs? What is the best approach to coordinating programs for young children? How do local administrators establish policies and practices that support early childhood teachers? How do teachers create engaging environments that foster healthy child development and learning? What can be done—at all of these levels, by all of these people—to ensure that programs are good enough to make a difference in children's lives?

We answer those questions. Existing research examines only one element of the system at a time—for example, how to create rich, hands-on experiences for young children, how quality rating and improvement systems work, what is the trajectory of child development, and the like. We take a different approach. We examine four early childhood systems from the statehouse to the classroom, probing the synergies, and the tensions, among the systems' elements. By exploring each program's history, its design and implementation, its successes and challenges, and its evolution over time, we show how to turn the idea of high-quality preschool into learning environments that make a difference for kids.

Our conclusions are based on a close-grained examination of four states—Michigan, North Carolina, Washington, and West Virginia—each of which has put in place a good early education system for a growing number of children.[4] The detailed descriptions and analyses of these initiatives will be useful to a variety of audiences:

- *Governors and legislators* can draw lessons from the discussion of how sound policy ideas are turned into legislation.
- *State early education administrators* can gain a deeper understanding of how to effectively manage early education programs and create linkages among the broad array of state agencies supporting children and families.
- *County administrators and school district superintendents* can learn how to prioritize early childhood education and see that it runs efficiently.
- *Principals and early education program directors* can see how well-crafted local policy and skilled management sustains good classroom practice.
- *Teachers* can understand why they are asked to follow certain practices and how they play a central role in changing children's lives.
- *Parents* can get a clear picture of what high-quality preschool looks like and why it's important.
- *Researchers* can broaden their perspectives to ensure their theoretical models include all the elements that matter.
- *Professors* can assign the book to college and postgraduate students who are studying child development and early learning, helping them connect the skills they are acquiring with the broader policy landscape.

We offer everyone with a stake in advancing early education an opportunity to learn from existing programs that demonstrate successful outcomes. The goal is not to provide a roadmap or single model to follow, for there is no one best strategy, but rather to present a range of successful examples. (The research methodology used in this book can be found in the online Appendix, available at tcpress.com.).

EARLY CHILDHOOD EDUCATION MATTERS

The preschool movement has been fueled by a remarkable confluence of research findings from across the scientific universe. The data point in the same direction: Good early education matters.[5] Studies of the well-known Perry Preschool and Abecedarian Project showed that access to a top-notch experience at a young age can have positive effects on children's life chances, with those effects evident decades later.[6] The ongoing studies of the preschool programs in New Jersey, Michigan, and Tulsa, Oklahoma, are identifying substantial and continuing effects. The evaluation of Michigan's state-funded preschool program indicates that it is reasonable to anticipate that this positive impact will persist through high school and beyond.[7]

Economists have translated those findings into the language of benefits and costs, and their work has confirmed that early education is a wise investment. Neuroscientists have established that the brain develops rapidly during the first years of life. Geneticists, who once believed that heredity is destiny, have shown that nurture as well as nature shape intelligence. These findings give the argument for early education the imprimatur of science. This impressive body of research has taken the argument for early education out of the realm of moral appeal and into the domain of evidence-based policymaking.[8]

THE POLICY IMPERATIVE

Early education has become a policy imperative nationwide. Polls have consistently shown that substantial majorities of both Republicans and Democrats back public funding for preschool and making early childhood education more affordable for working families.[9]

Lawmakers have responded. Forty-five states and the District of Columbia now support state-funded preschool. In the 2015–2016 budget year, 32 states and the District of Columbia raised their programs' funding. There was bipartisan support—the 32 states included 22 states with Republican governors and ten with Democratic governors, plus the District of Columbia. Total state preschool funding increased by $767 million, to a total of nearly $7 billion, a 12 percent increase over the previous year.[10]

During that legislative term, 39 states adopted legislation that expanded access, provided additional funding for teachers, or streamlined administration.

And even though the most dramatic changes have occurred at the state level, the federal government has also upped its investment. In 2016, Congress approved a $294 million increase in the Head Start and Early Head Start budgets designed to increase the number of hours and days of high-quality services. An additional $226 million was spent in 2014 to underwrite the Preschool Development Grant Program, which enables states to devise new or enhance current offerings. Funding for the Child Care and Development Fund, which underwrites state-administered child care, was $5.3 billion that year. That measure supports quality-improvement efforts and mandates that parents know what child-care choices are available to them.[11]

Dick Clifford, a senior scientist at the Frank Porter Graham Child Development Institute at the University of North Carolina at Chapel Hill, sees a profound historic shift. "The impact of what's happening to young children is like the effect of the Industrial Revolution on older children. Then, public schools became the norm. Now it is preschool."[12] The movement is one of the rare contemporary examples of an expanding public square. It aims to revive the ideal of the common good by persuading lawmakers and citizens to support a venture that benefits everyone.

However, rock-solid evidence, broad public support, and additional resources do not necessarily translate into policies that promote top-caliber early education. Sometimes the problem has to do with the law itself; at other times problematic management is the roadblock. That's what makes the four states whose initiatives we analyzed worth paying attention to— although they have taken different approaches and are confronting distinct challenges, each is on the road to high-quality early education.

QUALITY COUNTS

If the potential of early education is to be realized, the program has to be of high quality. The meaning of "quality" in early childhood education is well established:[13]

- Rely on pedagogy and curricula that address the social–emotional and physical, as well as the cognitive, dimensions of children's experiences.

- Prepare teachers to use engaging materials; to talk with, not at, children; and to design classrooms that pique children's natural curiosity to make sense of the world around them.
- Provide teachers with on-point mentoring and coaching for their entire careers in the field.
- Attend to children with diverse needs, including English language learners and youngsters with special needs.
- Engage families, children's primary educators, as partners in the education of their offspring.
- Provide sufficient classroom time for real learning to occur.
- Keep class sizes small and student–teacher ratios low.
- Use evaluation instruments that relate to the whole child; that measure structural factors, like the resources in the classroom; and that assess how teachers interact with their students.
- Design a mechanism to incentivize continuous improvement in preschools and hold accountable those who fall short of the quality benchmarks set out in quality rating systems.

But there are substantial variations with respect to these criteria, as they have been translated into practice, and consequently, the quality of early education varies greatly from state to state, as well as school district to school district, and even school to school. State report cards, issued annually by the National Institute for Early Education Research (NIEER), show that, while there has been considerable improvement in quality in recent years, many states do not meet NIEER's widely accepted benchmarks of quality: "Progress has been unequal and uneven," NIEER reports, "with some states taking large steps forward and other states moving backward."[14] The same variation holds true of appraisals of teacher-student interaction, based on the Classroom Assessment Scoring System (CLASS). Robert Pianta, Dean of the University of Virginia Curry School of Education and developer of CLASS, concludes that "superficial task demands, including giving directions and assigning routine tasks, predominate over children's involvement in appropriate conceptual or class-based activities."[15] A 2016 NIEER study finds, similarly, that the caliber of Head Start programs varies widely from state to state.[16]

What does it take to move high-quality early education up the list of policy priorities? The four case studies offer granular evidence about the approaches that have been adopted by early education champions, inside and outside government, at the state level and locally; that's what makes them useful for policymakers and practitioners elsewhere.

GETTING PROGRAMS OFF THE GROUND

Political scientist John Kingdon proposes a widely used model to describe political opportunity.[17] Whatever the policy problem—whether it is, say, regulating air quality or managing health care—getting an idea on the political agenda or making it a priority requires, first, persuading policymakers and the public that the problem is serious and pressing; second, demonstrating that the proposed solution is technically feasible, fiscally manageable, appealing to the public, and compatible with the lawmakers' values; and, third, promoting the widespread belief that this is an idea whose time has come. When these converge, a "window of opportunity"— a moment when success is within reach—opens. For preschool, that time is now.

In years past, preschool supporters relied mainly on moral arguments—"it's the right thing to do"—regarding what children deserve. Although that proposition is undeniably right, it was rarely persuasive in the political arena. The multiple strands of research now enable the advocates to reach beyond the congregation of the like-minded, seeking support from unlikely allies. Leaders from the corporate, foundation, and nonprofit worlds have been effective advocates. Local researchers have also played a major role, their studies cited as showing the effectiveness of the state's program. The Council for a Strong America epitomizes this "grass-tops" approach. It has drawn together leaders from business, the military, clergy, and sports as advocates for high-quality early education. The Council has members across the country and offices in 11 states, including two of the case study states, Michigan and Washington.

All politics is local, as the saying goes—no approach will work in all circumstances. Political strategies have been shaped by the local political and policy environment. While the goal—good early education—remains the same, the ways of reaching it vary widely among these states:

- Michigan has developed, and continues to expand, a high-quality preschool model for 4-year-olds from low-income families. Research showing the long-term benefits of the program has persuaded lawmakers to keep increasing its budget.
- Washington, which targets the very poorest youngsters, has adopted the Head Start model, enlisting doctors, nurses, and social workers to offer health care and social supports. Lawmakers, influenced by research showing the program's impact, have mandated that by 2018 the preschool program will have slots for

all eligible youngsters. The state also aims to bolster the quality of home-based child care through intensive coaching and rigorous quality standards.

- West Virginia has made preschool available to all 4-year-olds and has recently shifted to a 5-day, full-day model. The administration of its program is highly collaborative, with interagency teams at both the state and local levels.
- North Carolina initially focused on infants and toddlers, and later added prekindergarten. It is the only state that offers an array of birth-to-five services for poor children. It was the nation's first to devise a quality rating system, and it raises the salaries of teachers who hone their skills through additional training.

MAKING SURE THE PROGRAM IS EFFECTIVE

Getting a law on the books is hard enough, but making sure it is well implemented is even harder. The policy landscape is littered with well-intentioned programs that, for one reason or another, were failures in the field. Against these odds, the four states' efforts to build good early education systems are succeeding. Of course, there have been bumps in the road. To be useful to policymakers in states that are launching, revamping, or expanding early childhood education, and to the local administrators who are implementing the programs and working with children on a daily basis, it is just as important to understand the challenges these four states have encountered as to appreciate the successes.

None of the four states had all the answers out of the chute—no matter what the policy problem, that is never the case. There may be technical glitches in the law, or blurriness in the dividing line between social services and education agencies or between state and local agencies. Building an infrastructure is an iterative process. Achievements generate new puzzles. For instance, crafting a good quality rating system invites questions about how to make effective use of the system and spur improvement—how are capable, experienced trainers to be recruited? What mix of policy carrots, such as money to subsidize improvement, or sticks, such as decertifying unsatisfactory programs, will work best, and in what circumstances?

The key is adaptation, the willingness to learn from mistakes.[18] That is the ongoing story in each of these states. The case studies paint a picture of entrepreneurial administrators at both the state and local levels, responding to shifting circumstances, getting better over time. Their portfolio includes figuring out how to recruit good personnel and support quality instruction, how to keep the focus on results rather than simply following procedures, how to build trust and communications channels within and across agencies, and how to create a culture of continuous improvement. Administrators deliver feedback to state policymakers and advocates, and that feedback may prompt adjustments in the design of the program. Success, which is often equated with long-term gains in reading and math, may persuade lawmakers to provide additional funding for more slots and better programs. Preschools have gotten better in recent years, and much of the credit belongs to administrators who, laboring outside the limelight, can produce small miracles.[19]

The case studies specify key factors in building a strong early education system. One is coordinating the administration of various children's services. The case study states took different approaches—for example, establishing a separate child services department or creating an early education division within the education department. Each approach has its advantages and drawbacks. The pre-K–grade 3 linkage is more easily created if preschool and K–12 are housed under the same bureaucratic roof, but children's other needs are outside the agency's responsibility. A child services department, which includes preschool and a range of social and health supports, can span the array of children's needs but cannot directly shape pre-K–grade 3 policy.

Whichever model a state adopts, collaboration across bureaucratic lines is essential. Turf issues are likely to arise, and these should be addressed directly, so that the parties can establish a relationship based on mutual trust and respect. The joint work includes sharing data, aligning curricula and assessments, and integrating programs, most commonly state preschool and Head Start.

"Quality" must be defined if it is to be more than a slogan, and crafting a quality rating system is an important first step in articulating the elements of quality. Many states, including the four case study states, have devised specific standards guiding their early education programs. States that have yet to adopt quality standards can look to what has already been done. If the standards are to have bite, they must be backed by a structure of support: mentors and coaches who can show child-care and early education centers how to improve their practice. Necessary as well is financial support, including funding for teachers who return to school or for programs that move up the quality ladder, and a system of accountability for centers that don't meet the mark.

State dollars are the main revenue source for early education, and so having a dedicated source of state funding provides some assurance of stability. Combining, or braiding, multiple sources of revenue—Head Start, Early Head Start, the Temporary Assistance for Needy Families program (TANF)—can make more slots available and improve the quality of what's being delivered. When state administrators devise ways to simplify the overlapping paperwork requirements, teachers and local managers can spend more time on teaching, not filling out forms.

The decisions of local administrators give specificity to the state standards and shape the program's implementation in meaningful ways, making them another key piece of the puzzle. They develop strategies to recruit and retain teachers and administrators, which is particularly important in areas where early educators are paid substantially less than K–12 teachers, and migration from one system to the other is predictable. They strive to retain teachers with special skills, such as bilingual teachers, who are valuable in places where there are a substantial number of English language learners, but are often in short supply. In urban areas where space is at a premium, they must vet child-care centers and home care providers.

Administrators at both the state and local levels need to enlist parents, not only as partners in their children's education but also as collaborators in designing the program. Typically, policy is made top down, from legislature to administrators to teachers. That's the case in early childhood education, and it's a smart first step. But in turning policy into practice, a bottom-up approach is needed, one that starts with the classroom experience—the education of the child, as seen through the eyes of parents as well as teachers—and builds from there.[20]

We detail the path that each of the four states has adopted. Each is a work in progress, not a mission accomplished—there is no "mission accomplished" in the realm of continuous improvement. Policymakers and administrators can learn a lot from understanding what these states have achieved, and the challenges that lie ahead.

NOTES

1. Phillips, D. A., et al. (2017). *Puzzling it out: The current state of scientific knowledge on pre-kindergarten effects, A consensus statement.* Washington, DC: Brookings Institution. Retrieved from www.brookings.edu/research/puzzling-it-out-the-current-state-of-scientific-knowledge-on-pre-kindergarten-effects/;

Duncan, G. J., & Magnuson, K. (2013). Investing in preschool programs, *Journal of Economic Perspectives*, *27*(2), 109–132; Yoshikawa, H., Weiland, C., & Brooks-Gunn, J. (2016). When does preschool matter? *The Future of Children*, *26*(2), 21–35.

2. Wechsler, M., Melnick, H., Maier, A., & Bishop, J. (2016). *The building blocks of high quality early childhood education program*. Retrieved from learningpolicyinstitute.org/sites/default/files/product-files/LPI_ECE-quality-brief_WEB-022916.pdf

3. Phillips, D. A., et al. (2017); Duncan, G. J., & Magnuson, K. (2013); Yoshikawa, H., Weiland, C., & Brooks-Gunn, J. (2016).

4. To be sure, these are not the only states that have exemplary programs. These four states were selected for study because each meets at least eight of the 10 quality benchmarks of the National Institute for Early Education Research; each has been the subject of research that found positive outcomes for children; each has been able to expand its early learning programs without sacrificing quality; and, as a set, they vary in geography, demographics, and political context.

5. This section draws on Kirp, D. K. (2007), *The sandbox investment: The preschool movement and kids-first politics,* Cambridge, MA: Harvard University Press.

6. Schweinhart, L. J., Montie, J., Xiang, Z., Barnett, W. S., Belfield, C. R., & Nores, M. (2005). *Lifetime effects: The HighScope Perry preschool study through age 40*. Monographs of the HighScope Educational Research Foundation, No. 14. Ypsilanti, MI: HighScope Press; Campbell, F., Conti, G., Heckman, J. J., Moon, S. H., Pinto, R., Pungello, E., & Pan, Y. (2014). Early childhood investments substantially boost adult health. *Science*, *343*(6178), 1478–1485; Campbell, F. A., Pungello, E. P., Burchinal, M., Kainz, K., Pan, Y., Wasik, B. H., Sparling, J., & Ramey, C. T. (2012), . Adult outcomes as a function of an early childhood educational program: An Abecedarian Project follow-up, *Developmental Psychology,* *48*(4), 1033.

7. Phillips, D., Gormley, W., & Anderson, S. (2016). The effects of Tulsa's CAP Head Start program on middle-school academic outcomes and progress. *Developmental Psychology,* *52*(8), 1247–1261; Barnett, W. S., Jung, K., Youn, M-D., and Frede, E. C. (2013). *Abbott preschool program longitudinal effects study*. National Institute for Early Education Research; retrieved from nieer.org/wp-content/uploads/2013/11/APPLES205th20Grade.pdf; Schweinhart, L. et al. (2012). *Summary of great start program evaluation findings: High school graduation and grade retention findings*. Retrieved from highscope.org/documents/20147/43324/gs-rp-2012-report.pdf/af59eca6-7bcf-bdf1-736a-4d8170255318

8. Kirp, D. K. (2007). *The sandbox investment: The preschool movement and kids-first politics.* Cambridge, MA: Harvard University Press.

9. First Five Years Fund (2017). *2017 Poll*. Retrieved from ffyf.org/2017-poll/

10. Education Commission of the States (2016). *Fifty state review*. Retrieved from www.ecs.org/ec-content/uploads/01252016_Prek-K_Funding_report-4.pdf

11. U.S. Department of Health and Human Services, Administration for Children & Families, Office of Child Care (2016). *Fact Sheet*. Retrieved from www.acf. hhs.gov/occ/fact-sheet-occ

12. Kirp, D. K. (2007), p. 5.

13. Wechsler, M., Melnick, H., Maier, A., & Bishop, J. (2016), p. 1–3.

14. Barnett, W. S., Carolan, M. E., Squires, J. H., Brown, K. C., & Horowitz, M. (2015). *The state of preschool 2014*. Retrieved from nieer.org/sites/nieer/files/ Yearbook2014_full3.pdf.

15. Kirp, D. K. (2007), p. 40.

16. Barnett, W. S., & Friedman-Krauss, A. H. (2016). *State(s) of Head Start*. New Brunswick, NJ: National Institute for Early Education Research. Retrieved from nieer.org/headstart

17. Kingdon, J. (1995). *Agendas, alternatives, and public policies*. New York, NY: Harper Collins.

18. Bardach, E. (1977). *The skill factor in politics*. Cambridge, MA: MIT Press; Bardach, E. (2001). Political Implementation. In N. J. Smelser & P. B. Baltes, Eds., *The international encyclopedia of the social and behavioral sciences*. Oxford, England: Elsevier.

19. Barnett, W. S., Carolan, M. E., Squires, J. H., Brown, K. C., & Horowitz, M. (2015). *The state of preschool 2014*. Retrieved from nieer.org/sites/nieer/files/ Yearbook2014_full3.pdf

20. Elmore, R. (1982). Backward mapping: Implementation research and policy decisions. In W. Williams et al, *Studying implementation* (pp. 18–36). Chatham, NJ: Chatham House.

CHAPTER 2

Michigan
Quality From the Start

High-quality preschool is not a new concept for Michigan. The state is home to the Perry Preschool Project, one of the most well-known preschool programs in the country because of its proven long-term effects, and Michigan citizens and policymakers are aware of the potential benefits of a sound early education. Michigan is also home to the HighScope Educational Research Foundation, whose research, curricula, assessments, and training provide knowledge and tools for quality early education programs not just in Michigan, but nationwide. Additionally, Michigan boasts philanthropic foundations such as the Kellogg Foundation, the Frey Foundation, the C. S. Mott Foundation, the Skillman Foundation, the McGregor Fund, and the Colina Foundation, whose core missions include the improvement of early childhood education.

Michigan first funded preschool for at-risk 4-year-olds in 1985, with a small $1 million pilot project. Since then, the state has continued its investment in this young population, improving program quality, increasing funding, and expanding access. As the program has grown to serve 38,213 students,[1] reaching 51% of the eligible 4-year-old population,[2] studies have confirmed that participating students have better kindergarten readiness,[3] fewer grade repetitions,[4] better reading and math proficiency,[5] and higher high school graduation rates.[6]

A case of unlikely messengers, uncommon collaboration, and grit, Michigan offers important lessons on how to

- build and sustain a bipartisan early childhood coalition that weathers political shifts;
- thoughtfully restructure bureaucracies to facilitate collaboration and coordination across the early care and learning system;
- entrust program oversight and assistance to regional entities that have the capacity to support continuous improvement; and
- envision, embed, and engage local actors in maintaining quality preschool by setting clear state standards, monitoring processes

that inform implementation at every level of the system, and providing supports to foster program improvement.

Despite its successes, Michigan's progress remains fragile. Local providers' capacities to deliver the program vary considerably, and the budget appropriation process generates uncertainties, as do broader workforce and labor-market pressures.

This case study begins with an overview of Michigan's state-funded preschool program. It then proceeds to explore four dimensions of the Michigan story: political context, program administration and management, program quality, and next steps for the state. It concludes with key takeaways about Michigan's successes and challenges in implementing high-quality preschool.

STATE-FUNDED PRESCHOOL IN A NUTSHELL

The Great Start Readiness Program (GSRP), initially called the Michigan School Readiness Program, is Michigan's state-funded preschool program for 4-year-old children who have factors that place them at risk of educational failure (see Table 2.1). In fiscal year 1986, the Department of Education Appropriation Act designated $1 million to identify appropriate program models for the operation of preschool pilot projects. Fifty-three projects were funded, providing 694 part-day slots for 4-year-old children at risk of educational failure.

The pilot program was made permanent in fiscal year 1987 when Section 36 of the State School Aid Act and the Department of Education Appropriation Act provided $2.3 million in funding for early childhood programs, with programs beginning operation in September 1988.[7]

The state's preschool program continued to grow in the years that followed. By 2013–14, GSRP funded 48,075 part-day slots,[8] which served 31,952 4-year-old children.[9] (Children who attend full-day programs are counted as using two part-day slots.) In 2014–15, GSRP funded 63,248 part-day slots,[10] which served 38,213 4-year-old children (see Figure 2.A, online at tcpress.com).[11]

At the local level, 57 intermediate school districts are the grantees for GSRP and are responsible for program administration.[12] Intermediate school districts are government agencies generally organized along county lines, although some intermediate school districts cover more than one county.

Table 2.1. Key Facts About Michigan's Great Start Readiness Program

Element	
Number of children served	38,213 children in 2014–15[i]
Age	4-year-old children
Eligibility	Targeted for children in greatest need: • Family income below 250% of the federal poverty level ($60,750 for a family of four)[ii] • Families at or below 100% of the federal poverty level ($24,300 for a family of four) are referred to Head Start and may choose between the two programs.[iii] • When space is limited, children are prioritized locally based on risk factors. • A maximum of 10% of children may be from families above 250% of the federal poverty line who pay tuition on a sliding scale based on family income.
Length of program day	Determined locally: • Full-day (80% of children) • Part-day (20% of children)
Maximum class size	18
Teacher-child ratio	1:8 or better
Administration	• Department of Education, Office of Great Start administers at the state level • Intermediate school districts (government agencies generally organized along county lines) administer at the regional level
Setting	Programs are provided in a variety of settings: • Community-based organizations (must be awarded at least 30% of preschool slots) • Intermediate school districts • School districts • Charter schools • Private providers • Public agencies
Curriculum	Programs required to use a research-validated curriculum, including: • HighScope's Early Childhood Curriculum (used by 36% of providers) • Creative Curriculum (used by 60% of providers) • 4% of providers combine other approaches with Creative Curriculum[iv]

Table 2.1. Continued

Minimum teacher qualifications	Lead teachers must have: • Valid Michigan teaching certificate with an Early Childhood Education, or Early Childhood-General and Special Education, endorsement; or • BA in early childhood education or child development with a specialization in preschool teaching Assistant teachers must have: • AA in early childhood education or child development or the equivalent; or • Child Development Associate credential; or • Existing approval of 120 clock hours as a Child Development Associate credential equivalency[v]
Coaching for teachers	Early Childhood Specialists—experts with an MA and five or more years of relevant experience—conduct classroom visits on at least a monthly basis to support and mentor teaching teams.
Wraparound services	Children receive a variety of wraparound services, including developmental, hearing, and vision screenings.
Family engagement	• Program providers make a minimum of four family contacts per year, preferably two home visits and two parent-teacher conferences. • Each intermediate school district has parents participating in the regional Great Start Collaborative Parent Coalition, a network of key community advocates for early childhood. • Parents act as liaisons to local preschool advisory committees, which meet at least twice each program year.

Source: Michigan Department of Education. (2015, August 31). GSRP implementation manual. Retrieved from www.michigan.gov/mde/0,4615,7-140-63533_50451-217313-,00.html

i. Michigan's Center for Educational Performance and Information (2016). *Early childhood count, all ISDs, GSRP/Head Start blend and GSRP, all ISDs (2014--2015)* [Data file]. Retrieved from www.mischooldata.org/EarlyChildhood/EarlyChildhoodCount.aspx

ii. U.S. Department of Health and Human Services (2016, January 25). Poverty guidelines. Retrieved from aspe.hhs.gov/poverty-guidelines

iii. U.S. Department of Health and Human Services (2016, January 25); State of Michigan (2015, January 28). *Great Start Readiness Program income eligibility guidelines for Fiscal Year 2015-16.* Retrieved from www.michigan.gov/documents/mde/GSRP_Income_Eligibility_Guidelines_012815_480025_7.pdf

iv. Personal communication with Richard Lower, Director, Office of Preschool and Out-of-School Time Learning, Office of Great Start (2016, April 13).

v. This provision no longer exists; all teachers who received approval prior to 2011 are grandfathered.

As outlined in the GSRP Implementation Manual:

> [Intermediate school district] administrative policies and procedures document approaches to overarching aspects of the grant, such as community needs assessment, choosing and supporting subrecipients, slot distribution, community partnerships, recruitment, parent engagement, communication, record-keeping, staff credentialing, and program and fiscal evaluation. Administrative policies and procedures must also address systematic oversight of subrecipient practices.[13]

Intermediate school districts may operate the preschool programs directly, choose eligible subrecipients to operate the program, or take a hybrid approach. Subrecipients may be school districts, public school academies (i.e., charter schools), or public or private agencies; they may be nonprofit or for-profit entities. At least 30% of an intermediate school district's allocated slots must be awarded to community-based organizations—public, private for-profit, or nonprofit providers, such as Head Start agencies, community colleges, universities, day care centers, YMCAs, and faith-based organizations.[14]

Most Children Participate in Full-Day Programs

Michigan's state preschool programs are either part-day or full-day. Part-day preschool programs provide a minimum of 3 hours of teacher-child contact time per day, for at least 4 days per week, for a minimum of 30 program weeks. Full-day programs operate for at least the same length of day as the local school district's or public school academy's (i.e., charter school's) 1st-grade program, for a minimum of 30 weeks. Since the state allocates GSRP funds based on part-day slots, under the full-day option grantees use two part-day slots for each enrolled child.

A full-day program may be a GSRP-only program or a GSRP/Head Start blend program (see Table 2.2). An intermediate school district or its subrecipient partners with Head Start to create a "blend" within a classroom: A part-day GSRP slot and a part-day Head Start slot are blended to create a full-day slot for one child. All Head Start and GSRP policies and regulations must be applied to the blended slots, with the highest standard from either program given precedence.[15] For example, Head Start grantees must provide for developmental, hearing, and vision screenings of all Head Start children within 45 days of the child's entry into the program. This requirement goes beyond that of the GSRP requirement for developmental

Table 2.2. What a Michigan Great Start Readiness Program/Head Start Blended
    Program Looks Like

Blending defined	A GSRP/Head Start blended program combines a part-day GSRP slot with a part-day Head Start slot to create a full-day slot for one child.
Funding	Same per-slot amount as GSRP-only programs ($3,625 per child per part-day slot). GSRP/Head Start blends require two slots.
Length of program day	Blended programs must operate for at least the same number of hours a day as the local school district's or public school academy's 1st-grade program and must implement a full-day routine.
Length of program year	Must meet Head Start requirements. Programs that operate for four days per week must provide at least 128 days per year of planned class operations. Programs that operate for five days per week must provide at least 160 days per year of planned class operations.
Other requirements	All Head Start and GSRP policies and regulations must be applied to the blended slots, with the highest standard from either program given precedence.

Source: Michigan Department of Education (n.d.). *GSRP/Head Start blend: Meeting the standards.* Retrieved from http://www.michigan.gov/documents/mde/GSRP_Head_Start_Blend._Meeting_the_Standards._July_2014_467921_7.pdf

screenings; therefore, any children in a GSRP/Head Start blended program would also receive hearing and vision screenings, since this is the highest standard.

GSRP's strategy of blending GSRP and Head Start slots allowed the state to increase the number of children enrolled in full-day programs. In the 2011–2012 school year, 67% of children attended part-day programs and 33% of children attended full-day programs.[16] In the two years of expansion, the proportion of children in full-day programs grew to 67% in 2013 and 80% in 2014 (see Figure 2.B online).[17]

Eligibility Is Based on Poverty and Other Risk Factors

The state designed GSRP to target Michigan's most vulnerable 4-year-olds. Household income for all children is ranked from lowest to highest. The incomes are divided into quintiles based on how far a child's household income is below 250% of the federal poverty level. Children in the quintile with lowest household income are entitled to enroll before children in the quintile with the next lowest household income. Homeless children, those in the foster care system, and those who have an individualized education plan receive top priority.

A maximum of 10% of the children enrolled in GSRP may be from families above 250% of the federal poverty line. These families pay tuition calculated on a sliding scale, based on family income. Priority for these children is determined by risk factor: family income, diagnosed disability or identified developmental delay, severe or challenging behavior, primary home language other than English, parent(s) with low educational attainment, abuse/neglect of child or parent, and environmental risk. During the enrollment and intake process, local providers weigh the number and severity of risk factors.

Any child eligible for Head Start because of family income or other criteria is referred to Head Start, but families determine which program, Head Start or GSRP, best suits their needs. Families who select GSRP are enrolled through the GSRP prioritization process.[18] Children who are enrolled in a GSRP/Head Start blend classroom qualify for, and are concurrently enrolled in, both GSRP and Head Start.

Funding Has Steadily Increased Over Time

GSRP started as a $1 million pilot program in 1985 providing just under 700 part-day slots for 4-year-olds. The program grew to nearly $240 million in 2014 (see Figure 2.C online) providing more than 63,000 part-day slots serving 38,213 children. In its 30-year history, funding decreased twice, in 2001–2002 and again in 2009–2010, due to Michigan's loss of jobs in the automobile industry and its slow recovery from the Great Recession. The program's biggest expansion occurred when Governor Rick Snyder added $65 million to the budget in 2013 and again in 2014, essentially doubling the state's investment in preschool.

The Michigan Department of Education calculates per-child allocations on a part-day child basis. Each part-day child funded constitutes one preschool slot. As with the total investment for GSRP, the investment per slot has increased. In 1990, the part-day slot funding amount was $2,500; by 2015, it was $3,625. Children who attend full-day programs use two preschool slots, funded at a total of $7,250 per child for GSRP-only programs.[19] Although the per-slot allocation has grown over time, it has not kept up with inflation (see Figure 2.D online).

State funds are the main source of revenue for preschool, but some local programs combine state, federal, local, and private funding to cover the cost. For example, programs may blend federal Head Start funds and GSRP funds to create a full-day program.

Additionally, Michigan received a 4-year federal Race to the Top–Early Learning Challenge grant of $51.7 million for the period of January 2014–December 2017 to develop its early learning system.[20] (Table 2.A online lists the major sources of funding for GSRP and GSRP/Head Start blend programs.)

Aligning Curricula Across Standards and Grounding Curricula in Research

GSRP grantees are required to use a research-validated curriculum that aligns with the state's Early Childhood Standards of Quality for Prekindergarten. In the context of early childhood education in Michigan, a "curriculum" refers to "researched-based guidelines on how to set up the physical environment, structure activities, interact with children and their families, and support staff members in their initial training and ongoing implementation of the program."[21] GSRP's implementation guidelines advise grantees to develop children's interests and abilities through active learning experiences and to "reflect the value of play in the written philosophy statement, the comprehensive curriculum, and teacher-parent communication."[22]

Although the Michigan Department of Education does not mandate the use of any particular curriculum, 36% of providers use HighScope's Early Childhood Curriculum, 60% use Creative Curriculum, and 4% combine other curricular approaches with Creative Curriculum.[23] GSRP's implementation manual provides guidance on curriculum selection. The guidelines instruct programs to pay special attention to how a curriculum aligns horizontally with the state's early childhood standards and vertically with the state's infant and toddler standards of quality and its kindergarten-level content expectations.[24] Programs may choose their own curriculum and supplements, but the intermediate school district has final responsibility for ensuring the use of an approved comprehensive curriculum in each classroom and for guaranteeing that any supplemental curriculum is also appropriate.

POLITICS OF EARLY EDUCATION

In some states, support for preschool waxes and wanes with changes in the political climate, but Michigan has remained dedicated to supporting

GSRP despite notable shifts in the state's dominant political party.Throughout the history of the program, gubernatorial control over Michigan has switched between the two main political parties. Started under Democratic Governor James Blanchard (1983–1990), GSRP continued under Republican Governor John Engler (1991–2002), then Democratic Governor Jennifer Granholm (2003–2010), and now Republican Governor Rick Snyder (2011–).While the state Senate consistently has had a Republican majority, control of the House of Representatives has switched back and forth between the two parties. Despite the shifting political winds, support for GSRP has not wavered, not even during the state's economic crisis precipitated by the decline of the automotive industry in the 2000s.

Michigan's success in securing bipartisan support for state-funded preschool despite the political and economic shifts can be attributed to a confluence of events and efforts that include

- 20 years of steady education and coalition building across the research, advocacy, business, and political sectors;
- strong evaluation findings demonstrating the benefits of Michigan's preschool program;
- citizen engagement followed by a needs assessment; and
- a persuasive business case that has bipartisan appeal.

Building Momentum and Cultivating Champions

A persuasive program evaluation, combined with effective leadership and available resources, provided a window of opportunity for GSRP to expand. That expansion could not have happened without decades of groundwork by a broad coalition of supporters, inside and outside government.

There has been a purposeful effort by advocates to educate politicians on the importance of early education. Researchers have been vocal and regular communicators of their findings to governors, legislators, bureaucrats, and administrators.Year after year, local doctors and child development experts have testified at the state capitol on the importance of preschool to brain development. Advocates have held trainings at Michigan State University to bring newly elected legislators up to speed on education policy, including the importance of early childhood education.

Lawmakers have recognized the importance of collaboration among different sectors of the community. Early efforts included the passage of Section 643 of the Michigan Public Act 294 of 1998 (the Family Independence Agency budget bill), which provided $100,000 to leverage and match funds for a Ready to Learn leadership summit to examine how Michigan could develop a child care and early education system that would meet the needs of every child prior to kindergarten.[25] The summit brought together leaders from business, education, religion, government, health, labor, media, and philanthropy.

One year later, Section 641 of Michigan Public Act 135 of 1999 provided another $100,000 to leverage and match additional funds for follow-up efforts after the summit.[26] One of these efforts was the 2001 formation of the Ready to Succeed Partnership, led by a 33-member executive council consisting of legislators, funders, and leadership from Michigan 4C Association, Michigan Association for the Education of Young Children, Michigan Head Start Association, and Michigan's Children. The executive council supported the work of four smaller committees focused on parent education and support, professional development, public awareness, and partnerships. Together, the Partnership led the dialogue around building an early care and education system by:

- mobilizing and supporting expanded leadership involvement from multiple sectors;
- pooling investments to apply research and best practices in emerging community-based early childhood learning systems and policy development; and
- exchanging information across levels (e.g., state and local) and sectors (e.g., public and private), and across the continuum of political orientations.[27]

The Partnership boasted a roster of influential leaders, many of whom have continued to be pivotal figures through the most recent expansion, including then executive director of the Steelcase Foundation and current Office of Great Start Deputy Superintendent Susan Broman; former president of General Motors Foundation and current Congresswoman Debbie Dingell; former state school superintendent Michael Flanagan; and founder of The Center for Michigan and former publisher Phil Power. Former member of the Ready to Succeed Partnership's executive council and Early Childhood Director of Oakland Intermediate School District Joan Firestone commented on the importance of engaging these leaders:

> While much of the progress happened under Governor Granholm and Governor Snyder, a lot of the seeds were sown early on behind the scenes.

Most of us didn't feel like we had the power to make things happen without these more credible, connected champions behind the work. We had a lot of high-level connected people who early on saw this as an important thing to push forward.

But funding for GSRP was not always sacrosanct. In the last two years of Governor Granholm's administration, Michigan experienced budget shortfalls. Before the Senate went on legislative leave in summer 2009, the Senate passed a budget that eliminated about $105 million in funding for GSRP.[28] Matt Gillard, President and CEO of Michigan's Children, former State Representative, former Vice Chair of the House Appropriations Committee, former Chair of the House Appropriations School Aid Subcommittee, and former Chair of the Judiciary Subcommittee, recounted how early threats to preschool funding provided the impetus for the development of a strong grassroots movement:

That [Senate move to eliminate GSRP funding] was really the beginning of our big grassroots mobilization effort. At the time, I was working at the Early Childhood Investment Corporation, and they had this structure throughout the state of Great Start Collaboratives with parent coalitions—roughly 54 throughout the state. Through those efforts, we were able to mobilize a grassroots network of supporters around the state who got really anxious and were upset that there was even a proposal to eliminate GSRP funding. While those senators were on break during that summer, we had people in communities throughout the state going to parades and going to any organized events that were happening letting their legislators know that pre-K was important to them and [legislators] were crazy if they were thinking that they were going to be able to cut [the program]. So immediately when the senators got back in the fall and budget negotiations resumed, the pre-K cut was restored and pre-K was off the table. I really look at that as the beginning of the effort to mobilize grassroots support around pre-K.

Additionally, HighScope played a central role not only as a national research organization, but also as a community partner. According to Firestone, over the years, HighScope had several initiatives to educate citizens, policymakers, and civic groups about the importance of early childhood education. The organization launched Voices for Children campaigns in four states—Michigan, Ohio, North Carolina, and South Carolina—where HighScope staff trained citizens to go out to Rotary clubs and civic organizations and start spreading the message about the importance of early childhood education. HighScope also held convenings of state legislators where attendees would participate in workshops while simultaneously observing promising practices demonstration classrooms.

While grassroots and advocacy efforts were instrumental in saving the program, Michigan idled in recession, largely prompted by the decline in the automobile industry, leading to a $7.5 million cut to the program for the 2009–2010 fiscal year—the first funding cut for the program since 2001–2002.[29]

Notably, cuts to pre-K were not the only cuts to education. K–12 funding also suffered as Governor Granholm worked to keep the state fiscally afloat. These cuts and the palpable economic angst shaped the dominant narrative of pre-K champions: Pre-K is not just a moral issue; it is an economic issue. This would turn out to be the enduring message as the governor's office shifted from Democrat to Republican and the Republican party took control of both chambers of the legislature.

Thus, through a confluence of grassroots and grasstops efforts, early childhood entered the political bloodstream. These early efforts laid the groundwork for expanding investments in preschool.

The Power of Evaluation

Longitudinal evaluations showing the positive long-term impacts of GSRP contributed to the bipartisan support for the program. Since GS-RP's inception as a pilot project in 1985 (then called the Michigan School Readiness Program), evaluations of program quality have been both an impetus for policy change and the basis for increased investment. Even in the program's early years, policymakers were aware of the HighScope Perry Preschool Study. The study's lead researchers, Lawrence Schweinhart and David Weikert, actively educated policymakers on the study's results—high-quality early childhood care and education had substantial long-term effects on low-income 3- and 4-year-olds. While the Perry Preschool study was influential, the HighScope GSRP evaluation proved more important in maintaining support for the program because it was a study by local researchers focusing specifically on the state preschool program.

In 1994, the Michigan Department of Education awarded a grant to HighScope Educational Research Foundation to conduct a longitudinal evaluation of GSRP. Per the evaluation's design, HighScope invited urban and rural programs that served at least 100 children in the 1995–1996 preschool year and that knew that at least 100 additional children were not being served to participate in the study. HighScope observers rated the quality of each participating preschool classroom that year. The next fall, when these children arrived at kindergarten, they were paired with a comparison group of children who matched their demographic risk profile but had not been to any classroom-based preschool program (e.g., Head Start). The cohort consisted of 596 children in 1995–1996 (338 GSRP graduates and 258 non-GSRP graduates) from six districts.

After seeing early findings indicating better kindergarten readiness,[30] Lindy Buch, former state Director of Early Childhood Education and Family Services, who at the time was managing the implementation of the study, noted:

> One of my recollections is sitting with Larry [Schweinhart]. Again, he's a very patient teacher and he showed me the results at the different sites. He told me the results were different for different sites for the children's development, so I tried to figure out what the differences were with my knowledge of Michigan and its demographics. He said to me, "No, you don't have to know that. Look at what's in front of you. Keep looking at it." I looked and looked and, of course, the greatest impact on children was at those sites that had scored the highest on program quality. Larry was pretty excited about it because it fit the theory of change—that you'd get more change in child development if the preschool was of higher quality.[31]

The HighScope research confirmed the Department of Education's theory that quality preK (not merely offering preK) mattered, and it provided a research-driven rationale for future expansion.

HighScope continued to follow these students' progress throughout their schooling. Subsequent evaluations showed that students who had attended GSRP had fewer repetitions and better reading and math proficiency than students who did not attend GSRP.[32] In 2012, HighScope released its report on high school graduation and retention rates.[33] The study showed that 57.3% of the GSRP group graduated on time, compared to 42.5% of the non-GSRP group, a statistically significant difference. Effects were slightly more pronounced for students of color and were nonsignificant for White students.[34] The driving force behind the on-time graduation effect was found to be a significantly reduced retention rate for GSRP students over the course of their school career. That is, the GSRP group was significantly less likely to have been left back than the control group (63.2% of the GSRP group was never retained compared to 50.8% of the non-GSRP group).

Critics, including the politically conservative Mackinac Center for Public Policy, argued that allowing the programs to opt into the study, rather than randomly selecting participants, likely resulted in selection bias. Mackinac Center for Public Policy's Director of Research Michael Van Beek explained:

> The parents who enrolled their children in GSRP were (in the study's words) "likely more motivated regarding the early childhood education of their children." Since these parents were more involved in their children's education, it's possible that these Great Start students would have graduated high school at a higher rate than their peers anyway.[35]

Furthermore, because students were not randomly assigned to GSRP, families in the treatment and control groups may have varied on "soft skills" (e.g., organization, involvement with their child's education, communication ability) that are not captured by the risk factor analysis for the treatment and comparison group.

Many GSRP supporters, including HighScope itself, acknowledge that the longitudinal study had less than optimal rigor, but these shortcomings were not enough to undercut the study's persuasive impact. Policymakers on both sides of the aisle gave more weight to the study's homegrown nature than its perceived empirical shortcomings—it was a study conducted in the state, by highly regarded Michigan researchers, and on the very program that was up for debate. Ken Sikkema, former six-term Republican State Representative, two-term Senator, House Majority Floor Leader, and Senate Majority Leader, said:

> The HighScope study was critical for my involvement. This longitudinal research was critical in that it was very timely. When I read it, the light went off in my head. I said, "Hey, this 4-year-old GSRP program clearly makes a difference." I spent 20 years in the state legislature and voted for every education budget every year. I bet I voted on $300–400 billion of taxpayer spending on education and I never knew if it made a difference or not. But when I read [the HighScope longitudinal] study, I said, "Wait, this GSRP for 4-year-olds makes a difference." I don't know if 4th grade or 8th grade makes a difference, and we spend a billion dollars per grade in this state. But I knew [GSRP] made a difference. That was the trigger for my involvement.

In Michigan, policymakers, administrators, program administrators, and advocates cite the HighScope evaluation as undeniable proof that GSRP has a positive impact on children and is a worthwhile investment.

The Public Speaks: Engaging Citizens in Setting the Education Agenda

The HighScope evaluation generated widespread agreement on the importance of preschool and acknowledgment of GSRP's long-term impact. However, the state lacked a mandate for increasing its investment. The involvement of the Center for Michigan changed that. While the state suffered an economic decline, the Center for Michigan—a new "think and do tank" founded by former newspaper publisher and University of Michigan Regent Phil Power in early 2006—emerged and started to take an interest in early education.

Consistent with the center's approach of only taking on issues in response to public concern, the center launched a statewide public engagement campaign in which staff spoke with 7,000–8,000 people across the state, asking them which education issues were of highest importance. Early childhood education ranked at the top.

Discovering that the public supported preschool expansion, the center then reached out to policymakers, administrators, and advocates to determine just how much of an unmet need there was. Unable to find an answer, the center conducted Michigan's first census of 4-year-olds and determined how many children, not including Head Start enrollees, were eligible for but not being served by GSRP. The result: "30,000 forgotten 4-year-olds."[36]

A window of opportunity for preK expansion opened—here were a public mandate, a quantifiable unmet need, HighScope's latest findings, and economic pressure to make smart social investments. The only missing component, according to Power, was the right messengers. Matt Gillard, longtime advocate and current President and CEO of Michigan's Children, concurred. "We had this great grassroots movement, but we didn't have business folks leading the charge. They were able to get us over the finish line. The general public awareness and support was growing in a way that it would be hard to deny."

Business and Political Champions Emerge

Political leadership in Michigan has long shown an interest in supporting early childhood development, but efforts for significant state investment were greatly accelerated with the election of Governor Rick Snyder in 2010. Governor Snyder is a self-professed "nerd" governor, and at the time of his election he was the only governor in the United States who was also a certified public accountant. True to his background, he took a show-me-the-numbers approach to governance. Matt Gillard recalled:

When Governor Snyder came into office, the Republicans took over the House. Governor Snyder came in with a business background, and it was clear that he would have a business focus and that the business community would have an outside influence over his administration. So the Children's Leadership Council [a statewide coalition of 100 business leaders] formed with the idea that it would match business support up with the grassroots support that we had already grown and developed to bring another voice to the advocacy efforts around pre-K.

Governor Snyder built on the work of his predecessor, Governor Granholm, who in 2005 launched the Early Childhood Investment Corporation. Designed to provide statewide public–private governance and infrastructure support, the Early Childhood Investment Corporation includes individuals from the public, business, and philanthropic sectors. Speaking about the genesis of the Early Childhood Investment Corporation, Washtenaw Intermediate School District Superintendent Scott Menzel recalled:

> Governor Granholm was a big supporter of early childhood, but she never really had any money to play with during her time as governor. So [she] advocated for what [she] believed in, but the resources didn't follow. The stated purpose of the public–private partnership was to create a quasi-governmental unit that would be able to advocate for and advance early childhood initiatives in Michigan and generate additional investments, because we had no money. There was a notion that with a public–private partnership they would have some flexibility and freedom, that a governmental entity couldn't, to go out and find additional revenue and support.

Karen McPhee, Senior Advisor to Governor Snyder, also reflected on these earlier efforts:

> There was a growing awareness that was multi-stakeholder in its approach— [an awareness] of the importance of an investment particularly in preschool ... Business leaders in particular were starting to be engaged in the conversation, understanding early brain research and the importance of starting early so students have an equitable opportunity for a good start in school. So the dialogue was happening along the way, and there certainly was an investment in those efforts prior to Governor Snyder. He became convinced that it was one of those factors that clearly had evidence behind it. There was a lot of support for it—it was beyond conceptual and was absolutely rooted in re-

search, so he said this is something we really need to get behind in Michigan. We really need to help our families understand the importance and find the opportunity to access 4-year-old preschool.

Yet, within the advocacy community there was some concern that solely focusing on pre-K would derail attention and already sparse resources away from birth-to-age-3 early childhood efforts. Indeed, prior to the expansion, advocates had come to an agreement to work on a set-aside where at least 20% of any new early childhood funds would go to birth-to-age-3 efforts.[37] Matt Gillard, former legislator and current President and CEO of Michigan's Children, explained:

> From an advocacy perspective, the challenge became getting everybody who was focused on early childhood comprehensively just to focus on the pre-k component. At the time we already had $105 million going into our pre-k program, but we had very little if anything going into 0 to 3. So the advocacy community was really focused on getting us going on 0 to 3, and then this opportunity came with the governor focused on 4-year-olds. So Susan Broman at the Office of Great Start led the charge, and the rest of us—some of us reluctantly—got on board to keep everyone focused on this opportunity we had for this huge investment in 4-year-old pre-k.

In addition to these strategic concerns among education advocates, members of the K–12 community were concerned that they might lose some of their funding to intermediate school districts. Matt Gillard explained:

> Privately, we frankly had challenges from the public education community. This wasn't a priority and they were looking at K–12 issues that were severely underfunded. [The state legislature] had switched [the program's administration] to the intermediate school districts, so [members of the] K–12 community weren't necessarily excited about this money going to intermediate school districts instead of them.

Nevertheless, policymakers, administrators, advocates, and community members consistently stated that the expansion effort did not face any substantial opposition. Matt Gillard further explains:

> Much of the success of [GSRP's expansion] can be attributed to the fact that we did a good job of eliminating the opposition before it was able to manifest itself or able to really take hold. We had grown such a coalition of support from

both the business community and grassroots that it was really difficult for anyone to be publicly leading opposition to [GSRP].

Thus, support for expansion was largely bipartisan. John Bebow, President of The Center for Michigan, reflected:

> Early childhood, children's issues, and poverty issues are not Democratic and Republican issues. They are reality. In this state we have a very large portion of our children born into Medicaid. It's a fact and it creeps into all kinds of public policy no matter what party you're in, and that's what we're trying to impress upon all legislators. If you come at this from a partisan perspective, it's probably not going to work. You've got to find solutions. Right now Republicans and Democrats are both looking at early childhood as a potential solution.

Even the Mackinac Center for Public Policy, a conservative-leaning think tank, had only muted opposition to the expansion. The center was mostly concerned that the GSRP expansion would move children away from private providers into publicly funded providers and that evidence of GSRP's effectiveness was not persuasive.[38] In his legislative testimony on GSRP, Mackinac's Director of Research Michael Van Beek argued that the state should take a targeted approach to expanding GSRP by prioritizing the most disadvantaged children:

> Let me dissuade you of the notion that I am arguing that there are no benefits to preschool. Clearly, there are [benefits] since the vast majority of Americans choose to enroll their children in educational programs before kindergarten. . . . I am not convinced, based on the research that I have laid out before you today, that Great Start can deliver on these promises. If government is going to finance more preschool, a better approach would be to create small and targeted programs—to fund Perry Preschools in the neediest communities in Michigan.[39]

When reflecting on how a monumental investment in preschool became politically feasible in a Republican-controlled state, former Senate Majority Leader Ken Sikkema remarked:

> The return on the investment for this program was sevenfold—better employees, more stable families, and, of course, better education outcomes. So, this wasn't big government, this was small government. Sure, you have to spend an extra $130 million, but look at the return.

The state was at a pivotal moment in its history—it was genuinely wrestling with how to reset after its fiscal setback and where it should put its dollars to bounce back from the recession over the long-term. "Republicans care about getting bang for the buck," said Sikkema. "Most Republicans realize that you're going to spend some money and they care about showing that you're going to get something for it." In 2013, the Governor requested and the state legislature appropriated an additional $65 million in both fiscal years 2014 and 2015, bringing the total state spending level to $239 million and doubling the state's pre-K budget.

PROGRAM ADMINISTRATION AND MANAGEMENT

Governor Snyder also changed the administrative structure of the preschool program. At the state level, early care and education was consolidated into a single agency—the Office of Great Start—to bring coherence and coordination to the system. At the local level, GSRP was consolidated at the intermediate school district level to ensure sufficient capacity for the state's strategy of continuous improvement.

Consolidating at the State Level to Promote Collaboration and Coordination

In 2011, Governor Snyder issued an executive order establishing the Office of Great Start, which consolidated responsibility for many early learning and development programs under a single agency and placed it within the Michigan Department of Education. This was not Michigan's first attempt to improve services for young children through administrative restructuring, but it was the state's most comprehensive effort to facilitate collaboration and coordination across the early care and learning system. What is more, it was an example of putting the program before the politics.

While the creation of the Office of Great Start has been central to the historic expansion of GSRP, the Department of Education's efforts to consolidate early childhood administration and management had long been underway. In 2004, the department established the office of Early Childhood Education and Family Services and appointed Lindy Buch, a longtime department staffer, as its director. Buch had earlier managed the Michigan School Readiness program and the implementation of its longitudinal evaluation. According to the press release accompanying Buch's appointment:

The new office of Early Childhood Education and Family Services was created as part of the reorganization of the Department of Education in order to:

1. Unify in one office the various initiatives in early childhood education existing in the Department.
2. Give sharper focus to the importance of early childhood education in later school success.
3. Create a unified voice for the department in interacting with other agencies, within and outside state government, working to improve early childhood education in Michigan.[40]

Buch recounted the complex administrative history:

> When I arrived at the Michigan Department of Education, early childhood was part of the health unit; it then became part of several other units. One year we reported to six different directors—we were a part of Curriculum, we were part of School Improvement, and we were part of the Assessment program. We moved around, and then we were part of Special Education. We finally got to be our own unit around 1998. In 2004, we became our own office and then, last year [2011], we were joined by the child-care Head Start Collaboration offices from the Department of Human Services under a deputy superintendent as the Office of Great Start. The concerns of young children have gone from being buried within other k–12 priorities to being part of the department leadership team, to being part of the superintendent's cabinet agenda every week. That's a big change for us. The focus on early childhood systems has been building in Michigan. In other states, systems have both infrastructure and programs, and as early childhood program offerings have come and gone federally and with state funding, the state pre-k program has grown and has remained the largest state discretionary education program in the budget.[41]

With the creation of the Office of Great Start, then-Superintendent of Public Instruction Michael Flanagan of the Michigan Department of Education had full administrative control. The Department of Human Services' Office of Child Development and Care and the Head Start Collaboration Office were shifted to the Department of Education and joined its Office of Early Childhood Education and Family Services to form the new office.

The decision to place the Office of Great Start within the Department of Education represented a remarkable shift and a real political risk. As former State Superintendent Flanagan recalled:

Initially the Governor was going to put the Office of Great Start in the Department of Human Services. I met with him outside of our regular meetings and asked if we [Michigan Department of Education] could have the new office and associated funding. I think he knew that I wasn't an empire builder guy . . . I had been a superintendent in Wayne County—the biggest intermediate school district. [Governor Snyder] decided to give the Office of Great Start to the Michigan Department of Education. The reason that was a big deal is because [the Governor] doesn't control the Department—indirectly through budget stuff—but it's a separate entity. He could have put the Office of Great Start in the Department of Human Services to have full control, so it was a bit risky but I think he understood the merit.

The placement of the Office of Great Start in the Department of Education made policy sense. The Department of Human Services was overburdened with a heavy caseload, as many Michiganders were dealing with the aftershock of the Great Recession. Additionally, the Department of Education had the greatest expertise and, according to Flanagan, already had funding for early childhood. The Department of Human Services' nearly 10,000 employees were focused on administering supports for low-income residents, making it difficult for early childhood concerns to have a voice within the department. Flanagan continued:

[Governor Snyder] made Susan [Broman] a deputy and wanted it to be clear that this was different than other positions. Susan together with an advisory committee were just the right people to focus on quality standards and push us on the star quality rating and improvement system. It wouldn't have happened in the Department of Human Services. It would have gotten buried. They were overwhelmed with caseload. They wouldn't have been able to get up and running as quickly, and we just had the right people at the right time.

The Office of Great Start also helped overcome some of the challenges attributable to braiding and blending state funds with federal funds. Intermediate school districts may blend Head Start and GSRP funding to provide a full-day slot for a child, and the Department of Education provides guidance on braiding funds in instances in which different children in a classroom are funded by different sources, but other problems persist. For example, the definition of administrative costs is different at the state and the federal levels.

In this sense, aligning funding streams to leverage resources has not been easy; however, the Office of Great Start eased the intermediate

school district's burden. Washtenaw Intermediate School District Superintendent Scott Menzel explained:

> Bureaucratic rules at the state and federal level[s] make it difficult to do
> some of the things that make the most sense. But we are having conversa-
> tions with the right players at the table.... Cross-department, cross-agency
> conversations are made possible through the construction of the Office of
> Great Start.

In short, the Office of Great Start elevated the visibility of early childhood,
built connections among early childhood programs and between early
childhood and K–12, and provided guidance to local administrators on
how to manage funding streams.

Consolidating at the Local Level to Support Program Improvement and Coordination

At the local level, GSRP funds initially flowed directly to school districts,
with about 20% of the total budget reserved for a competition among non-
school-district providers. Beginning in 2011, intermediate school districts
became the grantees for GSRP, responsible for administering every aspect
of GSRP, including child recruitment, community needs assessment, fiscal planning, monitoring subrecipients, professional development, and
program evaluation. Each intermediate school district designates an early
childhood contact who "facilitates an [intermediate school district]–wide
plan with a vision to improve child outcomes, to minimize achievement
gaps, and help all stakeholders to see the 'big picture' of how GSRP stra-
tegically fits into the local Great Start Collaborative early childhood efforts."[42] The early childhood contact partners with specialists who are
charged with collecting, interpreting, and providing feedback on classroom data to promote continuous quality improvement. In smaller intermediate school districts, one person may be both the early childhood
specialist and the early childhood contact.

This regional approach was a long time coming. There had not been
sufficient capacity at the state level to monitor the quality of state-funded
preschools, and there was a built-in disincentive at the local level to accurately monitor capacity.

Washtenaw Intermediate School District Superintendent Scott Menzel
recalled:

We knew and the Department of Education knew that [the agency] could not guarantee through monitoring that everyone across the state was complying with all the rules and regulations, [such as] the curriculum requirements, the early childhood specialist requirements. So you would have districts that named an elementary school principal as the early childhood specialist who had no training, technically met the criteria, [but] never engaged with the program, so you didn't have some of those core [program] components in place. With the money now coming down to intermediate school districts, a lot more of that quality assurance is taking place because we're responsible for it. And we've said to our local districts, you can't continue to operate the program the way you want, you have to operate the program in compliance with the rules and regulations and what the expectations are.

It is not always fun to be the compliance police . . . but at the same time we make the argument that it's not just for the sake of compliance. Research indicates that doing certain things produces the kinds of results we want. Shooting from the hip and doing your own thing means that we can't guarantee the same kinds of results. And if we want our elected officials to continue to fund GSRP to the tune of roughly $248 million, then we have to continue to show results.

Speaking at the 2012 Conference for Early Childhood Research and Evaluation, Lindy Buch, former state Director of Early Childhood Education and Family Services, recalled that HighScope suggested this regional administrative approach in GSRP's early years:

In the very first set of recommendations in 1997, HighScope suggested that there were too many grantees, that they were too small, and that the regional intermediate school districts in Michigan should take over management of the program to provide better local oversight and have a big enough number of classrooms so that there could be professional support at the local level. I'm glad to say that that change occurred last year in 2011. Sometimes change is slow.[43]

There were also practical reasons why intermediate school districts made administrative sense. Other early education funds already flowed through them, so giving them oversight over GSRP improved the alignment across early education programs. The new administrative structure enabled intermediate school districts to coordinate GSRP and Head Start. According to Washtenaw Intermediate School District Early Childhood Director Alan Oman:

On paper [GSRP and Head Start] are not supposed to compete with each other, but you have a whole host of other factors that influence parents. If there's a state pre-K program that is operated by a school district and it's in the same building where my 2nd grader goes to school, why wouldn't I want my 4-year-old to go to the same building? Or if I live walking distance from the local state pre-K program, but they are telling me that I am only eligible for a Head Start program that is 15 minutes away by vehicle. Those are the kinds of things that impact parents.

Many intermediate school districts, including Washtenaw, have dealt with this issue by making themselves the grantees for both GSRP and Head Start. As Alan Oman explained:

We've been able to look at both sides of the coin. What we have developed is a single point of entry. Every parent who is looking to have their child placed in a public program fills out the same form and they can select a first, second, or third choice. If a parent chooses the state pre-k program, our staff contacts them and just makes sure that they are aware that Head Start may offer additional services. But if they choose state pre-k after knowing that, it's their choice.

Having intermediate school districts responsible for program administration at the regional level strengthens capacity for program monitoring and fosters coordination between GSRP and Head Start.

Together, creating the Office of Great Start at the state level and empowering intermediate school districts as program grantees at the local level set the administrative conditions for a quality pre-K program.

GETTING TO QUALITY

Since its early years, GSRP's theory of change has been that quality pre-K matters. As described by Lindy Buch, former state Director of Early Childhood Education and Family Services,

One thing that was important and guided us all the way was that you have to have a theory of change. Ours was that higher program quality matters for children's outcomes. You can measure both of those things [program quality and children's outcomes] and you should keep checking to make sure it is happening. Every time you learn more, you need to make sure that [your stan-

Ensuring High-Quality ECE Instruction

Putting the administration of the Great Start Readiness Program into the hands of intermediate school districts has created the opportunity for greater oversight of, and greater influence on, the instructional practices implemented in state pre-K classrooms. In Ionia County Intermediate School District, Cheryl Granzo, Director of Early Childhood Programs, has worked diligently to ensure that GSRP classrooms reflect state standards and embrace developmentally-appropriate practices. According to Granzo, when state pre-K was previously run through school districts, there was greater variability in the quality of the programming, as communities tended to perpetuate the practices they knew best rather than the latest understanding of best practices. When the Intermediate School District took the reins, however, there was an opportunity to shift practices and promote quality instruction tailored to the needs of young learners.

Doing so, however, took careful attention to relationships. Granzo described one meeting with a parent who was concerned because her child had not brought home worksheets from her pre-K classroom as she had the previous year. In their community, worksheets had been the norm. To help families understand the transition toward the types of high-quality instruction set forth in state standards, program administrators developed a box from which parents could select an activity to bring home for their child—a familiar routine for some families. Having this box enabled GSRP to implement a high-quality program in its classrooms, while also building trust with families. Granzo recognized that developing a shared understanding of the types of practices used in high-quality ECE classrooms takes time and strong relationships. She was able to phase out the box the following year.

Source: Interview with Cheryl Granzo, Director of Early Childhood Programs, Ionia County Intermediate School District (2015, September 29).

dards are] still up to date and you have to prove that the quality instrument actually measures your standards. Standards and assessments have to align and you have to prove that they align. You have to have that [alignment of quality, standards, and assessments] and state that as your theory of change—publicly and all of the time.

From early on, Michigan defined preschool quality through clearly articulated standards and aligned those standards with child outcomes. The state devised systems to monitor, assess, and track program quality. It promoted structural and process quality through a rating system that is intentionally linked to state standards. Further, it built in a system of continuous improvement through on-site coaching tailored to individual program needs.

Raising the Bar Through Quality Standards

Michigan was at the forefront of setting standards for early education. In 1971, Michigan's State Board of Education approved "Preprimary Objectives" to describe the learning and development expected for preschool- and kindergarten-age children in the affective, psychomotor, and cognitive domains.[44] The state used these objectives as it implemented programs for students with special needs before the federal government mandated such programs.

"Catherine Scott-Little [a national expert on early learning standards] once called us a 'pioneer' in the standards movement," recalled Buch. Reflecting on the integral role of standards in early education from the very beginning, Buch recalled:

> We collected descriptive data on how the program looked. We developed with HighScope a Program Quality Assessment where we reviewed the quality of the programs and we had not just a checklist to see if the program was being implemented with fidelity, but also a scale to see how good the program was. We had pretty extensive standards for the program. I found that all the way back to 1976 when we started doing preschool special education, Michigan had rules and guidelines for what preschool should be like, and we had learning standards from around 1998 for what children should be learning in early childhood programs.

This attention to articulation of standards has continued over the years; the State Board of Education and its agency and organizational partners review the standards on an ongoing basis. The State Board of Education approved the *Early Childhood Standards of Quality for Prekindergarten* in 2005 and revised them in 2013. The standards are divided into two major areas: early learning expectations for 3- and 4-year-old children and quality program standards for preK.[45]

The *Early Learning Expectations for 3- and 4-Year-Old Children* establish standards in nine domains:

1. Approaches to learning
2. Creative arts
3. Language and early literacy development

4. Dual language learning
5. Technology literacy (early learning and technology)
6. Social, emotional, and physical health and development
7. Mathematics
8. Science
9. Social studies

The standards apply to all 3- and 4-year-olds of all developmental backgrounds and abilities. Under each domain, the standards define subdomains, associated early learning expectations, emerging indicators, and examples of children's experiences and teaching practices to support the learning expectations.

The *Quality Program Standards for Preschool and Prekindergarten Programs*[46] establish standards for center-based classroom preschool programs for 3- and 4-year-old children in seven areas:

1. Program's statement of philosophy
2. Community collaboration and financial support
3. Physical and mental health, nutrition, and safety
4. Staffing and administrative support and professional development
5. Partnership with families
6. Learning environment, which contains four subdomains:
    a. curriculum
    b. relationships and climate
    c. teaching practices
    d. facilities, materials, and equipment
7. Child assessment and program evaluation

In addition to these standards, which apply to all pre-K programs for 3- and 4-year-olds, the Michigan Department of Education has developed specific GSRP standards for teacher qualifications, child-teacher ratios, and curriculum.

Lead teachers must have either a valid Michigan teaching certificate and an Early Childhood Education or Early Childhood-General and Special Education endorsement, or a bachelor's degree in early childhood education or child development with a specialization in preschool teaching. The pre-K student-teacher ratio is 8:1, and when a classroom enrolls its ninth child, it must also add an associate teacher. An associate teacher must have either an associate's degree in early childhood education or child development or the equivalent, or a valid classroom Child Development Associate's credential, or an existing 120-hour approval, if the teacher was grandfathered under the now-defunct Child Development Associate equivalency credential. A third adult must be present in any classroom where 17 or 18 children are enrolled.

GSRP grantees must use a research-validated curriculum that aligns with the *Early Childhood Standards of Quality for Prekindergarten*. The Department of Education's *GSRP Implementation Manual* provides a list of curricula among which programs may choose. The manual assists GSRP programs in selecting a curriculum that matches each program's student population and philosophy by providing guiding questions about the curriculum's scope and sequence, materials, learning experiences, and activities, among others. Two of the curricula, Creative Curriculum and HighScope, have created companion documents showing how each respective curriculum aligns with Michigan's prekindergarten standards.

Great Start to Quality: Establishing a Continuous Improvement System

To encourage program quality and ensure compliance with the standards, Michigan developed Great Start to Quality, a five-star rating and improvement system for all programs in the state's early care and education system. The system started in 2011 and was updated in 2013. Minimal licensing standards are the foundation of the rating system, and programs can climb a staircase of graduated improvements in quality. While participation is voluntary for licensed non-GSRP early childhood programs such as group child care homes, family child-care homes, center-based child care, and non-GSRP preschool programs, a program must have a three-star rating or higher to be eligible for GSRP funding.[47]

The Early Childhood Investment Corporation, a public–private partnership, implements Great Start to Quality on behalf of the state. As part of the quality rating and improvement system (QRIS), all programs complete a self-assessment survey that measures structural quality in five areas:

1. Family and community partnerships
2. Administration and management
3. Environment
4. Curriculum and instruction
5. Staff qualifications and professional development

An assessment specialist validates a random selection of all self-assessment surveys, as well as all programs that rate themselves as four- or

PROMOTING FAMILY ENGAGEMENT THROUGH HOME VISITS

Family partnerships are a key part of Great Start to Quality's conception of quality in ECE programs. In the rural community of Ionia County, home visits are an important strategy for building strong relationships with families and encouraging meaningful family engagement. Teachers visit all GSRP families in their homes at least two times per year and each visit lasts at least an hour, though it is not uncommon for them to last longer.

During the first home visit of the year, which typically occurs the summer before children begin the program, teachers and parents get to know each other and begin to build trust. Importantly, the first home visit offers a chance to discuss what parents hope their child will gain from pre-K. Parents select a developmental goal for their child, and the parents and teachers together discuss how teachers can support the child in achieving the goal over the course of the year. Cheryl Granzo, Director of Early Childhood Programs for Ionia County Intermediate School District, noted that the goals parents choose for their children tend to vary widely, from making a friend in their sparsely-populated community to learning letters or beginning to count.

Whatever the goal, the process of selecting it brings educators and families together and sets the stage for ongoing communication throughout the year. For social goals, the teacher may make a point of sending home periodic updates about the child's budding relationships with others in the class. For goals related to learning letters or numbers, the teacher may occasionally choose a picture featuring the child's emerging script to specially share with families. The first home visit also provides an opportunity for the teacher to answer parents' questions, review important paperwork such as the parent handbook, and conduct a developmental screening of the child. At the second home visit, educators and parents build on these earlier interactions, addressing parent concerns and sharing updates about the child's progress.

The relationships between educators and families are further reinforced through twice-annual parent-teacher conferences, focused on children's developmental progress, and through ongoing informal contact throughout the year. As Granzo noted, GSRP teachers sit down formally with each family at least four times a year, and if there's a need, more often.

Source: Interview with anonymous early childhood specialist and with Cheryl Granzo, Director of Early Childhood Programs, Ionia County Intermediate School District (2015, September 29).

Assessing Quality in GSRP Classrooms: A Coach's View

GSRP coaches play a critical role in assessing the quality of the pre-K classrooms. Using the Program Quality Assessment, coaches look beyond the nuts and bolts of classrooms to focus on the factors that lead to child growth and development. One early childhood specialist described the depth of how coaches assess quality in GSRP classrooms:

> The tool we use, the Program Quality Assessment, is very detailed when it comes to what we are working on in quality. It's not just "do you have nice, clean toys?" and it's not just "do you have a degree?" That's part of the [tool]. But I did an [assessment] in a classroom with of one of the specialists I am training and we were looking at everything: What's the level of conversation? What's the warmth in the environment? How is the classroom speaking to the community cultures that are represented in the classroom? Are there examples of something stereotypical that need to be addressed? Is multiculturalism evidenced in classroom diversity? We are looking at a ton of things that may not sound to an educator in a different realm, like a middle school teacher, as though they are important facets of education. . . . But we need to support the whole child.

Source: Interview with anonymous early childhood specialist.

---

five-star. Great Start to Quality also utilizes the Program Quality Assessment, a classroom-level program evaluation tool developed by the HighScope Educational Research Foundation, to assess the environment and adult/child interactions. An approved rater, who may also be an early childhood specialist who provides ongoing improvement support, conducts the Program Quality Assessment. A program's star rating is good for 2 years.

For GSRP programs, all of which must participate, Great Start to Quality is more than an accountability system; it is also a system for continuous quality improvement. All GSRP programs work with an early childhood specialist, who leads the GSRP teaching teams and uses the Program Quality Assessment to support continuous improvement efforts. The GSRP Implementation Manual explicitly outlines the specialized knowledge needed to fulfill this role:

> The early childhood specialist must have a graduate degree in early childhood education or child development, five or more years of relevant job experience (such as working with young children in a group setting, program planning and implementation, program evaluation, staff supervision/

development and program management), and specific professional development (such as curriculum development, program evaluation, program management, and staff development). An early childhood specialist supports no more than 15 teaching teams to ensure a manageable caseload. [48]

The early childhood specialist provides curriculum training on a daily basis and visits classrooms on a monthly basis to support and mentor teaching teams. At the beginning of the school year, the early childhood specialist conducts a baseline quality assessment using HighScope's Program Quality Assessment. The early childhood specialist then coaches teachers on areas that need improvement, such as adult-child interactions, learning environment, daily routine, curriculum planning and assessment, and parent involvement. Three times during the school year, the early childhood specialist runs data analysis team meetings where the participants discuss challenges identified through the data and the early childhood specialist provides teaching teams with strategies for improvement. Finally, the early childhood specialist conducts a follow-up Program Quality Assessment in the spring and submits those data to the state. Christine Maier, an Early Childhood Specialist for Oakland Intermediate School District (Oakland Schools), described the continuous improvement model:

> We contract with about 20 different masters-level people who are assigned to no more than 15 classrooms throughout Oakland County to evaluate classrooms, look at data, and set goals with teachers. There is always continuous improvement. [We] recheck the goals, provide support, reset goals. Every year there's resetting goals, and that's on the very ground level.

The qualifications and responsibilities of the early childhood specialist illustrate a solid commitment to professional development and create a measure of uniformity across the state. Intermediate school districts may deliver additional professional development for GSRP teachers, but variations in available resources and the commitment of the leadership among intermediate school districts leads to variation in the amount and depth of support that teachers can access.

For example, Oakland Schools, which currently receives the third largest amount of annual state funds,[49] has created a tiered early childhood professional learning system with a series of professional development options tailored to beginning, mid-career, and experienced teachers. A site director remarked that this rich tapestry of resources is a reflection of the committed leadership of Early Childhood Director Joan Firestone and her staff—a caliber of leadership that not all intermediate school districts

---

**ONE TEACHER REFLECTS ON THE IMPORTANCE OF
PROFESSIONAL DEVELOPMENT OPPORTUNITIES**

A GSRP teacher within Oakland Schools described the rich array of professional development available to her:

> We're given time to reflect every day after school on how the day went, what should we do differently tomorrow, what [child] interests did we notice and how can we use that to bring in an academic core subject, how can we keep the interest going and include the skills that we need to practice. We do that daily in an informal manner, and then we get Fridays for professional development, conferences, home visits, and paperwork. It is really important for teachers to have that time. You have to give teachers pay for it and give them that time.
>
> Where I grew as a teacher was the ability to go to these professional development trainings, either at the intermediate school district's office, or here [at the school], or at the yearly state conference in Dearborn. And [the intermediate school district] paid for me to attend. That is a big help and a big incentive to learn.
>
> We meet in staff meetings and break down into groups where teachers will talk and meet, and we will work on our goals for our building. [For example,] maybe the focus is on how to set up lessons for a particular kind of skill. There are opportunities for those of us who have gone to conferences to share with other teachers.

Source: Interview with anonymous teacher (2015, October 1).

have. A local early childhood director commented on the difference that bringing her early childhood program under the leadership of Oakland Schools has made to her practice:

> I believe the change came truly from the partnership with Oakland Schools. Before it was just me here filling out reports, figuring out implementation standards—we were doing appropriate practices, but we never had an on-site review. All of the districts were doing their own thing. When the state gave control over to the intermediate school district, we had a great bunch of women [at the intermediate school district level] who are extremely bright, policy focused, and focused on early childhood, so when they took it over, that all trickled down to us. As a director, I knew that I now had partners in them. For me it was a real benefit because I didn't feel isolated and I had a network.

Strong early childhood leadership in Oakland also makes it possible for directors and teachers to receive professional training at scale and at a lower cost. The local early childhood director continued:

> Before I was submitting things directly to the state. Now we submit our work to the intermediate school district and they send it to the state, which allows for another layer of accountability, and it allows the intermediate school district to take the lead to support training on data and curriculum. So instead of me partnering with HighScope, they can pool the money and fund it district-wide. [The intermediate school district] also has early childhood specialist meetings monthly and we dialogue about how to support our programs, what are you doing with data, how are you reflecting on data, how are you taking it back to the level. So everything they end up doing on the intermediate school district level ends up finding its way back to the classroom. I can see a direct shift in my practices now having that partnership.

Not all intermediate school districts have the funds or leadership to offer such comprehensive professional development. Although all GSRP programs have an annual professional development plan that is based on needs identified by the early childhood specialist during observations of teaching teams, there are no specific state requirements for training other than a mandate that the specialists offer classroom-based support.

Challenges to Quality: The Realities of Local Resources

While the Department of Education aims to create consistency among intermediate school districts, differences in fiscal resources, teacher workforce population, and leadership priorities result in substantial variation across localities. Like many states across the country, Michigan is far from homogeneous. Michigan is home to dense, urban areas such as Wayne County (Detroit) and neighboring metropolitan areas, including Oakland and Macomb counties. The state includes agricultural regions in the Lower Peninsula, as well as the mostly rural Upper Peninsula, which contains 29% of Michigan's land area but just 3% of the state's population. Variation exists even within intermediate school districts. Washtenaw County, for example, encompasses relatively wealthier, relatively homogeneous, and higher-performing districts, such as Chelsea, Manchester, Dexter, and Saline, as well as high-poverty, diverse, and low-performing Ypsilanti.

These regional variations are reflected in population density and demographics, as well as resources and support for GSRP. In some inter-

DATA-DRIVEN TEACHER PROFESSIONAL DEVELOPMENT IN OAKLAND COUNTY

In Oakland County, GSRP programs use data to better support children and educators. The county's GSRP classrooms use HighScope's child observation tool to assess children's development throughout the year. While the observation provides valuable information about the supports individual children need, Oakland County also uses the observation data to identify the supports its educators need. Using these assessment data, local GSRP administrators identify domains in which there are lower scores among children and set professional development goals for staff to better support children in those areas. One local GSRP administrator described how these data were recently used to inform professional development for educators:

> Last year, we looked at all the indicators and in our bottom-scoring areas, we had dialogue. That falls in the conflict resolution, social-emotional area for our kids. . . . [So,] last year's goal was "children will show growth in their ability to recognize and be able to express emotion. Children will have the ability to become aware of their own feelings, which will allow them to observe and explain the emotion to others." That became our focus for students, based on data.
>
> Then we turned and made it a professional development goal for adults. So teachers will have training about what we can do to support children in that area. [I asked] "What training do we need? How do we focus on that in our practices? And how can I support adults? Do I need funding to bring more training in?" As an example, we contracted with a mental health consultant to come in and do reflections with teachers. She'll observe in a classroom to get a sense of the functioning of the classroom and the interactions, and she'll provide feedback to the staff. . . . We try to find layers to adult growth to support the student growth.

Source: Interview with anonymous GSRP administrator.

mediate school districts, GSRP teachers receive the same pay as K–12 teachers, while in other intermediate school districts GSRP teachers are paid far less. Some districts within a given intermediate school district have buildings dedicated to early education, but others must scramble to find suitable space for a single classroom.

Consider Oakland Schools, the intermediate school district serving Oakland County. Located in the Detroit metropolitan area, Oakland Schools encompasses 28 school districts and 26 public school academies. The intermediate school district supports more than 48 local GSRP programs that serve more than 3,000 children in 317 schools.

Because it operates on such a large scale, Oakland employs an entire team—a director and five early childhood specialists—to support GSRP. Funding for these staff members comes partly from the administrative fee paid by each of the intermediate school district's subrecipients. With 48 subrecipients, even small fees represent a substantial revenue stream. Still, resources are insufficient for the level of support the intermediate school district leadership believes is necessary to foster high-quality pre-K programming, and so the intermediate school district supplements the GSRP funds with local dollars and brings on additional staff when needed. For instance, Oakland Schools leadership hired a behavioral consultant who specializes in mental health to support children in GSRP programs because providers reported that their local communities needed this resource.[50]

The situation in the Ionia County Intermediate School District is very different. Located in a rural region in western Michigan, halfway between Lansing and Grand Rapids, Ionia encompasses nine local districts and one public school academy, accounting for 28 schools. Its GSRP program includes only eight classrooms operated by the intermediate school district and another two classrooms operated by EightCAP, the parent agency of Head Start.

Cheryl Granzo, Ionia's Director of Early Childhood Programs, directs the program district-wide and also supervises classrooms. As Granzo described:

> I do two roles. I do the early childhood contact. I have to make sure I have [community] partners, I have to do the implementation plan and make sure all the monitoring pieces are in place. But as the supervisor, I have to do all the teacher evaluations, the teacher meetings, all the staffing. [If a teacher says] "I'm sick," [I figure out] who is going to fill in. I do all the hiring.

In Ionia, the intermediate school district, not the local districts, delivers GSRP programming. But the intermediate school district does not supplement the state funding, as Oakland Schools does. When the Ionia Intermediate School District assumed administrative control over GSRP, the intermediate school district no longer contributed general education dollars to the GSRP program, and neither did local school districts.[51]

With limited resources due to state funds being its only source, Ionia must keep teacher salaries low and offers only single-subscriber health benefits that do not cover teachers' families. The children of many Ionia teachers are enrolled in Medicaid.[52]

OAKLAND SCHOOLS' PROFESSIONAL DEVELOPMENT SYSTEM

Oakland Schools has created a tiered early childhood professional learning system. The bottom tier includes learning sessions for first-time teaching team members and administrators. Many of those sessions are prerequisites for other sessions in the middle and top tiers, targeted to teachers with more years of experience. Although Oakland does not require advancement through the tiered professional development system, many teachers take advantage of this "soft requirement."

Beginning teachers might choose to attend GSRP Boot Camp, a workshop on the Ages and Stages Questionnaire—a developmental screening parents complete with questions about how their child is learning and growing—or a workshop on HighScope's child assessment tool. One of the intermediate school district's popular offerings is the HighScope First 30 Days training, in which beginning teachers receive training and lesson plans based on the HighScope curriculum for the first six weeks of class. Oakland Schools developed this training in response to the fact that many teachers are not hired until shortly before the start of classes because intermediate school districts do not know how many slots they may have until the governor signs the state School Aid budget bill, typically in late June or early July.

More experienced teachers might choose to attend a workshop on conflict resolution, dual language learners, or home visiting. The most experienced teachers can study intentional teaching, an instructional approach that combines both child-guided and adult-guided classroom experiences.

In addition to these voluntary professional development sessions, Oakland Schools requires all teaching staff to have basic curriculum training by a certified trainer in the subrecipient's curriculum of choice (all but one classroom in the intermediate school district uses HighScope). Oakland Schools currently has a project underway that gives early childhood specialists and program directors an avenue to become curriculum trainers, which builds training capacity across the intermediate school district.

The intermediate school district has an assigned early childhood preschool consultant, a HighScope certified trainer, who oversees all of the intermediate school district's professional development efforts. Some of Oakland Schools' trainings are free, but others have a nominal cost (about $100) to cover food and materials. Oakland Schools also has a staff person who regularly checks the subrecipients' budgets to make sure that there is professional development money set aside.

Source: Interview with Christine Maier, Early Childhood Specialist, Oakland Schools (2016, March 16) and Oakland Schools Early Childhood Director Joan Firestone (2015, October 2); Oakland Schools. (2016, March 16). Professional learning for early learning staff 2015/2016 - Early childhood professional learning triangle. Waterford, MI: Oakland Schools.

WORKING TOGETHER FOR GSRP:
THE IMPORTANCE OF PARTNERSHIPS IN OAKLAND COUNTY

In Oakland County, GSRP, Farmington Public Schools, and the county early childhood department work together to make GSRP a success. There, state funding provides the bulk of the resources needed to run the program, but the school district provides in-kind support for a number of key program components, including classroom space and utilities, custodial staff, and assistance with fiscal oversight. Other program resources, such as secretarial staff, are paid for using a combination of GSRP, Head Start, and school district funds.

Locating GSRP classrooms in district facilities not only provides fiscal benefits, but also makes district resources more accessible to the program. For example, the district's Child Find program, which identifies and supports young children with special needs, is conveniently located in the same building as GSRP. Staff members concerned about a pre-K child's developmental progress can head right down the hall to access screening and on-site supports such as speech and occupational therapy. This partnership is crucial to the program's successful implementation. As one local administrator noted, "It's truly a partnership that they are offering these services within the district. If [state and district] funding sources were not here to have this program, it wouldn't be here."

Source: Interview with anonymous early childhood administrator.

Finding and retaining qualified preschool teachers has always been a challenge in rural Michigan, one that was exacerbated by the program's recent rapid expansion. Making matters worse, because GSRP teachers are so highly qualified, they can readily transition to higher-paying jobs as kindergarten teachers in the local school districts, where some teachers could see a salary increase of $10,000 or more.[53] Granzo talked about the long-term challenge of sustaining an underfunded program:

> For me, what I worry about is the ability to sustain it because we are not part of that local school district. They have no financial obligation to it. The intermediate school district does not have a financial obligation to it. So what happens when we come to the point that we can't stay within the grant? Even though there have been increases [in the state allocation per slot] it does not in any way, shape, or form meet what needs to be done. I can't require a more skilled teacher than your average elementary school teacher, and pay them significantly less, and not give them health care, and keep

them. $3,500–$3,600 per kid [per part-day slot] is just not going to cut it. I worry about how the program will be sustained in the future.

As the tale of these two intermediate school districts illustrates, while Michigan has set up systems that are intended to ensure all programs meet high-quality standards, local variations can greatly affect what is happening on the ground.

NEXT STEPS FOR MICHIGAN

Pre-K has been the primary focus of the Department of Education and state policymakers in Michigan, but the state plans to increase the number of child-care centers that participate in the Great Start to Quality system, expand birth-to-age-3 offerings, and improve the links between early education and K–12.

Increasing Participation in Great Start to Quality

Considering all early care and education providers across the state, not just GSRP, participation in the Great Start to Quality improvement system is low. Thirty-five percent of the participating programs are GSRP programs.[54] The state requires any program that wants to be considered for GSRP funding to go through the Great Start to Quality system, but of the 6,675 early childhood programs (child-care centers, preschool centers, group child-care homes, and family child-care homes), only 28% participate. The rest remain at what the Early Childhood Investment Corporation refers to as the "empty star" level (see Table 2.B online). These programs have met the bare-bones environmental, health and safety, and professional development licensing requirements,[55] and they can offer preschool, but they do not receive state funds because they do not participate in the quality rating and improvement system.

Some programs opt not to participate in the quality rating and improvement system because participating does not make business sense. Early Childhood Investment Corporation CEO Marijata Daniel-Echols explained:

A program could be the highest quality program in the state, have a waiting list of six months, charge people $5,000 a month and be cruising along on an empty star because [they think], "I don't need a star rating to stay in business. I don't want GSRP funding because I don't want government in my mix. I have paying customers so I don't need child-care subsidy payments because my clientele is all tuition based and I'm paying my bills." So there are some types of child-care providers who don't need a rating or want one because it makes no difference for their business.

Other programs stay out of the system because they cannot meet the standards. The Office of Great Start has used some of its Race to the Top–Early Learning Challenge funds to bring group and family providers who are not participating in the quality rating and improvement system into the fold. These providers are offered grants that can help them start the quality improvement process. As a result of these efforts, from January through June 2015, home-based provider participation in Great Start to Quality increased by 3.5%, bringing the statewide home-based provider participation rate up to 12.5%.[56]

Increasing and Strengthening the Broader Early Childhood System

There is growing recognition at the Department of Education that expanding birth-to-age-3 efforts and creating stronger early childhood services, aside from early learning, is the next order of business. Analogizing the importance of building in quality in the earliest years to the manufacturing industry, Deputy Superintendent Susan Broman remarked:

> We have a lot more work to do in the child-care subsidy program, children's health access, screening, assessment, home visitation. I'm not satisfied. I worked at Steelcase for 15 and a half years. It was a manufacturing environment that went through incredible trauma in downsizing, so I think about things a little differently. If you watch what they do in manufacturing—how they build quality in at the earliest point because it costs too much money not to—I wish that we thought about health and human services like that. We do pay by not building in quality all along the way—we just pay in different ways.

On the birth-to-age-3 front, there are budding district efforts to expand Early Head Start. Washtenaw County Intermediate School District, often seen as a microcosm of the state because of its diversity, recently began implementing the program. Although the district has the capacity to serve several hundred children, a lack of funding prevented the district from ramping up. The county now provides 36 slots—just a fraction of the need, according to Washtenaw Intermediate School District Early Childhood Director Alan Oman—but it is a start.

There are also efforts to improve the quality of child care statewide. Michigan is using its Race to the Top–Early Learning Challenge funds to improve program quality, family engagement, credentialing for providers, and business training for child-care providers. In its Race to the Top application, the state presented a plan to increase the number of online Child Development Associate credential programs through partnerships with five community colleges. Using Race to the Top funds, the state plans to increase the number of community college early childhood programs accredited by the National Association for the Education of Young Children from 7 to 13. As Michigan noted in its Race to the Top application:

> Michigan is focusing their training efforts on home-based providers because they serve a large number of children with high needs and they are the early childhood educators with the least amount of formal training. Providing training that will result in a Child Development Associate credential improves the quality rating for these providers.[57]

The Department of Education also proposed expanding its T.E.A.C.H. (Teacher Education And Compensation Helps) scholarship program to include home-based providers, enabling them to receive the training required for certification. The state also intends to use T.E.A.C.H. scholarships to enable early childhood educators with a bachelor's degree to become credentialed GSRP lead teachers. In its 2014 Race to the Top–Early Learning Challenge Annual Performance Report, Michigan reported that it had made progress toward these efforts in the grant's 1st year by "providing 66 T.E.A.C.H. scholarships to eligible providers for fall 2014 semester, including 41 scholarships to home-based providers and 25 scholarships to providers seeking certification to teach in GSRP."[58]

Advancing K-12 Alignment Efforts

In its Race to the Top–Early Learning Challenge grant application, Michigan promised to design a better-coordinated system through 3rd grade. The state has done a great deal to align early learning and K-12 standards. As described by Richard Lower, Director of the Office of Great Start's Office of Preschool and Out-of-School Time Learning:

> We have ensured that our standards align and we have crosswalks across all domains of K-12. We did that in 2013 intentionally so that we can ensure that any revisions didn't go out of scope. So the issue of having alignment between early childhood standards and quality is not so much an issue of

do they exist, are they valid, are they high quality—the main issue that I see is a lack of clear communication and understanding that standards exist to begin with.

But some educators persist in believing that early education is just babysitting. For that reason, the Department continues to encounter resistance to its attempts to integrate pre-K and K–12 standards. Lower continued:

> The problem is that people don't recognize that [early learning] standards exist and that [early learning] is not babysitting. There's an expectation that if standards do exist they should be aligned and they should set the foundation for a progression through K–12, and they do. But the issue is k-3 teachers and administrators, in particular, have no real understanding about the fact that early childhood has standards and that they are set at a high level—many times in several areas much higher than even when the kindergarten standards kick into place . . . I think that is the biggest barrier and it is going to be a key part of the k-3 classroom standards work.

However, Joan Firestone, Early Childhood Director of Oakland Schools, expressed concern that tighter alignment between preK and K–12 may result in the K–12 community pushing down developmentally inappropriate practices to the preschool level, compromising GSRP's well-developed standards. She was particularly concerned about the possibility of preK being folded into the K–12 funding system. Firestone explained:

> I would hate to see that. I don't care if we get more funding, but [as an intermediate school district director] I have no oversight at all for our K–12 programs in the way that I have oversight over GSRP. Our intermediate school district has kindergarten classrooms with 35 kids and one adult. We have kindergarten classrooms where the curriculum is not necessarily appropriate for kids at that age. If someone asks us for our opinion we could give it, but we can't impact that [because we don't hold the purse strings or make the rules]. Unless we have these rules for GSRP about class size, qualifications, staff, assessments, and curriculum, people will do inappropriate things.

Additional efforts to align preK practices with kindergarten expectations are taking place through the Department of Education's kindergarten entry assessment pilot. The kindergarten entry assessment indicates a child's level of readiness. The tool that is used, Teaching Strategies

GOLD, is an ongoing observational assessment covering the five essential domains of school readiness—language and literacy, mathematics, approaches toward learning, physical well-being and motor development, and social and emotional development—and it is aligned with the state's standards for children ages 3–5.[59] The assessment enables teachers and administrators to observe how individual children or groups of children are progressing toward Michigan's readiness standards.

One teacher described her process of observing a child and later inputting her reflections on that interaction into Teaching Strategies GOLD:

> The child pointed to a picture and told me that it was a picture of his family. When a student draws a picture I write on it and then I take a picture and email it to myself. I note that he is recalling what he drew, and I took pictures of him using the pencil grip because these are all notes in Teaching Strategies GOLD. We put a note in every dimension, so he's using his fingers and hands under fine motor skills with the 3-point grab. Teaching Strategies GOLD can be overwhelming to parents. But I try to explain to them that it is not a report card. We just show [the parents] where [the children] are and where we want them to be.

Initially, intermediate school district participation in the pilot was slow. One reason was teachers' understandable concern that, with the current stress on accountability, the results will be used to evaluate their performance. As Washtenaw Intermediate School District Early Childhood Director Alan Oman explained:

> Even within the Department of Education, there's a misunderstanding of what the purpose of the kindergarten entry assessment is. We have had legislators inadvertently refer to it as the kindergarten entry test or exam. As you know in education these days, testing is a hot-button issue. The other thing that is currently happening is a push for teacher evaluation being partly tied to the progress of their children. So we are very nervous about the idea of teachers being concerned about the assessment of their children and having children score really low at the beginning of the year and really high at the end of the year.

Notably, the Michigan Department of Education did not request federal funds for the implementation of the new assessment. It asked instead for funds to develop material that would help families understand the meaning of the kindergarten entry assessment results.[60]

Parents are not the only stakeholders that the Department needs to educate about the assessment. The Office of Great Start is also working with the Division of Accountability Services, which is not accustomed to using an observation-based assessment. As described by Richard Lower:

> The kindergarten entry assessment is under our assessment office, yet they don't have the content expertise of observational assessment. This is a whole new arena for them because they traditionally work in direct assessment in K–12. The upside of the nationwide trend around 3rd grade reading and retention has pushed the discussion about developmentally appropriate practices on the kindergarten entry assessment in Michigan.

Kindergarten teachers and principals also need a fuller understanding of how to conduct this type of assessment. As Lower noted, "There's a need to put additional resources in place to retrain a population of teachers who didn't get training in observation assessment and are trained in direct assessment."

Michigan has made great strides improving and expanding GSRP, the centerpiece of the state's current system of early childhood supports. But Deputy Superintendent Susan Broman, members of the business community, and members of the advocacy community recognize that much more needs to be done to meet the needs of the state's youngest citizens. That is why the state is expanding its early childhood portfolio—improving birth-to-age-3 programming, boosting participation in Great Start to Quality, expanding access to teacher training, and strengthening connections between preschool and K–12 through the use of standards and a kindergarten entry assessment.

KEY TAKEAWAYS

Michigan's Great Start Readiness Program is a state-funded, targeted preschool program for 4-year-old children who have factors that place them at risk of educational failure. Michigan serves 33% of its 4-year-old population and 51% of all eligible 4-year-olds through this program in public and private settings across the state. Research conducted by HighScope Educational Research Foundation has found positive short- and long-term effects on program participants, including better kindergarten readiness, stronger reading and math proficiency, reduced retention rates, and increased graduation rates. Key takeaways include the following:

Broad-based state legislative support coupled with local advocacy efforts and a focus on the many benefits of pre-K has enabled early education to stay above the political fray. Because pre-K was not seen as a political issue, the state was able to maintain a stable foundation of financial and legislative support even when political control of the legislature and governorship shifted from the Democratic to the Republican party. While statewide and local advocacy groups played a significant role in securing such support, so did the ongoing education of lawmakers, the availability of trustworthy research findings, and a public mandate. By keeping a focus on the wide-ranging benefits of pre-K, including improved educational outcomes and a skilled workforce, prekindergarten was understood as a win-win proposition on both sides of the aisle.

Centralizing the administration of early childhood programs encourages collaboration and coordination across the early education system. Preschool is only one of many state and federal programs designed to support the academic, health, and social development of young children. By establishing the Office of Great Start, Michigan brought the numerous programs together under a single administrative umbrella, making it possible to devise a unified vision and strategy for providing services. Even though the Office of Great Start is located in the Michigan Department of Education, there are still gaps between pre-K and the K–12 system. But the reorganization has made it easier to flag and address these gaps.

A strong role for regional government agencies strengthens capacity for program monitoring, support, and program alignment at the local level. By putting intermediate school districts in charge of local program administration, Michigan enabled programs to meet local needs while building in sufficient capacity to monitor programs and deliver support tailored to individual districts' needs. Regional administration has also fostered alignment and coordination across early education programs, such as Head Start and GSRP.

Clear, integrated standards and expectations for learning, measured by a quality rating system that integrates classroom-based support for continuous improvement, help foster program quality. Michigan has adopted a comprehensive system of standards that addresses structural elements, such as teacher qualifications, a research-based curriculum, and student–teacher ratios, as well as process elements, such as student–teacher interactions. Performance is measured through the state's Great Start to Quality rating system; onsite coaching, provided locally to every teaching team by experienced and qualified consultants, addresses weaknesses that the quality rating system reveals. This integrated and cohesive approach increases the likelihood that GSRP classrooms statewide maintain a level of quality and are engaged in a process of continuous improvement.

Disparities in local resources, capacity, and priorities can affect programming. Variation across regions in terms of qualified staff, classroom space, availability of supplemental funds, and leadership priority for early education has a tangible effect on programs. Although Michigan's Great Start to Quality system ensures a certain level of quality across the state, the state has not yet addressed regional inequities.

Though Michigan's state-funded preschool program remains a work in progress, it is strongly supported by parents, community and business leaders, and politicians of all political stripes. The program has increased access to quality preK for many of its most vulnerable 4-year-olds. The state continues to reevaluate how it can deliver more and better services to children, and to consider how a good preK program can be linked to an expanded initiative for infants and toddlers, as well as to the K–12 system.

NOTES

1. Figure includes students enrolled in Great Start Readiness Program (GSRP) and students enrolled in GSRP/Head Start blended programs.

2. French, R. (2012, September 25). Michigan's forgotten 4-year-olds: 30,000 children lose out on pre-k classes. *Bridge Magazine*. Retrieved from www.bridgemi.com/talent-education/30000-children-lose-out-pre-k-classes

3. Florian, J. E., Schweinhart, L. J., & Epstein, A. S. (1997). *Early returns: First-year report of the Michigan school readiness program evaluation*. Ypsilanti, MI: HighScope Educational Research Foundation.

4. Malofeeva, E.V., Daniel-Echols, M., & Xiang, Z. (2007). *Findings from the Michigan school readiness program 6 to 8 follow up study*. Ypsilanti, MI: HighScope Educational Research Foundation.

5. Xiang, Z., & Schweinhart, L. J. (2002). *Effects 5 years later: The Michigan School Readiness Program evaluation through age 10*. Ypsilanti, MI: HighScope Educational Research Foundation.

6. Schweinhart, L.J., Xiang, Z., Daniel-Echols, M., Browning, K., & Wakabayashi, T. (2012). *Michigan Great Start Readiness Program evaluation 2012: High school graduation and retention findings*. Ypsilanti, MI: HighScope Educational Research Foundation.

7. Michigan Department of Education (2015, May 28). *History of funding*. Retrieved from www. michigan.gov/documents/mde/GSRP_Funding_History_2015_490520_7.pdf

8. Michigan Department of Education (2015, May 28).

9. Michigan's Center for Educational Performance and Information (2016a). *Early childhood count, all ISDs, GSRP/Head Start blend and GSRP, all ISDs (2013–2014)* [Data file]. Retrieved from www.mischooldata.org/EarlyChildhood/EarlyChildhoodCount.aspx

10. Michigan Department of Education (2015, May 28).

11. Michigan's Center for Educational Performance and Information (2016b). *Early childhood count, all ISDs, GSRP /Head Start blend and GSRP, all ISDs (2014–2015)* [Data file]. Retrieved from www.mischooldata.org/EarlyChildhood/EarlyChildhoodCount.aspx

12. Michigan Department of Education (2016). *Great Start Readiness Program (GSRP) Public Act 85 of 2015 final 2015-16 state aid allocations*. Retrieved from www.michigan.gov/documents/mde/rptAllocList-2016_with_Transportation9.6.17_599860_7.pdf

13. Michigan Department of Education (2015, August 31a). *GSRP implementation manual, ISD administration of GSRP*. Retrieved from www.michigan.gov/documents/mde/ISD_Administration_of_GSRP_467935_7.pdf

14. School Aid Act of 1979, Mich. Comp. Laws § 388.1632d(13) (2016). Retrieved from legislature.mi.gov/doc.aspx?mcl-388-1632d

15. Michigan Department of Education (n.d.). *GSRP/Head Start blend: Meeting the standards*. Retrieved from www.michigan.gov/documents/mde/GSRP_Head_Start_Blend._Meeting_the_Standards_July_2014_467921_7.pdf.

16. Michigan's Center for Educational Performance and Information (2016c). *Early childhood count, all ISDs, GSRP /Head Start blend and GSRP, delivery schedule (2011-2012)* [Data file]. Retrieved from www.mischooldata.org/EarlyChildhood/EarlyChildhoodCount.aspx

17. Michigan's Center for Educational Performance and Information (2016d). *Early childhood count, all ISDs, GSRP/Head Start blend and GSRP, delivery schedule (2013-2014)* [Data file]. Retrieved from www.mischooldata.org/EarlyChildhood/EarlyChildhoodCount.aspx; Michigan's Center for Educational Performance and Information. (2016e). *Early childhood count, all ISDs, GSRP/Head Start blend and GSRP, delivery schedule (2014-2015)* [Data file]. Retrieved from www.mischooldata.org/EarlyChildhood2/EarlyChildhoodCount.aspx.

18. Michigan Department of Education (2015, August 31b). *GSRP implementation manual, recruitment and enrollment*. Retrieved from www.michigan.gov/documents/mde/Recruitment_and_Enrollment_August_2014_466772_7.pdf

19. Michigan Department of Education (2015, August 31c). GSRP Implementation manual, funding. Retrieved from www.michigan.gov/documents/mde/Funding._August_2014_466768_7.pdf.

20. United States Department of Education & United States Department of Health and Human Services (n.d.). *Race to the Top-Early Learning Chal-*

lenge grantee abstract. Retrieved from www2.ed.gov/programs/ racetothetop-earlylearningchallenge/abstracts/miabstract.pdf

21. Michigan Department of Education (2015, August 31d). *GSRP implementation manual, curriculum.* Retrieved from www.michigan.gov/documents/mde/Curriculum_437968_7.pdf

22. Michigan Department of Education (2015, August 31d).

23. Personal communication with Richard Lower, Director, Office of Preschool and Out-of-School Time Learning, Office of Great Start (2016, April 13).

24. Michigan Department of Education (2015, August 31d).

25. Family Independence Agency Budget Bill, 1998 Mich. Pub. Acts § 643, www.legislature.mi.gov/documents/publications/MPLA/1998/pa294.pdf

26. Public Sector Consultants (2000, October). *The second year: Michigan ready to succeed: Dialogue with Michigan, preliminary report to the legislature.* Lansing, MI: Public Sector Consultants.

27. Public Sector Consultants (2000, October).

28. Interview with Matt Gillard, President and CEO of Michigan's Children (2016, May 4).

29. Michigan Department of Technology, Management, and Budget (2011, August 4). *Is Michigan's economic recovery real? Re-thinking the one-state recession.* Retrieved from www.michigan.gov/documents/cgi/cgi_census_OSR_Pres_11-0804_359979_7.pdf; Michigan Department of Education (2015, May 28).

30. Florian et al. (1997).

31. Buch, L. (2012, October). State prekindergarten works: The story of Michigan's Great Start Readiness Program, 1985–2012. *Proceedings from the Annual Conference for Early Childhood Research and Evaluation 1.*

32. Malofeeva et al. (2007); Xiang & Schweinhart (2002).

33. Schweinhart et al. (2012).

34. As for graduation within 5 years, the study found a non-significant difference between the GSRP percentage (64.1%) and the control group percentage (60.3%).

35. Van Beek, M. (2013, March 4). Great myths about Great Start. *Michigan Capitol Confidential.* Retrieved from www.michigancapitolconfidential.com/18334.

36. French (2012, September).

37. Gillard (interview) (2016, May 4); Interview with Mina Hong, Senior Policy Associate, Michigan's Children (2016, May 4).

38. Interview with Michael Van Beek, Director of Research, Mackinac Center for Public Policy (2016, May 5).

39. Van Beek, M. (2013, March 5). *Testimony of early childhood education.* Retrieved from legislature.mi.gov/documents/2013-2014/CommitteeDocuments/House/Education/Testimony/HCT_EDUC-3-6- 2013(Michael Van Beek-Mackinac Center for Public Policy).pdf

40. Michigan Department of Education (2004, October 15). *Dr. Lindy Buch to head up new office in Department of Education* [Press release]. Retrieved from www.earlychildhoodmichigan.org/articles/10-04/ MDE10-15-04.htm

41. Buch (2012, October).

42. Michigan Department of Education (2015, August 31a).

43. Buch (2012, October).

44. Michigan State Board of Education. (2005). *Early childhood standards of quality for prekindergarten.* Lansing, MI: Michigan State Board of Education. Retrieved from www.michigan.gov/documents/mde/ECSQ_OK_Approved_422339_7. pdf

45. Michigan State Board of Education (2005).

46. Michigan State Board of Education (2005).

47. School Aid Act of 1979, Mich. Comp. Laws § 388.1632d(4)(j) (2016).

48. Michigan Department of Education. (2015, August 31e). *GSRP implementation manual, early childhood specialist.* Retrieved from www. michigan.gov/documents/mde/Early_Childhood_Specialist_437969_7. pdf.

49. Michigan Department of Education (2016).

50. Interview with Joan Firestone, Early Childhood Director, Oakland Schools (2015, October 2).

51. Interview with Cheryl Granzo, Director of Early Childhood Programs, Ionia Intermediate School District (2015, September 29).

52. Granzo (interview) (2015, September 29).

53. Firestone (interview) (2015, October 2).

54. Lower (personal communication) (2016, April 13).

55. Bureau of Community and Health Systems Child Care Licensing Division (2014, January 2). Licensing rules for child-care centers. Retrieved from www. michigan.gov/documents/lara/ BCAL_PUB_8_3_16_523999_7.pdf

56. Michigan Department of Education (2015a). *Michigan is already off to a great start on its "Race to the Top."* Lansing, MI: Michigan Department of Education. Retrieved from www.michigan.gov/documents/ mde/RTTELC_Midyear_Report2015_Highlights_504317_7.pdf

57. State of Michigan (n.d.). *Michigan Race to the Top–Early Learning Challenge application for initial funding.* Retrieved from www2.ed.gov/programs/racetothetop-earlylearningchallenge/applications/michigan.pdf

58. State of Michigan (2015, June). *Michigan Race to the Top–Early Learning Challenge 2014 annual performance report.* Retrieved from www2.ed.gov/programs/racetothetop-earlylearningchallenge/2014apr/miapr2014.pdf

59. Michigan Department of Education (2015b). *Fall 2015 kindergarten entry assessment: Everything you need to know.* Retrieved from www.michigan.gov/documents/mde/Everything_You_Need_To_Know_About_ KEA_488297_7. pdf

60. United States Department of Education & United States Department of Health and Human Services (n.d.). *Race to the Top–Early Learning Challenge technical review form.* Retrieved from www2.ed.gov/programs/racetothetop-earlylearningchallenge/applications/2013-michigan-comments.doc

CHAPTER 3

West Virginia
Pre-K for All

West Virginia is perhaps best known for its coal and natural gas production, but among early education insiders, the Mountain State is increasingly known for a very different enterprise: preschool. The state's preschool program, West Virginia Pre-K (WV Pre-K), is one of only a handful of universal preschool programs nationwide, and West Virginia recently became one of six states whose preschool policies meet all 10 of the National Institute for Early Education Research's quality standards.[1]

West Virginia first funded public preschool in 1983, but the state significantly increased its investment with the creation of a universal program in 2002. Since then, the state has invested substantial time and resources into building its preschool program, expanding access and improving quality. The program has grown to serve more than 15,000 children—reaching three-quarters of the 4-year-old population—and an evaluation of the program has suggested it has positive impacts on children's school readiness at kindergarten entry.[2]

With a program built upon enterprising vision, sustained support, unrivaled collaboration, and commitment to local control, West Virginia offers important lessons on how to

- generate and maintain political support to sustain a long-term vision for state preschool;
- design and implement a preschool program that suits the state's needs and context;
- feasibly and sustainably fund a universal preschool program;
- build governance structures that foster interagency cooperation at both the local and state levels; and
- design and implement a quality improvement process that balances state standardization and local flexibility.

WV Pre-K has become an anchor of the state's early childhood efforts; however, this progress has not been without challenges. Among them:

a limited state budget, turf wars among collaborating agencies, and the difficulty of developing a data system to support continuous quality improvement in a decentralized program.

This case study begins with an overview of West Virginia's state preschool program and then explores four dimensions of the state's story: the political context, program administration and management, program quality, and next steps for the state. It concludes with key takeaways from West Virginia's experience implementing universal pre-K.

STATE-FUNDED PRESCHOOL IN A NUTSHELL

West Virginia initially authorized school districts to run publicly funded preschool programs in 1983, but the state's early childhood efforts received a significant boost in 2002 with the creation of a voluntary universal preschool program for all 4-year-olds and for 3-year-olds with special needs.[3] West Virginia Pre-K is designed to support school readiness for all of the state's young children—a commitment that is exemplified by its emphasis on universal access and inclusion for children with special needs.[4] Although many other state and federal programs serving young children exist in West Virginia, WV Pre-K is the largest of the state's early childhood efforts; in 2012, for example, the program received 85% of West Virginia's total early childhood investment.[5]

Access to Preschool Is Universal

WV Pre-K offers universal access to preschool. No waitlists are allowed for the state preschool program; all 4-year-olds and all 3-year-olds with an identified special need must be offered placement in a WV Pre-K classroom if their families decide to enroll them.[6] The state officially implemented this universal access policy in the 2012–2013 school year, following a decade of capacity building and enrollment growth (see Figure 3.A online).

Because WV Pre-K is voluntary, the state does not expect to serve 100% of eligible children. Instead, it has steadily worked toward serving 80% of 4-year-olds, a target that was set early in the program's history to gauge implementation.[7] The state is rapidly approaching that goal; in 2013–2014, the latest year for which a participation rate is available from the state, West Virginia served an estimated 75% of its 4-year-olds.[8] This participation rate is high relative to other states; the National Institute for Early Education Research ranks West Virginia fifth in access to preschool for 4-year-olds and seventh in access for 3-year-olds.[9] In 2014–2015, WV Pre-K enrolled 15,472

Table 3.1. Key Facts About West Virginia Pre-K

Element	
Number of children served	15,472 children in 2014–2015[i]
Age	4-year-old children and 3-year-old children with an identified special need
Eligibility	Universally available
Length of program day	Determined locally:[ii] • Full-day (93% of classrooms) • Part-day (7% of classrooms)
Maximum class size	20
Teacher-child ratio	1:10 or better
Administration	• The Department of Education, in cooperation with the Department of Health and Human Resources, administers the program at the state level. • School districts, in cooperation with other local early childhood stakeholders, administer the program at the county level.
Setting	School districts collaborate with a variety of partners to offer preschool classes: • Head Start (61%) • School districts alone (21%) • Center-based child care (15%) • Head Start and center-based child care (3%)
Curriculum	Counties select from three state-approved choices:[iii] • Creative Curriculum for Preschool (used by 97% of classrooms in 2008–2009)[iv] • HighScope Preschool Curriculum and Assessment • HighReach Curriculum for Pre-K

i. Unpublished data from the West Virginia Department of Education (personal communication, November 6, 2015).

ii. Full-day programs are 24 or more hours per week; part-day programs are 14–23 hours per week.

iii. West Virginia Department of Education. *Official multiple list*. Retrieved from wvde.state. wv.us/materials/2010/2011/UniversalPre-K.html

iv. Templeton, R., Dozier, J., & Boswell, L. (2009). *Universal access to pre-k in West Virginia*. Retrieved from sites.google.com/a/wvde.k12.wv.us/wv-universal-pre-k-county-administrators-summer-institute-2009/Home/july-9-2009/universal-access-to-pre-k-in-west-virginia

Table 3.1. Continued

Minimum teacher qualifications	Lead teachers must have: • West Virginia teaching license with early education or preschool special needs endorsement • Professional teaching certificate with early childhood, preschool education, or preschool special needs endorsement, or • BA in child development, early childhood, or occupational development with early childhood emphasis. Assistant teachers must have: • High school degree and • Early Childhood Classroom Assistant Teacher Authorization (requires Child Development Associate credential or equivalent coursework).
Coaching for teachers	Determined locally
Wraparound services	Children receive a variety of wraparound services, including: • Health, vision, dental, and hearing screenings for all children and • Additional screenings and support services determined locally.v

Family engagement	Programs must offer:
	
	• Minimum of two face-to-face parent-teacher conferences each year.
	
	• Additional outreach, including:
	
	  – parent communication through newsletters, phone calls, home visits, and/or email;
	
	  – encouragement for parents/guardians to participate in classroom activities;
	
	  – communication and support services for families who speak a language other than English.

v. Barnett, W. S., Carolan, M. E., Squires, J. H., Brown, K. C., & Horowitz, M. (2015). *The state of preschool 2014*. Retrieved from http://nieer.org/sites/nieer/files/Yearbook2014_full3.pdf

Source: Office of Early Learning, West Virginia Department of Education. (n.d.). *Overview of West Virginia Universal Pre-K: WVBE Policy 2525—West Virginia's universal access to a quality early education system, 2014–2015*. Retrieved from https://wvde.state.wv.us/oel/docs/wv-prek-overview.pdf; W. Va. Code R. §§ 126-28-1-22 (2015), available at http://apps.sos.wv.gov/adlaw/csr/ruleview.aspx?document=9959

children. This figure includes more than 14,000 4-year-olds, 1,400 with identified special needs, and approximately 930 3-year-olds with identified special needs.[10] Dual-language learners account for a small portion of West Virginia's preschool-age population and WV Pre-K enrollments.[11]

Most Programs Are Full-Day

WV Pre-K operating schedules are determined locally, but state policy requires providers to operate at least 14 hours per week and 128 instructional days per school year (minimum 4 days per week). A large majority (93%) of state preschool providers offer full-day programs, or 24 or more hours of instruction per week (see Figure 3.B online). All WV Pre-K providers offer at least 4 days of instruction per week during the academic year, and 16% of classrooms offer 5 days of instruction.[12] Beginning in the 2016–2017 school year, state preschool providers were required to offer at least 25 hours of instructional time each week for the length of the school year.[13]

WV Pre-K Is a Collaborative Endeavor

County boards of education are primarily responsible for the provision of state preschool.[14] However, state policy requires that county boards contract with community partners such as Head Start grantees, center-based child-care providers, and private preschool providers to jointly run at least half of their classrooms.[15] In West Virginia, these classrooms are known as "collaborations" or "collaborative settings." Nearly 80% of WV Pre-K's classrooms are collaborative, but the form of these collaborations varies among and within counties based on the contracts negotiated between county boards of education and local partners.[16] Strategies for collaboration range from shared administration of classrooms to subcontracting a state preschool classroom to a community partner. The state took a pragmatic approach when it decided to require local collaborations; these partnerships are designed to ensure that county boards of education engage with other early care and education providers to fully utilize existing capacity and resources for preschool before opening new classrooms.[17]

As a result of these collaborations, West Virginia provides state preschool in a variety of settings, including public schools, child-care centers, private preschools, and community-based organizations.[18] This mixed delivery approach offers choices for families and helped to sustain the program's rapid growth throughout the 2000s.[19] Counties determine the exact distribution and location of WV Pre-K classrooms based on their needs and the existing mix of local preschool providers.[20]

Counties Select from State-Approved Curricula

West Virginia policy requires that state preschool classrooms employ a research-based curriculum and assessment system. Each of the state's counties selects a system from a state-approved list. Most counties (97%) use Creative Curriculum for Preschool, although HighScope Preschool Curriculum and Assessment and HighReach Curriculum for Pre-K are also approved.[21] Counties are also permitted to use supplemental curricular materials, so long as they are evidence based and "support the philosophy and techniques of the comprehensive curriculum."[22]

WV Pre-K Relies on Multiple Funding Streams

West Virginia finances its state preschool program primarily through a combination of state and federal funds. The state school aid funding formula determines the state allocation for WV Pre-K each year and has offered a relatively stable source of support for the program over time (see Figure 3.C online). State school aid funds are disbursed to districts on a per-pupil basis for children ages 4 and over enrolled in a public school program; as a result, the state's total investment in WV Pre-K has grown throughout the program's history, mirroring enrollment trends (see Figure 3.1).[23]

These state investments comprise the majority of the funding for the program; in fiscal year 2012, West Virginia contributed over $86.2 million in state school aid to WV Pre-K, nearly two-thirds of total funding.

In addition, the program draws on several federal funding streams, including Head Start, Child Care Development Fund, Temporary Assistance for Needy Families, Title I, and Part B of the Individuals with Disabilities Education Act (see Table 3.2). Funds from these sources totaled over $48.4 million in fiscal year 2012. Federal contributions increase the pool of available funds considerably, accounting for about one-third of the program's support.[24] These federal funding streams entirely support the enrollment of 3-year-olds with special needs in WV Pre-K due to age restrictions in the state funding formula.[25] For 4-year-olds, federal funds are combined with state funds—a process often referred to as blending or braiding—at the local level to enhance the implementation of the program. Local contributions, which are not required, comprise 1% of overall funding for WV Pre-K.[26]

Figure 3.1. State Spending on West Virginia Pre-K Has Risen with Enrollment (measured in 2015 dollars)

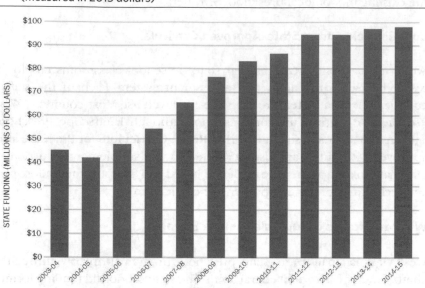

SCHOOL YEAR

Note: Figures do not include federal or local contributions.

Source: Data from the National Institute for Early Education Research annual report, *The State of Preschool.* See West Virginia data from 2004–2015 *Yearbooks.* For individual-year publications, see http://nieer.org/publications/annual-state-pre-k-reports-state-preschool-yearbooks

By combining multiple funding streams to support the program, West Virginia has come closer than many states to achieving parity between per-pupil spending in public pre-K and K–12. In 2012–2013, the total expenditure per child in WV Pre-K was approximately $9,170; that same year, the total per-pupil expenditure for West Virginia's K–12 students averaged $11,132.[27] This strategy of braiding and blending funding streams has made a universal program affordable for the state, but some advocates and administrators have expressed concerns that changes to the Head Start Performance Standards could create fiscal problems for the program. The draft Performance Standards require Head Start grantees to prioritize serving younger children in areas with public preschool programs for 4-year-olds, a change that could diminish the amount of federal funding available for WV Pre-K in the future.[28]

Table 3.2. West Virginia Pre-K Is Funded Primarily by State and Federal Sources

Funding Source	Description[i]	Funding Amount
State	State funds make up the majority of West Virginia Pre-K funding and come mainly from the state school aid formula. These funds are distributed on a per-pupil basis to school districts.	$86 million in 2012–2013 from state school aid
Federal	Providers rely on funding from various federal sources to support West Virginia Pre-K enrollment, including: • Head Start • Federal child-care programs • The Individuals with Disabilities Education Act (IDEA), Part B • Title I	$48.4 million in 2012–2013 from: • Head Start: $36.7 million • Federal child-care programs: $5.4 million[ii] • IDEA, Part B: $4.2 million • Title I: $2.1 million
Local	Local spending on state preschool varies by county, and has traditionally been limited.[iii]	$1.2 million statewide in 2012–2013; amount varies by county.

i. Interview with Janet Bock-Hager, Virginia (Ginger) Huffman, Rhonda Fisher, and Lisa Ray, West Virginia Department of Education Coordinators on October 23, 2015; Interview with Melanie Clark, Program Manager, Family Child Care Regulations, West Virginia Department of Health and Human Resources, and Melissa Smith, Early Care and Education Specialist, West Virginia Department of Health and Human Resources on October 19, 2015.

ii. Includes funds from the Child Care Development Fund, Child Care and Development Block Grant, and Temporary Assistance for Needy Families.

iii. Some districts provide in-kind support for the program, and these contributions may not be fully captured in the estimated funding amount.

POLITICS OF EARLY EDUCATION

West Virginia Pre-K emerged from the final days of the 2002 legislative session, championed by the Chair of the West Virginia Senate Education Committee, Lloyd Jackson. The program represented the culmination of years of discussion about early childhood education in the state, although the program's form—a universal preschool program for 4-year-olds—was unexpected. WV Pre-K has continued to benefit from strong political support and legislative leadership since its inception, deeply entrenching the program in West Virginia's political and educational landscape. Although West Virginia's state politics have experienced a dramatic shift in recent years—in 2014, Republicans gained control of the state legislature for the first time since 1931—WV Pre-K remains firmly ingrained in the state.[29]

Growing Support for Early Childhood Education

In the years before the passage of WV Pre-K, political leaders in West Virginia became increasingly supportive of early childhood education and interested in the positive impact it could have in the rural, high-poverty state.[30] By 2002, when WV Pre-K passed, the list of supporters for early learning initiatives included leaders in the West Virginia Senate, Governor Bob Wise, and the State Superintendent of Schools. Although widespread, support was not universal; some members of the legislature, both Republicans and Democrats, including the Chairs of the House Education and Finance Committees, were initially resistant to making significant public investments in early childhood education.[31] As one advocate noted:

> We've never run into anyone who's said, "We don't like the idea of young children getting off to a good start." Ever. On any side of the spectrum. Where the problem comes is the funding issue. They're all for it, at some level, as long as somebody else can pay for it.

Even so, Senator Lloyd Jackson, the author of the universal preschool bill, notes that West Virginia generally "had very supportive governors, very supportive legislators, and great support from outside."

Several non-state organizations facilitated the growing interest in, and support for, early childhood education by introducing West Virginia's political leaders to the research base on early childhood education. Senator Jackson, for example, credits two key organizations with introducing him to literature on the benefits of early childhood interventions, saying:

> I was active in the Southern Regional Education Board and the Education Commission of the States. Both organizations were becoming heavily interested in early childhood education. [The staff at the Education Commission of the States] was really interested in the brain development piece and the folks at the Southern Regional Education Board were particularly interested in early childhood as it relates to poverty, a problem that plagues far too many of us in the South.

Through his engagement with staff at these organizations, Senator Jackson came to appreciate the importance of the early years and the key role early childhood programs could have in improving educational outcomes in West Virginia. Senator Robert Plymale, another influential early education advocate in the state legislature, similarly credits the Southern Regional Education Board and a national organization, the National Conference of State Legislatures, with introducing him to the benefits of early childhood education.

Although he found the research base compelling, Senator Jackson also cites his personal experience as a father in helping to shape his interest in early learning:

> My kids were probably among a small handful of kids in Lincoln County who had [the opportunity to attend pre-K] because of the resources we had. I thought that was incredibly unfair. I saw the advantages that my children had that other children just didn't get and I just knew we could do it. Other states had started doing it and I thought we could, too.

This growing support for early childhood initiatives among West Virginia's leaders helped to set the stage for early care and education policymaking in the state.

A Need for Action: Legislative Champions Emerge

As support for early childhood was growing, West Virginia's educational system was experiencing demographic changes that imparted a sense of urgency in the discussion of education proposals and influenced the shape of the state's eventual early childhood program.[32] Throughout the 1990s, West Virginia counties had been experiencing declining enrollments in public schools; the problem was particularly acute in certain areas, such as McDowell County, that were "losing enrollment almost overnight," according to Senator Jackson. These declining enrollments presented a problem for school districts, which receive state funding on a per-pupil basis and therefore "need as many kids as they can get in their seats in October" when the annual headcount takes place. In an effort to stabilize enrollment counts, some school districts began enrolling 4-year-olds in public preschool. While serving these preschool-aged children meant maintaining level funding for schools, the circumstances also created, as Jackson described, "a real competition between Head

Start and schools for the enrollment of 4-year-olds." This strain was elevated further by the concerns of private child-care providers, who feared adverse financial impacts from declining 4-year-old enrollments.[33]

The early childhood proposal that dominated West Virginia's policy conversation in the late 1990s and early 2000s was West Virginia Educare. The program, which had no relation to the Educare Learning Network's widely known birth-to-5 early education model, was started as a pilot in 1998. Through the program, West Virginia offered grants to create local consortia that would identify and address the needs of children in their communities from birth to school entry; the West Virginia Educare grants were also known as "glue money" because they brought early childhood stakeholders together.[34] Advocates and legislators made several attempts to expand and codify the program, including a 2002 proposal to implement it statewide. As the discussion around West Virginia Educare developed that year, two issues emerged. First, although the program had many supporters it also had skeptics, which left the program politically vulnerable. As one former state administrator said, "The concern I had was that we were creating totally new programs out of whole cloth; we were ignoring existing programs—both education and child care." Second, and perhaps more important, the West Virginia Educare proposal was perceived by the legislature as prohibitively expensive. According to the Senator, "We said, 'We can't afford that right now. We can't pull that off right now.' But we knew we needed to do something."

With West Virginia Educare appearing increasingly untenable and the end of the legislative session fast approaching, Senator Jackson introduced legislative language to create a universal preschool program for 4-year-olds, embedded within a broad-ranging education reform bill. Although early childhood initiatives were popular among many legislators, they also tended to generate opposition from members of the House of Delegates, who were reluctant to make significant investments in the programs. In Jackson's words:

> [The legislature] understood it was important to have early childhood programs. They got it. They understood the message. They just, like most legislatures, didn't want to get stuck with a big price tag they couldn't pay.

The universal pre-K proposal succeeded largely due to intensive political negotiations in the legislature on the last day of the 2002 session.[35] The content of these negotiations remains largely unknown to the public, although the proposal likely benefited from its relatively low initial cost, its effort to maximize the use of existing federal funds, and its association with the larger education reform bill, which included teacher pay raises and other policies that appealed to education interest groups.[36]

The passage of the universal pre-K proposal created a program that dramatically increased access to preschool while solving several of the early childhood challenges West Virginia faced. In particular, the law required education agencies to work collaboratively with other early care and education stakeholders, including Head Start and child-care providers, to offer state preschool—a feature designed to take advantage of existing program capacity, diffuse tension among providers, and maximize resources for the program. The law affirmed the eligibility of county boards of education to receive state school aid dollars for 4-year-olds, a funding strategy that avoids annual appropriations battles and provides relative fiscal and political stability for the program. Importantly, however, the bill explicitly prohibits districts from using state school aid funds for younger children, eliminating the possibility of funding 3-year-old enrollments with state school aid, a political compromise that continues to disappoint some early childhood advocates.[37] The bill also legislated a 10-year implementation timeline for universal pre-K. This gradual rollout averted a precipitous increase in state and district expenditures, making the proposal more politically palatable, while helping districts avoid deficits—a problem that some districts had encountered with the rapid rollout of full-day kindergarten two decades earlier.[38] Phasing in the program also offered time to build implementation capacity at the state and local levels. And, while the bill assigned ultimate oversight of the program to state-level agencies, it maintained a meaningful role for localities, holding county boards of education directly responsible for the provision of state preschool.[39]

Many state administrators, advocates, and policy makers acknowledge Senator Jackson's important role as champion of West Virginia's universal preschool program. The extent of his role is underscored by the surprise of early childhood insiders at the passage of universal pre-K. Kay Tilton, former Director of the Early Care and Education Division at the Department of Health and Human Resources, explained:

> I didn't know it was coming. Cathy [Jones, the Department of Education's Early Childhood Coordinator] said she didn't know it was coming. We were all on the phone saying, "What is this bill that passed?"

Tilton's sentiment is echoed by other members of West Virginia's early childhood circles and highlights the importance of legislative leadership in securing universal pre-K for the state. As Cathy Jones said:

I believe with all my heart that whether it's in a small town or on the state or national level, you have to have a champion. A champion who can bring people together. Senator Jackson was that person.

When Senator Jackson proposed universal pre-K for West Virginia, there was already a growing consensus around the desire and need for expanded support for early childhood education in the state. Seeing the chances of a West Virginia Educare expansion dwindle during the 2002 legislative session, Jackson seized the opportunity to champion a more politically and fiscally feasible alternative: universal pre-K.

Building WV Pre-K: A Decade of Continuous Leadership

WV Pre-K has benefitted from continued political support and leadership throughout its history. In the years since the program's initial passage, political support for state preschool, and early childhood initiatives more generally, has continued to expand. Governor Earl Ray Tomblin, who was President of the Senate when WV Pre-K was created, co-authored a 2015 op-ed for *Forbes* with a call to action on early childhood initiatives for state leaders, saying:

> Now more than ever, the nation is looking to its leaders on all levels to roll up their sleeves and get things done. Communities thrive when leaders invest in smart, evidence-based programs with proven success. Quality early childhood education is a shining example.[40]

Today, WV Pre-K is broadly popular among the public and counts Governor Tomblin, the State Superintendent, and leaders from the state Board of Education among its supporters. This well of political support has helped maintain momentum for effective implementation and fostered the deep entrenchment of the program in West Virginia's educational landscape.

Despite expanded support, continued legislative leadership has been particularly vital, especially for guiding the program through its decade-long phase-in. After Senator Jackson left the state legislature in 2003, Senator Robert Plymale took up the leadership role, continuing to champion state pre-K by addressing complications that arose throughout implementation. As Senator Plymale explained:

> One of the reasons why I think we've had the continuity [in pre-K] is because we haven't changed as much in [legislative] leadership—up until re-

cently—and we've been able to keep the pedal to the metal to make sure we keep driving this.

For instance, Senator Plymale spearheaded an effort to provide state funding to develop educational pathways for early childhood educators.[41] More importantly, Senator Plymale and his colleagues in the Senate successfully protected the program from attempts to excise it from the school funding formula in 2003 and 2004—an effort that was led by the chair of the House Education Committee, Jerry Mezzatesta—and succeeded in getting preschool included in a bill to provide supplemental funding for districts experiencing enrollment growth. Then–President of the Senate Earl Ray Tomblin aided these efforts; as former State Superintendent of Schools Steven Paine explained, "At the time, the President of the Senate was Earl Ray Tomblin, who's now our Governor, and he supported Robert Plymale strongly." Political threats to the program have receded over time, driven by a number of factors, including the growing popularity of WV Pre-K and Mezzatesta's departure from the legislature.[42] Paine described the importance of legislative leadership for the program, saying:

> Robert [Plymale] was the visionary. And Lloyd [Jackson]. They both clearly saw that you just keep building the policy structure to support the high-quality program and eventually it'll come around.

Researchers also played an important role in assuring WV Pre-K's expansion. The Center for Business and Economic Research at Marshall University in Huntington, for example, produced state-specific analyses about the long-term economic benefits of early childhood investments, findings that were compelling to state leaders. As Senator Plymale explained, "The Center for Business and Economic Research was a major player because they did a research piece that made it [the research] a little more credible from a West Virginia standpoint." Program administrators have also called on other research organizations, such as the National Institute for Early Education Research at Rutgers University, to visit the state and discuss the evidence base on early childhood education with policymakers.[43] This ongoing discussion of research has continued to build momentum and support for early childhood programs, including state preschool, over time.

After more than a decade of implementation, WV Pre-K has become institutionalized in West Virginia, insulating it from the politics that so often surround large-scale early childhood investments.

PROGRAM ADMINISTRATION AND MANAGEMENT

The administration and management of WV Pre-K reflect the design features set forth in the universal pre-K law. Interagency groups form the core of the governance structure at both the local and state levels, helping to coordinate administration across several agencies and levels of government. Further, the program's administration maintains an important role for local leadership, promoting adaptation to suit local needs.

WV Pre-K Governance: Designed for Collaboration

West Virginia's education agencies have central roles in implementing WV Pre-K. At the state level, for example, the Board of Education codifies universal pre-K policy. Locally, county boards of education are ultimately responsible for the provision of the program. At the same time, the program's governance structures are designed to support the mandate for collaboration by involving various early childhood education stakeholders.

Cooperation at the State Level to Support Local Implementation. From WV Pre-K's inception, state law has mandated that the Department of Education share oversight of the program with the Department of Health and Human Resources, which administers child-care subsidies and houses the Head Start State Collaboration Office. Specifically, the pre-K bill dictated a role for both departments in developing state pre-K policy and approving counties' plans for implementing the program.[44] For Senator Jackson, this joint oversight was a crucial response to the tensions that had been building across the state; in his words, "[The legislature] wanted to be sure Head Start had a real role, that the Department of Health and Human Resources had a voice in this." To foster this shared leadership, the state created the Universal Pre-K Steering Team, a key element of the program's governance structure (see Figure 3.2).

The Universal Pre-K Steering Team is an interagency body tasked with leading much of the day-to-day implementation of WV Pre-K. This Steering Team has four members, representing the key state agencies involved in the WV Pre-K program:[45]

- the Office of Early Learning, which oversees pre-K to 5th grade within the Department of Education;
- the Office of Special Education, which is responsible for programs for children with special needs within the Department of Education;

Figure 3.2. State-Level Governance for West Virginia Pre-K Is Highly Collaborative

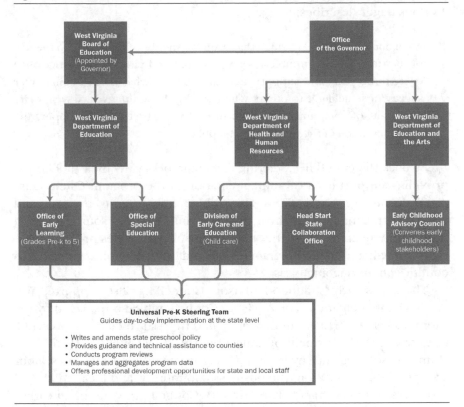

Source: W. Va. Code R. §§ 126-28-4, 126-28-18 (2015), retrieved from http://apps.sos. wv.gov/adlaw/csr/ruleview.aspx?document=9959; Interview with Janet Bock-Hager, Virginia (Ginger) Huffman, Rhonda Fisher, and Lisa Ray, West Virginia Department of Education coordinators on October 23, 2015; Interview with Steven Paine, former State Superintendent of Schools on October 19, 2015.

- the Division of Early Care and Education, which oversees child-care licensing, regulation, and subsidies within the Department of Health and Human Resources; and
- the Head Start State Collaboration Office, which is housed in the Department of Health and Human Resources and supports collaboration between Head Start, Early Head Start, and other programs.[46]

Janet Bock-Hager, the Office of Early Learning's current Steering Team representative, notes that this team is the "agent to support and deliver policy." The Steering Team is tasked with a number of important duties. As Bock-Hager describes:

> All of our decisions go through that team. We model collaboration to the rest of the state. We also troubleshoot and go out and visit every district once every three years and support them and look at what they're doing, offer suggestions, highlight to others when they're doing things very well. We're that agent of communication from district to district to help support the implementation of the universal pre-k policy.

As Bock-Hager outlines, Steering Team members view their function as providing support for local implementation of the program. One county pre-K director reported, "We've always been able to go to the state and ask for clarification on anything." The Steering Team is a source for such insights; the team manages the state pre-K policy, provides program oversight through a triennial program review, and offers technical guidance to counties on an ongoing basis.[47]

The state's Early Childhood Advisory Council has also supported WV Pre-K's implementation. The Advisory Council, which is managed by the cabinet-level Department of Education and the Arts, includes representatives from the Department of Education, the Department of Health and Human Resources, the governor's office, early childhood advocates, labor groups, higher education, the business community, and local child-care providers, among others.[48] The Advisory Council grew out of an earlier group known as PIECES (Partners Implementing an Early Care and Education System) that was formed to shepherd the state pre-K program to full implementation. The council was conceived of as a way of inviting people to the table "to guide policy, to have input, to negotiate changes" regarding West Virginia's preschool policy in the program's early years, according to Cathy Jones, one of the council's initial members.

In 2010, PIECES was replaced by the Early Childhood Advisory Council, which fulfills Head Start's mandate for a state advisory council. The Advisory Council oversees efforts to create a high-quality system of care and education for children from birth to age 8 in the state.[49] Unlike the Steering Team, which handles the myriad details in the pre-K program's implementation, the Advisory Council helps to "provide a view of the [early childhood] system as a whole" and drive the state's broader vision, according to Gretchen Frankenberry, the Advisory Council's Executive Manager. For example, the Advisory Council recently partnered with West Virginia's Early Childhood Planning Task Force to develop a proposal for a comprehensive birth-to-age-5 system in the state.

Figure 3.3. County Collaborative Teams Oversee Implementation at the Local Level

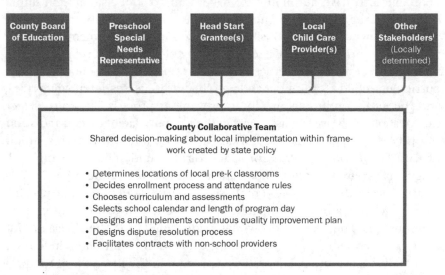

i. "Other stakeholders" may include parents, principals, classroom teachers, private preschool providers, representatives of early intervention services, and staff from child-care resource and referral agencies, among others.

Source: W. Va. Code R. §§ 126-28-4 (2015). Retrieved from apps.sos.wv.gov/adlaw/csr/ ruleview.aspx?document=9959

Both the Steering Team and the Early Childhood Advisory Council are designed to support West Virginia's mandate for collaborative implementation of the pre-K program by providing a forum for regular communication and cooperation among early childhood stakeholders.

Building Infrastructure for County-Level Collaboration. As at the state level, close cooperation between education agencies, Head Start, child care, and other early childhood stakeholders is essential for the program's implementation at the local level. Each of West Virginia's 55 counties has an interagency team, known as a county collaborative team, that oversees local implementation of the state pre-K program. As Figure 3.3 illustrates, each county's collaborative team includes, at a minimum, representatives from the county board of education, preschool special needs, child care, and Head Start; county teams also typically include a parent, a representative from early intervention services, and multiple private child-care providers, among others.[50]

Counties are required to follow state policy regarding the pre-K program, but also have autonomy to make numerous decisions with implications for the program's implementation. County collaborative teams are the primary body responsible for these local management decisions, providing a forum for joint decisionmaking at the local level. Within the framework set by the state, these teams determine the preschool calendar, curriculum, child recruitment and enrollment processes, attendance rules, and the local continuous quality improvement process. They also select the location of all pre-K classrooms in their county, facilitate contracts and resource-sharing agreements, and design the county's dispute resolution process for providers.[51] Pre-K providers directly undertake some other elements of program administration, including staff recruitment.[52]

Because of the program's emphasis on local leadership, county teams were largely responsible for managing WV Pre-K's 10-year rollout in their communities. The state set few statewide targets for the phase-in, but did require counties to create an implementation plan that included the launch of at least one collaborative classroom in the first year of the program; counties also resubmitted their implementation plans to the state for reapproval every two years until the program reached full implementation in 2012. Not all county teams were equally proactive during this time. Some counties waited until 2012 to go universal, although many others used the rollout to build capacity.[53] As one local Head Start administrator said:

> We have worked it [the implementation of universal pre-k] through very thoroughly. The state was very wise. They gave us 10 years to implement universal pre-k. That was really important. We had to do it in stages. We couldn't just say "okay, two years from now we're all going to be universal: go do it."

The 10-year timeline was generally perceived as an achievable timetable, giving counties the time to develop strong pre-K programs before being required to offer universal access.

County collaborative teams also promote relationship building between early childhood stakeholders across the state. For instance, representatives of Birth to Three, West Virginia's early intervention services, are typically included on county collaborative teams and play a critical role in referring 3-year-olds with special needs to WV Pre-K, although the programs remain distinct. The strength of these ties between WV Pre-K and other birth-to-5 programs varies, but the state has begun to recognize a need to strengthen them, as one state administrator explained:

We've got more work to do, but we're at least recognizing that we need to start talking that language [about birth to 3] more often and showing how those dots connect.

Given the key role county collaborative teams possess in shaping the program, WV Pre-K can look markedly different across counties. While acknowledging the importance of consistently strong implementation, the state also embraces this diversity of programs; WV Pre-K is built on a belief that each county is unique and that local staff are best suited to identify the county's needs. Amy Wolfe, a board member of the West Virginia Association for Young Children, summed up the state's approach to pre-K in this way:

The creation of those local collaborative teams that understood their funding stream so well could, if given the right tools and the right framework to work within, really develop programs that maximize each other's strengths as well as each other's resources.

The pre-K system is designed to empower counties to implement the program that best suits the needs of local families.

Administration and Management Challenges

WV Pre-K's strategy of gradual implementation gave the state ample time to encounter and largely address some of the obstacles associated with scaling a state pre-K program, including providing transportation and resolving turf battles among early childhood providers and agencies at the local level.

Transportation for Preschool Students. In West Virginia's large rural counties, providing transportation for state preschool students is a significant concern. West Virginia's state pre-K policy classifies transportation as a support, rather than a required service.[54] Although transportation is not mandated, state administrators acknowledge that it is a key element of the program in many parts of the state. As one state administrator said, "Transportation is not required, but a lot of counties figured out how to do it because they recognized that, for the kids who needed [pre-K] most, you've got to get them there." However, providing transportation can be a logistical and financial puzzle. As Melanie Clark, Program Manager for Family Child Care Regulations at the Department of Health and Human Resources, points out,

COLLABORATION IN ACTION: KANAWHA COUNTY

Kanawha County is West Virginia's most populous, home to the capital city, Charleston, and around 10% of the state's total population.[i] Although these factors make it something of a metropolitan outlier in a largely rural state, the county's pre-K program offers a clear illustration of the potential of WV Pre-K's collaborative model.

In Kanawha County, nearly all state pre-K classrooms are run collaboratively.[ii] WV Pre-K is offered at public school sites, where classrooms are funded by both Head Start and the county board of education, and at center-based child-care sites, where classrooms are funded by braiding child-care subsidies and county board of education dollars. Regardless of the setting in which pre-K is offered, all parents in Kanawha County enroll their children through a universal online application and all of Kanawha's WV Pre-K participants are tracked using a single data system, which was customized for use by the county. Further, the salaries of staff, including teachers, family service workers, and the county pre-K coordinator, are paid using a combination of funds from Head Start and the county board of education. This unique braiding strategy ensures that all children receive access to all program resources, including family service workers, regardless of whether their circumstances would traditionally qualify them for such supports.[iii]

This integration of services, so seamless that only a handful of people in the county can differentiate Head Start and pre-K participants, illustrates a complex and highly integrated approach to fulfilling the pre-K mandate. Carol Fleming, the county's Director of Preschool, explained "[Collaboration] can be a little complex, but it works. I think the key is having one central point. . . . Instead of having three people manage money, you have one central point and one central director. I think that is important." This strategy has enabled the county to offer comparable experiences for all students, regardless of their financial situation. As Fleming describes, "Our goal here, when we blended this program, was to treat all children the same and to make sure all children received the same services."

i. U.S. Census Bureau, Population Estimates, 2015 county total population estimates, factfinder.census.gov/faces/nav/jsf/pages/index.xhtml

ii. Office of Early Learning, West Virginia Department of Education. (n.d.). *Overview of West Virginia Universal Pre-K: WVBE Policy 2525—West Virginia's universal access to a quality early education system, 2014–15*. Retrieved from wvde.state.wv.us/oel/docs/wv-prek-overview.pdf

iii. Interview with Carol Fleming, Director of Preschool, Kanawha County Schools on October 20, 2015.

"[T]ransportation is so expensive, especially for that young of children." The Rural School and Community Trust reports that K–12 schools in West Virginia spend $7.40 on transportation for every $1 invested for instructional expenses, the highest of any state in the nation.[55] There are also safety concerns specific to the transportation of children as young as 4 years old, including the need for supervision during the bus ride.

Despite these impediments, many counties have found ways to offer transportation to WV Pre-K students, often through collaborative agreements. In some areas, such as Kanawha County, the county collaborative team has completed waivers allowing pre-K students to ride the local elementary school buses, avoiding a significant expense by leveraging existing busing routes. Other counties have been more creative in their solutions. Clark describes one county's unique transportation arrangement:

> There was a county where the county school system collaborated with Head Start for transportation. The Head Start provided the buses, the bus driver, and the bus aide, and the county supplied all the gas and maintenance for those buses. And that way they picked up all pre-K children within the county.

These types of in-kind agreements are common across West Virginia, with its highly collaborative and localized system of governance. Not all counties provide transportation, but those who do see the benefit. As one child-care provider in a rural and highly impoverished West Virginia county said, "I believe that a lot of children get to pre-K that would not if they didn't have that transportation."

Making Collaboration Work: Overcoming Turf Wars. WV Pre-K relies heavily on collaboration to function, an arrangement that rests upon a complex web of interagency and interpersonal relationships. As Bill Huebner, the former Director of Head Start State Collaboration and a member of the first Universal Pre-K Steering Team, said, "My mantra throughout my time working in the state was 'it's all about relationships.'" Building and maintaining these collaborative relationships among partners at the local level has complicated program implementation. The pre-K program emerged in an era when tensions were building between Head Start and public schools in some West Virginia counties over the enrollment of 4-year-olds—a challenge that was compounded by the concerns of private child-care providers, some of whom anticipated "the school bus coming to take [their] children."[56] Promoting collaboration among these stakeholders has been a central focus of WV Pre-K's implementation.

During the program's early years, the Universal Pre-K Steering Team played an important role in fostering trust among collaborating partners. From the program's start, the Steering Team traveled extensively throughout the state, convening face-to-face meetings to address conflicts among partners and troubleshooting everything from reimbursing programs for student meals to ensuring Head Start standards were implemented in blended classrooms.[57] In addition to helping counties tackle these implementation challenges, the Steering Team provided a model of collaboration for counties. As Geraldine Sawrey, a former administrator in Cabell County, explained:

> One thing that was very important about our program, and I think to other people across the state, too, was the modeling that went on at the state level for what was supposed to happen. [Members of the Steering Team] didn't speak from just their perspective. They all knew what was at stake, and if the Department of Health and Human Resources person was out to talk to you about pre-k, they were saying the same thing as the Department of Education person or the Head Start person. They were singing from the same hymnbook, off the same page. They really modeled at the state level what needed to be done.

The Steering Team bolstered the legitimacy of the policy model put forth by the legislature by providing an example of collaboration and helping to foster the rapport needed for successful cooperation.

Leadership at the county level has also facilitated collaboration. As Amy Wolfe, a board member of the West Virginia Association for Young Children, noted:

> That these agencies all work together and communicate with each other and make the best effort to improve everybody's experience—it's remarkable. And I think that leadership is to be credited with that. You know, there were people who saw this as possible. Instead of being territorial, they found a way to make the best things happen for each stakeholder in the equation.

In some counties, local leaders and administrators acted as program advocates, helping to generate buy-in among local stakeholders. In other cases, counties with strong cultures of collaboration shared their expertise with others, acting as peer mentors. In one case, a county pre-K administrator helped foster dialogue in a neighboring county that was struggling with handling paperwork in developing a shared pre-K enrollment process:

> They want[ed] to do two enrollment packets; [they were saying] every parent must do two enrollment packets—one for Head Start and one for the county. And I said, "Why? Why are you making parents do double work?" "Well, we [the county board of education] want the originals." I said, "Okay, why can't you make a copy? Why can't they [Head Start] make you a copy? If they need the originals, why can't you just have a copy? That's what I do." And after we went back and forth, they got it down to [where] the parent only has to do one enrollment packet.

Addressing these practical details facilitates effective collaboration among organizations with competing regulations. Local leaders have been critical to the success of the program's collaborative model.

Sources in the state also indicate that the existence of a widely shared vision for pre-K in West Virginia has made collaboration easier to achieve. Talking to WV Pre-K staff, the importance of focusing on young children and families is a consistent refrain. In the words of one local center director, "Our priority was children and families. We didn't have any political agendas. You have to put those behind you and work for the good for all." Her sentiment was echoed by a county-level administrator who said that from the start, "we [the county collaborative team members] all understood we were there for the benefit of the kids." This commitment to serving the state's children is invoked most often when providers and administrators encounter difficulties, such as managing the numerous, sometimes competing regulations applied to collaborating programs. As one child-care center director, who runs WV Pre-K classrooms in partnership with the local board of education, explained:

> You know, we're a center that tries our best to always be compliant with all the regulations, even though they're innumerable some days. But we still try to comply because we know the bottom line is that it's for the safety and the health and the well-being of the children.

Janet Bock-Hager, a Department of Education Coordinator and Steering Team member, affirmed this perspective: "Especially when counties are struggling, we try to remind them of all of the benefits that these things can potentially provide for them, through collaboration."

Most in the state consider the worst of these battles over, although many, including former Cabell County administrator Geraldine Sawrey, also readily acknowledge that program partners "still have those territorial things from time to time" and that the need for ongoing relationship building has continued throughout the life of the program. The relationship between child-care providers and local education agencies, for example, remains a source of tension in some areas, with some child-care providers believing that WV Pre-K has caused centers to close. As one private child-care center director explained:

> I like the collaboration that I've experienced because I feel that it has bumped up the quality of my program overall, but I know there are centers across the state that have closed because they've lost their 4-year-olds. . . . It's happened in counties I know and that's scary.

While WV Pre-K achieved universal access in 2012–2013, the program continues to grow and evolve through policy revisions, personnel changes, and quality improvement efforts. As a result, forging strong relationships and fostering effective collaboration is an ongoing process.

GETTING TO QUALITY

Quality has been a focus of the state pre-K program since its inception. As Senator Jackson, one of the program's champions, argued, "You need quality. . . . We need to be doing everything we can to be sure these kids are learning, are being stimulated, are getting prepared for what's coming." County-led continuous quality improvement plans have emerged as the heart of WV Pre-K's quality promotion strategy in recent years. While recognizing the importance of this local involvement, state officials have also established robust quality standards and technical assistance channels to support local teams in delivering a strong program. The result is a system designed to balance state standards with local flexibility.

Setting the Stage for Local Success: State Standards and Support

Although West Virginia's quality improvement strategy is focused primarily on county efforts, state agencies serve an important role in creating the conditions for success at the local level by developing robust state quality standards and offering multiple channels for technical assistance.

LEARNING THROUGH PLAY

During free choice time in one WV Pre-K classroom, the class buzzes with activity. In one corner, four children don costumes and pretend to shop, while one of the classroom's two teachers, tiara-clad, engages them in conversation about their purchases. In the classroom's library area, children work together to solve puzzles, practicing cooperation and problem-solving skills. Others stand at the classroom's easels, mixing up new colors of paint to use and developing their creativity, fine motor skills, and scientific thinking in the process. These playful activities, chosen by children and guided by their teachers, provide engaging opportunities to learn and develop important skills and knowledge.

Source: Classroom visit in anonymous West Virginia county.

A Commitment to Policy Development: Building Robust State Standards. From the start, West Virginia's pre-K leaders gave careful attention to the development of a strong state pre-K policy with robust quality standards to guide the implementation of the program. West Virginia's state pre-K policy, commonly known as Policy 2525, was written in 2003. The Steering Team endeavored to make the policy exhaustive. As Cathy Jones, a former Department of Education coordinator and one of Policy 2525's original architects, said, it included "everything from ratios . . . [to] developmentally appropriate practice." In drafting the policy, the state drew on models from national organizations, including the National Association for the Education of Young Children and the National Institute for Early Education Research. It also took West Virginia's existing early childhood infrastructure into account. As Jones described, the drafting committee considered the state's context:

> [I]f we involved our Head Start and child-care partners, what would be a reasonable expectation for personnel, teacher credentials, what would be a reasonable expectation as far as how this is funded. And how we didn't step on the toes of what was already out there.

Jones and her colleagues also drew on their own expertise as early childhood practitioners throughout the process:

> We tried really hard to put in Policy 2525 things that we believed as practitioners of early childhood were important, [such as] developmentally ap-

propriate practice. We even went so far as to talk about things like what materials needed to be in the classroom. What a schedule should look like. What shouldn't be there.

The result was a policy that outlined, in generous detail, a vision for state preschool with clear expectations for classrooms and practitioners. For example, the policy required the use of curricula that draw on "a wide variety of learning experiences, materials and equipment, and instructional strategies" and the creation of learning environments that incorporate learning centers, nonstereotypical images, and materials that are organized, labeled, and accessible to children.[58] The policy also explicitly prohibited instructional practices that are considered inappropriate for preschool-aged children, such as "the use of student desks, worksheets, [and] long periods of sitting."[59]

West Virginia's dedication to policy development focused on program quality has continued. Over time, members of the Steering Team and their associated agencies have taken advantage of their ability to "crack open policy" and "bring stakeholders together" to enhance the quality of WV Pre-K by elevating the standards, according to Clayton Burch, the West Virginia Department of Education's Chief Academic Officer, who oversees the Division of Teaching and Learning. Policy 2525 has been revised seven times since 2003, with an eighth revision likely to follow the approval of new federal Head Start requirements.[60] Many of these amendments have been designed to increase program quality and ensure the policy's alignment with state and federal code. Past changes include raising the bar for teacher credentials, expanding the minimum number of operating hours, and updating the requirements for counties' continuous quality improvement efforts.[61] In addition to official policy revisions, state administrators have intermittently published policy guidance to clarify expectations for county and program staff.

At present, Policy 2525 requires classes of no more than 20 children, lead teachers with at least a bachelor's degree in early childhood education, ongoing family engagement, and a variety of additional supports, such as meals and health screenings. The policy also emphasizes the role of developmentally appropriate curriculum and assessment that supports the development of the whole child in WV Pre-K classrooms. For example, under Policy 2525, pre-K curricula are expected to "valu[e] exploration, creativity, and construction as the child's primary learning approaches" and "provid[e] them [children] with opportunities to make meaningful choices." The policy also calls for a curriculum that integrates development across all domains and "build[s] on what children already know."[62]

MEAL TIME AS LEARNING TIME

Mid-morning in one West Virginia Pre-K classroom, eight children wash their hands and wander to the table, where a family-style breakfast awaits. Encouraged by the teacher to begin the meal, one child reaches for a bowl of cereal and pours milk from a pint-sized pitcher before passing it to her neighbor, who was patiently waiting her turn. Across the table, a boy takes a helping of fruit and bread, deciding against cereal for breakfast this morning. As the children fill their plates, teachers sit down with them at the table to strike up conversation—"What did you do before you came to school today?" "How many apple slices will you eat this morning?"—and offer gentle reminders to say please and thank you to their classmates.

Though this meal is important for nourishing the children for the day to come, it offers other benefits as well. As one WV Pre-K administrator noted, "Meal time is part of early childhood [programs]. It's instructional time." In the Pre-K classroom, teachers purposefully use child-sized table-ware to give children the opportunity to build their fine motor skills and offer children a chance to choose what to eat from among multiple dishes so they learn independence and self-help skills. The teachers sit with the children during meals to model conversation and seize the opportunity to introduce new words and foods into children's repertoires. Young children learn through exploration and activity, and thoughtfully-structured meals like this one present a chance for valuable learning.

Source: Classroom visit in Kanawha County; Interview with Janet Bock-Hager, Virginia (Ginger) Huffman, Rhonda Fisher, and Lisa Ray, West Virginia Department of Education coordinators, on October 23, 2015; W. Va. Code R. §§ 126-28-11 (2015). Retrieved from apps.sos.wv.gov/adlaw/csr/ruleview.aspx?document=9959.

Further, the policy has maintained clear examples of the types of activities that are discouraged in preschool classrooms, such as extended periods of sitting or teaching content in isolation.[63] The state has carefully vetted each of the three approved comprehensive curriculum and assessment system options to ensure they align with this approach.[64] The policy also outlines clear expectations for environmental design, classroom routines and transitions, ongoing family engagement, and child guidance.[65]

The quality standards in Policy 2525 are complemented by the state's early learning standards, which were developed to guide instruction in WV Pre-K classrooms. The standards outline what young children should know and be able to do across seven content areas: social and emotional development, English language arts, mathematics, science, the arts, health and physical development, and approaches to learning.[66] The standards are research based and designed to apply to children ages 3 to 5, regardless of setting; they are also aligned with the Head Start Early Learning Outcomes Framework, state kindergarten standards, and West Virginia's formative assessment for preschoolers, the Early Learning Scale.[67] The Early Learning Scale is an ongoing observational assessment in which teachers note and record examples of individual student behavior and work across 10 items, including self-regulation, oral language, and play. It is administered during three assessment windows over the course of the pre-K year for each child and is designed to gauge children's development over time, inform instruction in pre-K classrooms, and facilitate communication with parents.[68]

State Support for Quality Improvement. Despite the high standards laid out in state policy, WV Pre-K administrators still occasionally observe practices that are at odds with the program's vision of quality, as one state administrator explained:

> We can make all these rules and have these grand plans at the state level, but that does not mean that developmentally appropriate practice is occurring in the classroom, so you need to constantly be on that ground level.

As Cathy Jones, former Early Childhood Coordinator at the West Virginia Department of Education, recalled, she would sometimes enter classrooms to see "developmentally inappropriate practice, teachers who are having children sit for long periods of time doing worksheets" after "specifically putting into policy that worksheets aren't allowed." In response, West Virginia state administrators have created multiple channels to support quality improvement and encourage instructional practices that are aligned with the program's philosophy.

County-level pre-K staff receive training and guidance throughout the year through a series of workshops and seminars provided by the Leadership System of Support. As part of this system, the Steering Team invites new county collaborative team members to an administrator workshop each fall and runs an annual conference known as the Leadership Institute that convenes county pre-K leaders and provides a forum for sharing program data and expertise.[69] In addition, state administrators conduct a review of each county's program at least once every three years. This review ensures that each county's classrooms align with state and federal policy, offers individualized technical assistance, and provides additional input for the local continuous quality improvement process.[70] The program review includes an audit of program documentation, classroom observations, and a conference with state and county staff to discuss results.[71] State and regional agencies also offer a variety of instructional resources for counties. For example, the Department of Education offers six online professional development courses that counties can offer to WV Pre-K teachers, and West Virginia's eight Regional Education Service Agencies provide a variety of professional development opportunities for counties in their service areas.[72] The state also provides reference materials—including policy crosswalks, administrative checklists, and implementation guides—to support counties.

Beyond these formal support structures, counties benefit from ongoing dialogue with experts and peers across the state. West Virginia's early childhood community is strong and well connected; many of the key actors involved in pre-K at the state and local levels know each other, which helps to foster open communication among stakeholders. As Bill Huebner, a former member of the Steering Team, explained:

> West Virginia's not that big of a state. We all knew one another. We all kind of traveled the circuit of different meetings, collaborative meetings. We had had discussions about collaboration quite a bit, long before WV Pre-K came our way.

These interactions, combined with more formal support and robust quality standards, are designed to set the stage for local success in implementing a high-quality program.

Local Leadership on Quality Improvement

Starting in the mid-2000s, West Virginia began to rely on a county-led continuous quality improvement process as its primary strategy for monitoring and promoting quality in state preschool classrooms.[73] Under this model, local administrators create plans to collect and analyze data to monitor progress and inform decisions related to program improvement. As Janet Bock-Hager, WV Pre-K Coordinator, describes, continuous quality improvement plans offer "a system to check on yourself" using data and a means "to utilize [data] to make good data-driven decisions."

At their most basic, West Virginia counties' continuous quality improvement plans lay out a strategy to collect and submit fiscal, program, child outcome, and classroom observation data to the state, as well as a process to use these data to develop school readiness goals, plan for staff development, and identify new objectives for the county's quality improvement

TEACHING AND LEARNING IN A WV PRE-K CLASSROOM: THE RESTAURANT PROJECT

Many preschool classrooms follow familiar routines, transitioning between children's arrivals, free-choice play, circle time, meals, and outdoor time at predictable intervals, a practice that supports children's security and independence at school.[i] While the day may follow a well-established schedule, the activities and interactions that occur in preschool classrooms are anything but monotonous. In one WV Pre-K classroom, over the course of several days, students were engaged in play- and project-based learning, undertaking a restaurant project that integrated diverse concepts and dynamic learning opportunities under a single theme.

The restaurant project emerged from several children's interest in cooking, which they demonstrated by "cooking" spaghetti and other foods in the dramatic play area during free-choice time—an element of the pre-K routine that provides children with the opportunity to make meaningful choices throughout their day. The teacher, recognizing and engaging with the children's interest, planned and presented a number of activities to explore cooking throughout the week. One day, children were offered the opportunity to make their own snack of caprese kabobs and applesauce. Among other things, preparing snacks offered chances to hone their fine motor skills, practice sharing and taking turns, and describe the world around them—competencies that span several domains of West Virginia's early learning standards.[ii] Later, students created a restaurant in the dramatic play area, taking orders, "cooking" a variety of foods, and serving "customers"—demonstrating an emerging understanding of writing and building their conversation and social skills.[iii] When the students decided they would like to create a menu for their restaurant, the teachers provided scaffolding for the activity, offering pictures and props to stimulate students' thinking about the menu, facilitating the discussion and the decision-making process, and working with students to type out the final product. Several days later, the restaurant project culminated with an opportunity to make breadsticks, one of the items featured on the students' menu. During the activity, the entire class took turns rolling out the dough, while the teacher engaged the children in conversation about the process—how the dough felt, looked, and smelled, and how it changed as they rolled it out. Throughout the project, teachers documented students' efforts and created a pamphlet to share the class's activities with the students' families.

The restaurant project embodied many of the characteristics that West Virginia state policy establishes for pre-K curriculum and instructional practice. It engaged children actively in their learning; responded to individual interests and needs; incorporated a variety of learning experiences, materials, and strategies; and emphasized interaction between and among teachers, children, and their families.[iv] The project activities were also language-rich and highly interactive, two characteristics of high-quality early education programs.[v]

i. See W. Va. Code R. § 126-28-15 (2015).
ii. W. Va. Code R. § 126-440-3 (2015).
iii. W. Va. Code R. § 126-440-3 (2015).
iv. W. Va. Code R. § 126-28-15 (2015).
v. Wechsler, M., Melnick, H., Maier, A., and Bishop, J. (2016). *The building blocks of high-quality early education programs.* Palo Alto, CA: Learning Policy Institute.

efforts. County teams also assess local needs, establish goals and priorities, and select assessment tools.[74] Because these decisions are made at the local level, continuous quality improvement plans offer significant local flexibility.

The flexibility of the plans is illustrated by the diversity of tools that counties use to assess quality and track improvement. State preschool providers were formerly required to conduct classroom observations using the Early Childhood Environment Rating Scale, a widely used observational tool that encompasses seven dimensions of quality, including classroom activities, interactions, and program structure.[75] The state recently altered this requirement, instead requiring an annual health and safety checklist and permitting counties to choose assessment instruments to best suit their context.[76] One state administrator explained:

Let's say a county just demolished a room and redid it, then they're allowed to use the Environment Rating Scales because that would help them with setting up the classroom. Maybe they have a new teacher, so this year they would rather see how the teacher is interacting with the children, so maybe they would use the Classroom Assessment Scoring System this year for that particular teacher. Or they might use a continuous quality improvement tool based on the curriculum that they're implementing. They just always have to be thinking and planning, looking at where their weaknesses are and moving forward.

As the administrator describes, many counties continue to rely on quality assessment instruments that are well known in the early childhood space, including curriculum-based assessments, the Early Childhood Environment Rating Scale, and the Classroom Assessment Scoring System, an observational assessment that emphasizes classroom management and instructional and emotional support.[77] Counties also use West Virginia-specific tools, including the health and safety checklist and an observational walk-through, which is designed for use by administrators who are not familiar with early childhood settings, to help monitor classroom quality. County Pre-K administrators report the latter tool being particularly helpful since many principals lack specialized training in early childhood education. As one former Pre-K administrator explained:

> The administrators that were school principals—having pre-k in their building was very foreign to them. They just thought, "Well if I walk by and they're playing they must be fine." Or, worse, "If I walk by and they're sitting at tables and doing pencil, paper, then everything must be fine." So we really needed to make sure that people did understand what high quality looked like. And there was a document that came out of the state—it was a principal walk-through form, they called it. And of course it wasn't just for principals—it could be used in Head Start and child-care settings—but it was aimed at principals because they typically had absolutely no background in early childhood education. And so [the tool explained,] when you walk into an early childhood classroom, this is what you should see.

These classroom-level data are complemented by data from the previously described Early Learning Scale, West Virginia's required observational child assessment. The data from these different tools are available to guide quality improvement at the classroom, district, and state levels. For example, county pre-K coordinators leverage the results of observations and assessments to provide feedback to teachers and other staff. As one local administrator described, "I am always looking at—what are our low points? What areas do we need to have additional professional development in? What areas, when I go out and visit classrooms, do I see teachers struggling?"

Under West Virginia's preschool policy, all counties must also use data to inform their staff development plans, although counties differ in exactly how the data are applied.[78] Counties have the flexibility to engage teachers on topics that they identify as relevant using methods that they choose, whether a speaker, workshop, or individualized coaching. Many counties employ several of these formats for professional development throughout the year. As Janet Bock-Hager, Pre-K Coordinator, explains:

There are some counties that do some of their mandatory trainings in the beginning of the year, [where] it's more of a session bringing in a professional speaker or something like that. A lot of counties are kind of doing those, but they're also doing some individual mentoring and support based on individualized data. We encourage them to do that as part of their continuous quality improvement, but to do it in conjunction with the direct supervisor of the staff person.

Many in the state celebrate this local flexibility in designing continuous quality improvement plans because, as Amy Wolfe, a board member for the West Virginia Association for Young Children, explained, "conversations have become more nuanced and more local in terms of meeting local needs." Though the state offers regulations, tools, and resources that shape county efforts, there remains an important local role in implementing continuous quality improvement.

Collaboration as Quality Improvement

Local-level collaboration is another force for quality improvement in West Virginia's system. In particular, collaboration can improve the quality of all providers in the system by encouraging the sharing of quality standards and expertise across programs, a process that Amy Wolfe has seen play out throughout the state:

When you think about child-care centers, Head Starts, and public schools, each of those entities has its strengths. Say one entity is known for being good at providing developmentally appropriate practice for young children and another entity is good at providing standards-based curriculum and using assessment to inform their practice. And another entity is good at providing professional development for their teachers. Instead of those things being at odds, I think by coming together in the way that they have in West Virginia, everyone has benefitted. The developmentally appropriate practice group has learned about assessment and curriculum from the agency that had that as a strength. . . . By bringing the entities together, it's improved child-care centers, it's improved Head Start, it's improved public schools. Because each of those groups has a lot to learn from the others and if they just remained isolated and separate then they never would have had that opportunity to be challenged, to take on that other perspective and to do their work in a different and better way.

USING DATA TO INFORM CONTINUOUS QUALITY IMPROVEMENT:
EXAMPLES FROM TWO COUNTIES

While all West Virginia counties are engaged in continuous quality improvement for WV Pre-K, each county's process is distinct due to significant local flexibility. Continuous quality improvement is, by definition, a dynamic and multi-faceted process, but a brief snapshot of the decisions two counties have made regarding classroom assessment and planning for professional development help to illustrate the varied approaches that define WV Pre-K's locally informed continuous quality improvement landscape.

As in other counties, Kanawha County, the state's largest, uses several tools to gauge the quality and implementation of WV Pre-K. Carol Fleming, the county Director of Preschool, enumerates several core pieces of the county's continuous quality improvement system:

> Teachers are evaluated every year by their principals, administrators, directors, so that's included in part of the continuous quality improvement [plan]. We also have the walk-through. . . . The principals do that with the education managers . . . .Then with . . . the child assessment, that's how we determine who needs what, you know, basically in the classrooms. And we try to provide [those materials] ongoing, so that we don't wait until the end of the year and then [say] "you needed this, you needed that."

In addition, education managers administer the Classroom Assessment Scoring System twice a year in each of the county's pre-K classrooms.

Among other uses, these data, plus a staff survey, inform professional development opportunities for pre-K teachers. As a large county, Kanawha is able to offer different trainings for new and experienced teachers, in addition to trainings appropriate to teachers of all experience levels. For example, during one professional development day, new pre-K teachers might receive training on the CLASS assessment tool or PATHS, the county's supplemental social-emotional learning curriculum, while more experienced educators may participate in professional development around behavior management and effective uses of technology in the classroom.[i]

Clay County, a smaller, more rural county, has selected a different approach to classroom assessment. Pam Mullins, county Director of Preschool, explains:

USING DATA TO INFORM CONTINUOUS QUALITY, CONTINUED

I use observations if I'm out here [in a school] and see something that's going to help my continuous quality improvement plan. We're going to continue to use the Environment Rating Scales for, like, a new teacher. . . . We also use a Creative Curriculum checklist to make sure that we have enough supplies and that the schedule looks good. . . . And I have a retired teacher who we've just contracted as an instructional coach.

In addition, the county tracks data from the required formative assessment of students, and principals at local elementary schools conduct walk-throughs using the state-developed checklist.

The county pre-K coordinator relies on conversations with staff and the results of the Early Learning Scale to plan ongoing professional development to meet the needs of pre-K teachers and their students. Time is reserved every Friday for planning and professional development, which is typically organized around the developmental domains laid out by the state's Early Learning Standards. The county also encourages teachers to attend trainings provided by the Regional Education Service Agency.[ii]

i. Interview with Carol Fleming, Director of Preschool at Kanawha County Schools, on October 20, 2015.
ii. Interview with Pamela Mullins, Director of Preschool, Clay County Schools on October 21, 2015.

This sharing of expertise has been extensive, particularly because in West Virginia, the most stringent applicable quality standard is applied in collaborative classrooms.

Further, state administrators encourage pre-K providers to engage in joint training and professional development opportunities with collaborative partners. For instance, in counties that collaborate with the local Head Start grantee, public pre-K teachers may be invited to participate in Head Start professional development opportunities, and vice versa. Partners have also benefitted from the infusions of cash that have accompanied a collaborative funding structure.[79] By promoting the sharing of expertise and resources across programs, the state's collaborative approach has been a key strategy for promoting quality across pre-K classrooms.

Challenges to Quality Improvement

Although WV Pre-K has benefitted from state and local efforts, the state has encountered several obstacles to quality improvement, including the need for a statewide data system and developing an early childhood workforce.

Building a Unified Data System. Data collection and analysis are central components of WV Pre-K's continuous quality improvement approach, offering a means to identify opportunities for growth and analyze progress. As one administrator put it, the program's quality improvement efforts are "all about the data." To provide teachers, districts, and state agencies with the means to collect and analyze program data, West Virginia recently launched a tailored statewide pre-K data system. It is part of the broader K–12 data system and is comprehensive, including individual child assessment, health, and attendance data, as well as program assessment information. All WV Pre-K students, even those served in collaborative settings, are entered into the system and will remain there throughout their public school careers.[80]

The creation of this data system has been one of the state's greatest successes in recent years. As one state administrator noted:

> The best thing that ever happened, not only in terms of the children with disabilities, but [also] in terms of the growth of our system, is the ability within the state to have the [data] platform. Now, when you look at that, you've got the school readiness profile. You have our child assessment data. You have health and safety. You have the classroom piece. And it's all tied together within our data system because we were able to put that on our own platform and we can tweak that as we go through our process.

This linked data system is a powerful tool for supporting the development of continuous quality improvement processes across West Virginia's pre-K classrooms. Lisa Ray, an Office of Early Learning Coordinator, explained, "[W]e're saying to teachers, 'you need to be using individual child data to drive your instruction.' And then at the county level, you use your classroom data to guide your professional development." Through the system, teachers can create reports on each child's progress to share with parents, while local and state administrators can access aggregated data for program monitoring and strategic planning.

The data system will likely yield benefits for the program, but creating it presented a challenge. For one, there were technical barriers to overcome—one teacher mentioned that her class's assessment data disappeared for a time during one data migration—which the state managed with the assistance of a dedicated programmer. Pre-K administrators also had an uphill battle to extend access to all staff in West Virginia's decentralized and highly collaborative system. As Rhonda Fisher, a coordinator for the Office of Early Learning, explained:

> One of the challenges was just getting access to people who weren't district employees. [The programmers said,] "You mean you want us to give access to child-care workers?". . . With the contracts, with the authorizations they get, they aren't county employees, but they're county schoolteachers. It was very hard to get that concept across.

The problem has become less acute with time, as the Office of Early Learning's programmers have come to understand the program's collaborative model and developed strategies to limit the possibility of a data breach.[81]

Although the state's data system has progressed, more work remains, particularly to incorporate other early care and education programs into the system. West Virginia is currently in the process of planning for an integrated early childhood data system serving all of the state's birth-to-5 programs.[82]

Developing an Early Childhood Workforce. When WV Pre-K started, the state did not have a robust supply of qualified teachers for pre-K classrooms, a challenge that the state began to address soon after the program's passage. As Amy Wolfe, board member of the West Virginia Association for Young Children, explained:

> One of the challenges of bringing this to fruition was that there wasn't a workforce that had the educational requirements to do this, so they [the state] were able to gradually bring people up to the level of education necessary over time.

The strategy to raise workforce qualifications was two-pronged. As a first-level response, West Virginia allowed teachers in collaborative settings to be grandfathered under new personnel policies. Typically, grandfathered staff are authorized to remain in their current positions, but may not work in any other state pre-K classroom until they earn the necessary credentials (a bachelor's degree in early childhood or a related field for lead teachers and a high school degree plus specialized training for assistant teachers).[83] This strategy offers staff an opportunity to pursue additional training while simultaneously preventing serious personnel shortages when new requirements take effect. The proportion of teachers who remain grandfathered today is fairly small.[84]

At the same time, West Virginia created programs to support professional development within the existing teacher workforce. As Melanie Clark, a Program Manager at the Department of Health and Human Resources, describes, "[A]bout the time that we were having these qualifications put forth, we brought T.E.A.C.H. into West Virginia." Through T.E.A.C.H.—the Teacher Education and Compensation Helps program—child-care providers pursuing higher education degrees in early childhood can receive scholarships in exchange for a commitment to remain with their employers for a specified period following degree completion.[85] The state also offers the Apprenticeship for Child Development Specialist, a four-semester program that combines coursework and on-the-job training, culminating in a certificate that is equivalent to a Child Development Associate.[86]

Although programs like T.E.A.C.H. and the apprenticeship program have trained hundreds of providers, these programs largely rely on student access to brick-and-mortar educational institutions, which is not feasible for all providers. The state launched e-learning courses for early childhood educators to begin to address this challenge.[87] Because courses are offered for free online, they are more accessible to educators in the state's rural areas than programs that rely on traditional classroom models, and in addition they offer increased flexibility to participants. Even so, some areas of the state lack high-speed internet access, a prerequisite for participation.[88]

Once teachers are trained and hired, West Virginia Pre-K programs sometimes struggle to retain qualified teachers, largely due to low compensation. The challenge tends to be more pronounced in collaborative settings, which typically offer lower pay and fewer benefits than public schools. As a Department of Health and Human Resources administrator explained:

> There is some discrepancy in reimbursement to staff. You know, in a board of education setting, they're going to be paid at a certain level with certain benefits. Whereas in child-care centers it is typically a lot lower, maybe minimum wage.

The average child-care wage in the state is $8.00 per hour, while a typical public pre-K teacher earns $27.19.[89] As the required credentials for preschool teachers in public schools and collaborative settings have become more similar, the incentive to leave child-care centers for employment in public schools has increased. The director of one private child-care center understands the motivation for such a move, saying, "[T]hey would have benefits, which they don't have here, and they would be paid for 40 hours a week, not 34. There definitely is that desire to, there'd be a reason for them to leave." In response, several of the state's scholarship programs include efforts to boost the wages of child care and Head Start instructors; both T.E.A.C.H. and the Apprenticeship for Child Development Specialist require employers to offer a modest bonus or wage increase after participants complete their credentials.[90]

Some counties have also taken action to address these wage differentials by supplementing the pay of teachers in child-care centers or Head Start classrooms to match that of the public school teachers. As one administrator explained:

> That's why sometimes a county will say, "We will just pay for your staff to meet the same level of income, so you don't have turnover in your programs." Because that's where you see shifts occur—they get some of this training and then they realize that they could be working for the Board of Education.

The effect of these salary supplements can be observed in state teacher compensation data; teachers in collaborative pre-K settings on average earn $19.18 per hour—more than double the average wage for a child-care worker.[91] However, even child-care workers receiving supplements frequently lack benefits and may not work a 40-hour week. Further, wage supplements are part of the collaborative agreements that Head Start grantees and private child-care centers individually negotiate with county boards of education and as a result, are not universally available. As one private child-care center director said, "[C]hild care is not a lucrative business in the state of West Virginia."

NEXT STEPS FOR WEST VIRGINIA

Although West Virginia has achieved much in WV Pre-K's 14-year history, state and local leaders acknowledge that program improvement must continue. As the Chief Academic Officer for West Virginia public schools, Clayton Burch, said, "We never want someone on our State Board of Education to ever think that the work's done." The state's upcoming priorities include managing the transition to five-day full-day preschool, strengthening the state's birth-to-5 system, and further aligning early education programs.

Transitioning to Five-Day, Full-Day

In 2013, Governor Earl Ray Tomblin championed the passage of an education reform bill requiring that state pre-K programs expand instructional time to offer at least five hours of instruction, five days per week by the 2016–2017 school year.[92] Despite legislative challenges to the provision during the 2015 and 2016 legislative sessions, Governor Tomblin has continued to support the change, writing, "I believe offering five-day-per-week programs for early childhood education is critical to meet the developmental needs of our state's students."[93] The change will impact a significant number of WV Pre-K classrooms; currently, only 16% of classrooms offer five days of instruction per week.[94]

Several local providers and administrators expressed concern that this transition to "five-day, full-day," as it is referred to in the state, will create staffing and resource issues. Today, most programs offer four days of instruction per week. During those four days, most teaching staff remain in their classrooms all day—promoting continuity of care for children and forgoing daily planning time in favor of an entire day for planning and professional development each Friday. Adding a fifth day to the pre-K week will require new personnel schedules that accommodate planning hours and expanded instructional time, while maintaining teacher-child ratios.

Because the state is not offering additional funding to support the change, counties must meet their expanded need for staff using existing resources. Many counties have yet to find a workable solution; as one administrator shared, "We're having some problems trying to figure out how to pay for that extra day and how to pay for planning. Teachers have to have planning periods and right now our teachers of 4-year olds have Fridays to plan." The challenge may be most acute for private child-care providers who run state pre-K classrooms but typically operate on narrow margins. As one center director argued, "we're being directed by law to have a 5-day, full-day program. . . . There's got to be money that funds that extra day." This change is made more complex by the highly decentralized nature of the program, which makes one-size-fits-all guidance difficult. One local administrator predicts that solutions to the challenge "will be by county."

The Universal Pre-K Steering Team has already begun helping counties plan for the rollout of the new requirement, holding sessions to discuss the change at the annual Leadership Institute and organizing a multi-county pilot of 5-day, full-day programming to develop strategies and models that other counties might use to adapt their programs. While counties have not yet settled on their plans for moving to 5-day, full-day programs, one state preschool provider expressed optimism, saying, "We're resilient and we're creative and we're intelligent and we will find a solution. Inventions come because there was a need."

Strengthening West Virginia's Birth-to-5 System

After more than a decade focused on achieving the goal of universal access to state preschool, West Virginia has begun efforts to focus on other elements of its early childhood system. As Senator Robert Plymale explained, "In West Virginia, the demographics are so bad in the early years—prenatal to 3—that if we don't change that and put more dollars into that, in the long run, we'll pay for it. It is the best investment you can make."

The state has been exploring options for strengthening its birth-to-5 system through the Early Childhood Planning Task Force, which was convened by Governor Tomblin in May 2013 to create a development plan for West Virginia's early childhood system. Partnering with the state's Early Childhood Advisory Council, the Task Force involved more than 1,200 West Virginians in its planning process through interviews, focus groups, community forums, and an online survey. The group's efforts were supported by a combination of state and private funds.[95]

The Task Force's Development Plan, released in fall 2014, calls for expanded access to and participation in the state's existing early childhood programs, including Birth to Three, child-care subsidies, home visiting, and pre-K. It also articulates a need for system-level improvements, including an integrated data system, a statewide quality rating and improvement system, financial incentives for high-quality programs, and a unified system of governance. Drawing on the state's success with progressive pre-K implementation, the task force proposed a 10-year timeline to achieve its vision for the state's early childhood system.[96]

The development plan has not yet been implemented. While there is broad agreement among state leaders that what happens before school entry is as important as what happens in school, the state's precarious budgetary position makes any substantial new investment unappealing for policymakers.[97] Faced with a declining coal industry and falling gas prices, the state has already begun to experience budget cuts, including an across-the-board cut to education spending.[98] Implementing the Task

Force's plan would likely require a new line item in the state budget, a significant political and fiscal lift in the current fiscal climate. At the same time, however, Governor Tomblin has demonstrated his continued support for early education by investing in planning for an integrated early childhood data system.

Advancing Alignment in Early Care and Education

In recent years, West Virginia has invested in building a pre-K to 5th grade approach to early learning, with support from members of a pre-K to 3rd grade national working group, including Harvard's Graduate School of Education and the Center on Enhancing Early Learning Outcomes.[99] This work has resulted in several important changes to the state's early learning infrastructure. The state created the Office of Early Learning to oversee grades pre-K to 5 and unify the work already occurring around elementary instruction, 3rd-grade reading proficiency, school readiness, and early learning workforce development.[100] West Virginia also recently reclassified both pre-K and kindergarten as "early learning readiness grades" or grades whose primary goal is to help children develop positive dispositions to learning and to prepare children for learning in 1st grade and beyond.[101] Rather than having developmentally inappropriate practices "push down" into pre-K from later grades, West Virginia aims to "push up" developmentally appropriate practices into later grades. Clayton Burch, the state's Chief Academic Officer, explained how the success of WV Pre-K has impacted the state's approach to kindergarten:

> We've been able to drive improvements, even in our environments in kindergarten. All of a sudden you start having these rich preschool environments because you're collaborating with Head Start and the Department of Health and Human Resources and you're trying to weave together each other's policies and federal requirements. So, we had this really strong monitoring system and expectations for things like the environment, teacher-child ratios, assistant teachers, that ended up carrying on as a conversation into kindergarten. We said, "Wait a second. If we have all these rich things we expect in preschool, why wouldn't we have these same things in kindergarten?"

This perspective is also reflected in the state's education policies, which emphasize formative assessment, developmentally appropriate practice, and personalized learning throughout students' public school careers.[102]

West Virginia's campaign for grade-level reading provides another il-

---

ENCOURAGING EARLY LITERACY IN A RURAL WEST VIRGINIA COUNTY

In one rural West Virginia County, local education leaders have sought to engage families and the community in building the literacy skills of their youngest learners. The county sponsors and extensively promotes the Imagination Library, an international initiative that mails free books to children to foster print-rich home environments. Participation in the initiative has been robust, reaching more than half of the target population in the county. There are also frequent literacy activities at community events. For example, at the local high school's annual block party, there was a community read aloud by a costumed volunteer. Thanks to support from a local business, after the reading, each child in attendance received a free copy of the book to take home. These family and community activities complement the county's formal early childhood programs, including universal pre-K and evidence-based home visiting, to encourage early literacy.

Source: Interview with anonymous local administrator.

---

lustration of how the state is continuing to foster alignment between early childhood and the early elementary grades. As Clayton Burch, the state's Chief Academic Officer, explained, "Right now the big rock is still literacy. It is really the dire need to figure out how to break the cycle of poor literacy." West Virginia launched Leaders of Literacy: Campaign for Grade-Level Reading in 2014,[103] a campaign that aims to close the literacy gap—to double the number of low-income students who read proficiently at the end of 3rd grade by 2020—by providing counties funding to implement locally designed early literacy plans.[104] Rather than focusing solely on reading during 3rd grade, the campaign encourages counties to consider how early childhood and early elementary interventions can support children's literacy development.[105] Burch elaborated:

> The nice thing is that he [Governor Tomblin] recognized that in order to [improve literacy], you have to have a comprehensive literacy system from birth to 3rd grade. . . . It was really nice to see in state code an initiative like that, that says "listen we're going to focus on a whole comprehensive system. We can't expect that they [children] get to school and somehow we're going to close that literacy achievement gap by 3rd grade in school by itself."

Despite a tight fiscal climate, the Governor appropriated $5.7 million to the campaign in his 2016 budget, a sign of how high literacy ranks among the state's educational and political priorities.[106] Three-quarters of the Governor's appropriation will be funneled directly to West Virginia's counties, which are just beginning to implement their early literacy plans.[107]

KEY TAKEAWAYS

West Virginia Pre-K is a voluntary universal program aimed at bolstering school readiness among participants. The program serves 75% of West Virginia's 4-year-olds, and 3-year-olds with special needs, at public schools, private child-care centers, and Head Start sites. The state employs a highly collaborative model to run the program, which was developed over a decade, and relies on both state and local input to succeed. Key takeaways from West Virginia's experience include:

Champions help generate and sustain support for implementing long-term early childhood commitments. The work of a political champion spurred WV Pre-K's creation, while a broad well of support for the program, continuous legislative leadership, and an ongoing dialogue about the early childhood evidence base have helped maintain the program's momentum and drive it to full implementation.

WV Pre-K was designed to suit West Virginia's context. The program's design is pragmatic and capitalized on political and fiscal opportunities specific to West Virginia. For example, the program's strong role for collaboration and reliance on the state funding formula transformed difficulties facing the state—competition among providers, a tight state budget, and declining K–12 enrollments—into assets for the universal pre-K program. A high degree of local flexibility also gives counties space to meet their unique needs.

Funding is important for feasibility. WV Pre-K's funding strategy maximizes the use of existing resources by braiding multiple funding streams at the county and provider levels, thereby expanding the pool of funds available to support a universal program. The program's inclusion in the state school aid formula also avoided a substantial new budget line item at its inception and has provided a stable source of financial support over time.

Developing interagency administrative structures at the state and local levels can enable effective collaboration among programs. The Universal Pre-K Steering Team, Early Childhood Advisory Council, and county collaborative teams provide forums for communication and cooperation among early childhood stakeholders, including local education agencies, Head Start, child care, and others. Cooperation and coordination among these groups are at the core of WV Pre-K's model.

Building a coherent state framework can support the creation of quality programs at the local level. West Virginia has invested time and resources in codifying its conception of quality and developing channels for technical assistance to anchor and orient the work of county-level teams. This approach balances state standards with local flexibility to provide a program that best suits the needs of children and families across the state.

Since WV Pre-K was established in 2002, West Virginia has displayed a strong and steady commitment to developing the program, over time expanding both access and quality. While the state has encountered barriers in the implementation of WV Pre-K, West Virginia has persisted in its efforts to build a program that serves the needs of all of its young children.

NOTES

1. Barnett, W. S., Friedman-Krauss, A. H., Gomez, R., Horowitz, M., Weisenfeld, G. G., Clarke Brown, K., & Squires, J. H. (2016). *The state of preschool 2015.* Retrieved from nieer.org/sites/nieer/files/2015 Yearbook.pdf

2. Office of Early Learning, West Virginia Department of Education (n.d.). *Overview of West Virginia Universal Pre-K: WVBE Policy 2525—West Virginia's universal access to a quality early education system, 2014–15.* Retrieved from wvde.state.wv.us/oel/docs/wv-prek-overview.pdf; Wong, V. C., Cook, T. D., Barnett, W. S., & Jung, K. (2008). An effectiveness-based evaluation of five state pre-kindergarten programs. *Journal of Policy Analysis and Management, 27*(1), 122–154.

3. Barnett et al. (2016).

4. W. Va. Code R. §§ 126-28-2, 126-28-5, 126-28-8 (2015). Retrieved from apps.sos.wv.gov/adlaw/csr/ruleview.aspx?document=9959

5. Figures represent state funding for early care and education programs serving children from birth to age 5. Collective Impact, LLC. (2013, October). *State and federal expenditures: Early childhood programs, West Virginia* (Briefing paper for the West Virginia Early Childhood Planning Task Force). Retrieved from www.wvecptf.org/docs/CI-State-and-Federal-Expenditures-Report.pdf; West Virginia Early Childhood Planning Task Force. (2014, October). *Building a system for early success: A development plan for West Virginia's early childhood system.* Retrieved from www.wvecptf.org/docs/WVECPTF%20Development%20 Plan_single%20page.pdf

6. Office of Early Learning, West Virginia Department of Education (n.d.).

7. Interview with Lloyd Jackson, Vice President of the West Virginia Board of Education, on October 20, 2015.

8. Participation rate represents the proportion of kindergarteners enrolled in WV Pre-K the previous school year. The estimate does not include children who were served in private preschool settings. Office of Early Learning, West Virginia Department of Education (n.d.).

9. Barnett, W. S., Carolan, M. E., Squires, J. H., Brown, K. C., & Horowitz, M. (2015). *The state of preschool 2014*. Retrieved from http://nieer.org/wp-content/uploads/2016/08/Yearbook2014_full3.pdf

10. In some instances, older or younger children may be permitted to enroll in WV Pre-K if it is determined to be in the best interests of the child; in 2014–15, there were approximately 485 out-of-age enrollments in the program. Unpublished data from the West Virginia Department of Education (personal communication November 6, 2015).

11. In 2014–2015, 185 dual-language learners were enrolled in the program. Barnett et al. (2016).

12. Office of Early Learning, West Virginia Department of Education (n.d.).

13. S.B. 359, 80th Leg., Reg. Sess. (W.Va. 2013).

14. West Virginia's school districts are geographically contiguous with its counties, meaning that each district is associated with a single county. These county-districts are the level at which local administration for WV Pre-K occurs.

15. W. Va. Code R. § 126-28-4 (2015). Retrieved from apps.sos.wv.gov/adlaw/csr/ruleview. aspx?document=9959

16. Office of Early Learning, West Virginia Department of Education (n.d.); Interview with Janet Bock-Hager, West Virginia Department of Education Pre-K Coordinator, on January 25, 2016.

17. S.B. 247, 75th Leg., Reg. Sess. (W. Va. 2002).

18. Family child-care providers are not eligible to provide state preschool.

19. Bock-Hager interview (2016, January 25); Interview with Carol Fleming, Director of Preschool at Kanawha County Schools, on October 20, 2015.

20. W. Va. Code R. § 126-28-4 (2015), retrieved from apps.sos.wv.gov/adlaw/csr/ruleview. aspx?document=9959

21. Templeton, R., Dozier, J., & Boswell, L. (2009). *Universal access to pre-k in West Virginia*. Retrieved from sites.google.com/a/wvde.k12.wv.us/wv-universal-pre-k-county-administrators-summer-institute-2009/Home/july-9-2009/universal-access-to-pre-k-in-west-virginia; West Virginia Department of Education. *Official multiple list*. Retrieved from wvde.state.wv.us/materials/2010/2011/UniversalPre-K.html

22. W. Va. Code R. § 126-28-15 (2015). Retrieved from apps.sos.wv.gov/adlaw/csr/ruleview.aspx?document=9959

23. See nces.ed.gov/whatsnew/conferences/statsdc/2014/pdf/VII_C_Barkley_Handout2.pdf for a description of West Virginia's state school funding formula. Jackson interview (2015, October 20); Interview with Pamela Mullins, Director

of Preschool, Clay County Schools on October 21, 2015.

24. Collective Impact, LLC. (2013, October). *State and federal expenditures.*

25. Collective Impact, LLC. (2013, October). *State and federal expenditures.*

26. Collective Impact, LLC. (2013, October). *State and federal expenditures*

27. Collective Impact, LLC. (2013, October). *Estimating costs of expanding early childhood services* (Briefing paper for the West Virginia Early Childhood Planning Task Force). Retrieved from www.wvecptf.org/docs/CI-ExpansionCosts-Final.pdf; U.S. Census Bureau (2013). *Public education finances: 2013* (Census Bureau publication no. G13-ASPEF). Washington, D.C.: U.S. Government Printing Office.

28. Head Start Performance Standards, 80 Fed. Reg. 35,429 (proposed June 19, 2015) (to be codified at 45 C.F.R. chapter undef); Interview with Barbara Gebhard, Assistant Director of Public Policy, Zero to Three and former Deputy Director, West Virginia Governor's Cabinet on Children and Families on October 20, 2015; Interview with anonymous participant on November 11, 2015.

29. Hunt, J. (2014, November 5). Republicans will control both chambers of state Legislature. Charleston Gazette Mail. Retrieved from www.wvgazettemail.com/rticle/20141105/DM05/141109591/1276; Wilson, R. (2014, November 4). Party switch gives Republicans control of West Virginia Senate. *Washington Post.* Retrieved from www.washingtonpost.com/blogs/govbeat/wp/2014/11/05/party-switch-gives-republicans-control-of-west-virginia-senate/

30. Unless otherwise indicated, sources for this section are Jackson interview (2015, October 20); Interview with Robert Plymale, West Virginia Senator on October 22, 2015.

31. Bushouse, B. K. (2009). *Universal preschool: Policy change, stability, and the Pew Charitable Trusts.* Albany, NY: State University of New York Press; Interview with Steven Paine, former State Superintendent of Schools on October 19, 2015; Plymale interview (2015, October 22).

32. Bushouse (2009).

33. Many private child-care providers rely on 3- and 4-year-old enrollments to offset the higher costs of infant and toddler care; they worried that losing 4-year-olds could elevate providers' costs beyond parents' ability to pay, forcing child-care centers to close.

34. Bushouse (2009).

35. Bushouse (2009).

36. Bushouse (2009).

37. Bushouse (2009); Jackson interview (2015, October 20); Gebhard interview (2015, October 20).

38. In West Virginia, state school aid funds are allocated based on an October headcount, but funds are not disbursed until the following summer; when the state expanded full-day kindergarten, it led 17 districts to enter a deficit. Bushouse (2009); Plymale interview (2015, October 22).

39. S.B. 247, 75th Leg., Reg. Sess. (W.Va. 2002); Jackson interview (2015, October 20). See also Bushouse (2009).

40. Bentley, R., & Tomblin, E. R. (2015, May 13). Quality early childhood education is a smart investment for policy makers. *Forbes.* Retrieved from www.forbes.com/sites/realspin/2015/05/13/quality-early-childhood-education-is-a-smart-investment-for-policy-makers/#745f70af1080

41. Plymale interview (2015, October 22).

42. Bushouse (2009); Plymale interview (2015, October 22).

43. Interview with Cathy Jones, former Early Childhood coordinator West Virginia Department of Education, on September 28, 2015.

44. S.B. 247, 75th Leg., Reg. Sess. (W. Va. 2002).

45. Although the Steering Team officially has four members, other staff from the Department of Education, Head Start, and the Department of Health and Human Resources play an important role in supporting the program's day-to-day implementation.

46. Office of Early Learning, West Virginia Department of Education (n.d.).

47. W. Va. Code R. §§ 126-28-4, 126-28-18 (2015). Retrieved from apps.sos.wv.gov/adlaw/csr/ruleview. aspx?document=9959

48. See earlylearning.wv.gov/about/Pages/Council-Membership.aspx for a complete list of representatives on the Early Childhood Advisory Council.

49. See earlylearning.wv.gov/about/Pages/default.aspx for more information about the history and goals of the Early Childhood Advisory Council.

50. W. Va. Code R. § 126-28-4 (2015).

51. W. Va. Code R. § 126-28-4 (2015).

52. Mullins interview (2015, October 21).

53. Interview with Janet Bock-Hager, Virginia (Ginger) Huffman, Rhonda Fisher, and Lisa Ray, West Virginia Department of Education coordinators, on October 23, 2015.

54. Children with special needs are ensured transportation regardless of whether their district offers the service for other preschoolers.

55. Johnson, J., Showalter, D., Klein, R., & Lester, C. (2014, May). *Why rural matters 2013–14: The condition of rural education in the 50 states.* Retrieved from www.ruraledu.org/user_uploads/file/2013-14-Why-Rural-Matters.pdf

56. Helen Post-Brown cited in Bushouse (2009), 87.

57. Jones interview (2015, September 28); Interview with Bill Huebner, former Director, West Virginia Head Start State Collaboration, on October 16, 2015; Interview with Kay Tilton, former Director, Division of Early Care and Education, West Virginia Department of Health and Human Resources, on October 19, 2015.

58. W. Va. Code R. § 126-28-11 (2003). Retrieved from apps.sos.wv.gov/adlaw/csr/ruleview. aspx?document=1786.

59. W Va. Code R. § 126-28-11 (2003).

60. W. Va. Code R. § 126-28-1 (2003) (amended 2005, 2007, 2009, 2010, 2012, 2014, 2015). Retrieved from apps.sos.wv.gov/adlaw/csr/ruleview.aspx?document=1786; Bock-Hager, Huffman, Fisher, and Ray interview (2015, October 23).

61. Bock-Hager, Huffman, Fisher, and Ray interview (2015, October 23). See also W. Va. Code R. §§ 126-28-4, 126-28-16, 126-28-18 (2015), retrieved from

apps.sos.wv.gov/adlaw/csr/ruleview.aspx?document=9959; W. Va. Code R. §
26-28-16 (2012), retrieved from apps.sos.wv.gov/adlaw/csr/ruleview.aspx?doc-
ument=8617; W. Va. Code R. §§ 126-28-7, 126-28-16 (2009), retrieved from
apps.sos. wv.gov/adlaw/csr/ruleview.aspx?document=1734; W. Va. Code R.
§ 126-28-3 (2007), retrieved from apps.sos.wv.gov/adlaw/csr/ruleview.aspx?
document=1784.

62. W. Va. Code R. § 126-28-15 (2015). Retrieved from apps.sos.wv.gov/
adlaw/csr/ruleview. aspx?document=9959.

63. W. Va. Code R. § 126-28-15 (2015).

64. W. Va. Code R. § 126-28-15 (2015). See www.naeyc.org/dap for an overview of developmentally appropriate practice.

65. See W. Va. Code R. §§ 126-28-9, 126-28-10, 126-28-13, 126-28-14 (2015).
Retrieved from apps.sos. wv.gov/adlaw/csr/ruleview.aspx?document=9959 for
the specific guidelines regarding these topics.

66. W. Va. Code R. § 126-44O-3 (2015). Retrieved from apps.sos.wv.gov/
adlaw/csr/ruleview. aspx?document=9733.

67. W. Va. Code R. § 126-44O-3 (2015); W. Va. Code R. § 126-28-15 (2015).

68. Office of School Readiness, West Virginia Department of Education.
(2012). *An overview of the WV Pre-K child assessment system.* Retrieved
from static.k12.wv.us/oel/docs/WV%20 Pre-K%20Child%20Assessment%20Sys-
tem%20Overview%201%2012.pdf; Riley-Ayers, S., Frede, E.C., & Jung, K. (2010).
Early Learning Scale: Technical report. Retrieved from nieer.org/wp-content/
uploads/2012/03/Early_learning_scale_tech report_Sept_2010.pdf

69. West Virginia Department of Education. (2015). *West Virginia Universal
Pre-K Leadership Institute.* Retrieved from drive.google.com/file/d/0BytJXpD-dz-
1jaTJMa0NnWGYxaGs/view

70. Bock-Hager, Huffman, Fisher, and Ray interview (2015, October 23).

71. W. Va. Code R. § 126-28-18 (2015).

72. Bock-Hager, Huffman, Fisher, and Ray interview (2015, October 23).

73. Bock-Hager interview (2015, January 25).

74. W.Va. Code R. § 126-28-18 (2015).

75. See ers.fpg.unc.edu/early-childhood-environment-rating-scale-ecers-r for
more information on the Environment Rating Scale-Revised.

76. W. Va. Code R. § 126-28-18 (2015); W. Va. Code R. § 126-28-18 (2012). Retrieved from apps.sos.wv.gov/ adlaw/csr/ruleview.aspx?document=8617.

77. See teachstone.com/classroom-assessment-scoring-system/class-domains
-dimensions/ for more information on the Classroom Assessment Scoring System. Bock-Hager, Huffman, Fisher, and Ray interview (2015, October 23); Interview with Amy Wolfe, West Virginia Association of Young Children board
member on October 16, 2015; Interview with anonymous participant in October, 2015.

78. W. Va. Code R. § 126-28-18 (2015).

79. Bock-Hager, Huffman, Fisher, and Ray interview (2015, October 23).

80. Bock-Hager, Huffman, Fisher, and Ray interview (2015, October 23).

81. Bock-Hager, Huffman, Fisher, and Ray interview (2015, October 23).

82. Interview with Gretchen Frankenberry, West Virginia Early Childhood Advisory Council Executive Manager on October 23, 2015.

83. W. Va. Code R. § 126-28-16 (2015), retrieved from apps.sos.wv.gov/adlaw/ csr/ruleview. aspx?document=9959; Bock-Hager, Huffman, Fisher, and Ray interview (2015, October 23).

84. Bock-Hager, Huffman, Fisher, and Ray interview (2015, October 23).

85. T.E.A.C.H. Early Childhood West Virginia (n.d.). *Fact sheet*. Retrieved from www. wvearlychildhood.org/resources/Teach_fact_sheet.pdf

86. See www.wvacds.org/About_ACDS.html for a detailed description of the Apprenticeship for Child Development Specialist model.

87. See www.bc.edu/research/intasc/researchprojects/eLearning/efe.shtml for information about studies of the effectiveness of e-learning courses delivered through this program.

88. Interview with Melanie Clark, Program Manager, Family Child Care Regulations, West Virginia Department of Health and Human Resources and Melissa Smith, Early Care and Education Specialist, West Virginia Department of Health and Human Services on October 19, 2015. See www.wvgs. wvnet.edu/broadbandmaps/ for West Virginia broadband access maps.

89. Collective Impact, LLC. (2013, November). *Early childhood programs wage and benefit comparison* (Briefing paper for the West Virginia Early Childhood Planning Task Force). Retrieved from www.wvecptf.org/docs/CI-Wages-and-Benefits.pdf

90. Early Childhood West Virginia (n.d.). *Fact sheet*. Retrieved from www. wvearlychildhood.org/resources/Teach_fact_sheet.pdf. See www.wvacds.org/ About_ACDS.html for details about the Apprenticeship for Child Development Specialist model.

91. Collective Impact, LLC. (2013, November).

92. S.B. 359, 80th Leg., Reg. Sess. (W.Va. 2013). See also Quinn, R. (2016, January 23). Senate committee furthers bill to remove preschool day requirement. Charleston *Gazette Mail*. Retrieved from www.wvgazettemail.com/news/20160123/ senate-committee-furthers-bill-to-remove-preschool-day-requirement

93. Quinn (2016).

94. Office of Early Learning, West Virginia Department of Education (n.d.).

95. West Virginia Early Childhood Planning Task Force. (2014, October). *Building a system for early success: A development plan for West Virginia's early childhood system*. Retrieved from www. wvecptf.org/docs/WVECPTF%20Development%20Plan_single%20page.pdf

96. West Virginia Early Childhood Planning Task Force (2014).

97. Bock-Hager, Huffman, Fisher, and Ray interview (2015, October 23).

98. Burnette, D. (2016, January 12). Revenue woes in oil, coal states squeeze K–12. *Education Week*. Retrieved from www.edweek.org/ew/articles/2016/01/13/revenue-woes-in-oil-coal-states-squeeze.html

99. See sites.google.com/a/wvde.k12.wv.us/wvde-prek-cqi-advisory-council/ for details on the West Virginia Department of Education Advisory Committee on a Comprehensive Approach to Early Learning.

100. Email communication with Monica DellaMea, Director of the Office of Early Learning,West Virginia Department of Education on February 12, 2016.

101.W. Va. Code R. § 126-42-5 (2014). Retrieved from apps.sos.wv.gov/adlaw/ csr/ruleview.aspx?document=9313

102.W. Va. Code R. §126-42-5 (2014).   .

103. See wvde.state.wv.us/leaders-of-literacy/overview.html for an overview of the Leaders of Literacy campaign.

104. West Virginia Department of Education. (2015, June 18). *State literacy campaign continues to move forward,* retrieved from wvde.state.wv.us/ news/3182/; Quinn, R. (2015, July 20). Campaign aims to double low-income students' reading proficiency rates. *Charleston Gazette Mail.* Retrieved from www.wvgazettemail.com/article/20150720/GZ01/150729954/1101

105. Quinn (2015); Bock-Hager interview (2015, January 25). See wvde.state. wv.us/leaders-of-literacy/overview.html for an overview of the Leaders of Literacy campaign focus areas.

106. Quinn (2015).

107. West Virginia Department of Education. (n.d.) *Spring/Summer 2015 timeline to support county implementation of the WV Leaders of Literacy: Campaign for Level Reading.* Retrieved from http://wvde.state.wv.us/leaders-of-literacy/static/doc/timeline-to-support-county-implementation.pdf

CHAPTER 4

Washington State

Pre-K and Child Care for the Whole Child

Washington State is home to a small but high-quality public preschool program that serves more than 10,000 of the state's most vulnerable children. Washington's Early Childhood Education and Assistance Program (ECEAP) stands out for the extensive wraparound services that have been integral to the program since its inception in 1985, when it was among the few state-funded pre-K programs in the country.[1] A 2014 evaluation by the Washington Institute for Public Policy showed that ECEAP students made impressive test score gains in both reading and math that persisted through 5th grade, bucking the common trend of test score "fade-out" seen in many large-scale programs.[2]

Washington's preschool implementation is noteworthy for many reasons:

- The "whole child" preschool model that the state initially chose has endured, despite tough economic times.
- A bipartisan, united coalition has created the political will to expand funding for early learning.
- Grants from the federal government and foundations have catalyzed long-term investments in quality and program alignment.
- Administration at the state level has been streamlined by consolidating programs in a cabinet-level Department of Early Learning.
- The state recently began efforts to expand access to quality early learning by investing in the workforce for child care as well as preschool.

For all its strengths, Washington's state preschool program is quite small. Although state law mandates that there be enough preschool slots to serve all income-eligible children by 2020, there will be significant challenges to this expansion along the way.

This case study begins with an overview of Washington's state-funded preschool program. It then delves into three parts of Washington's early learning landscape: political context, state administration and management, and program quality. Finally, it concludes with next steps for the state.

STATE-FUNDED EARLY EDUCATION IN A NUTSHELL

Washington's state preschool program, which was launched in 1985, was modeled after Head Start. The two programs have similar eligibility requirements and serve similar groups of children.

Like Head Start, the state preschool program provides all enrolled children and their families with an array of extensive wraparound services (see Table 4.1). Parents are involved in their youngsters' education through conferences with teachers. Each site has a family support worker and a health advocate, as well as access to nutrition and mental health consultants to advise staff and parents about children's specific needs. Families may also receive services such as developmental and health screenings for children and referrals for housing or legal services that occur outside of the formal instructional day.[3] The state preschool program provides a gateway to these services that take place off-site.

Preschool Serves the Most Vulnerable Children

Washington policymakers designed the state preschool program to focus on the very poorest children in the state. Youngsters are eligible if their families earn no more than 110% of the federal poverty level (in 2016, this is $26,730 for a family of four).[4] Children with special needs are also eligible, as are those receiving Child Protective Services.[5] Four-year-olds and children from the poorest families have the highest priority.

In 2014–2015, the state preschool program served 10,091 children, an increase of 15% from the previous year.[6] Head Start served another 11,387 children.[7] An additional 8,482 preschool-aged children received special education services, which may include preschool, through the Individuals with Disabilities Education Act (IDEA).[8]

In state preschool, 4-year-olds made up 71% of the enrolled students in 2014–2015. About one-third of all enrolled children in the pre-K program were dual-language learners, most of whom spoke Spanish or Somali. The majority of students were Latino (39%) or white (36%). Ten percent had an individualized education plan.[9]

Table 4.1. Key Facts About Washington's Early Childhood Education and Assistance
    Program

Element	
Number of children served	10,091 children in 2014–15[i]
Age	3- and 4-year-old children
Eligibility	Targeted for children in greatest need: • Family income under 110% of the federal poverty level ($26,730 for a family of four)[ii] • Enrolled in Special Education • Involved in the child welfare system
Length of program day	Determined locally: • Part day (81% of all children) • Full day (13% of all children) • Extended day (6% of all children)
Maximum class size	20
Teacher-child ratio	1:10 or better
Administration	The Washington Department of Early Learning administers the program and contracts directly with local providers.
Setting	Programs are located in a variety of settings: • Public schools (57%) • Child care centers (12%) • Head Start facilities (12%) • Nonprofit organizations (9%) • Faith-based facilities (4%) • Other (5%)
Curriculum	Providers are required to use a research-based, developmentally appropriate, and culturally relevant curriculum. • 87% of teachers use Creative Curriculum for Preschool • 13% of teachers use HighScope Preschool Curriculum and Assessment[iii]

Table 4.1. Continued

Minimum teacher qualifications	Lead teachers must have: • AA with 30 credits in early education or • Teaching degree or • Washington State teaching certificate with an endorsement in early education Assistant teachers must have: • 12 college quarter credits in early childhood education or • State Early Childhood Education Certificate or • Child Development Associate credential
Coaching for teachers	All classes are required to have a coach; coaches and teachers are encouraged to meet once a week.[iv]
Wraparound services	Children receive a variety of wraparound services, including: • Health care coordination, such as health care referrals and follow-up, and • Health, dental, and vision screenings
Family engagement	Programs must provide: • Minimum of 3 hours of documented family support per year • Information about community resources and referrals to housing, energy, legal, and health services • Parent education on topics such as child development, leadership, and advocacy skills

i. Data reflect the number of slots, or the children that could be served at any given time.

ii. U.S. Department of Health and Human Services. (2016, January 25). *Poverty guidelines*. Retrieved from https://aspe.hhs.gov/poverty-guidelines

iii. Washington Department of Early Learning. (n.d.). *Preschool essential elements: Supporting strong curricula*. Retrieved from http://www.del.wa.gov/publications/eceap/docs/curriculum.pdf

iv. Ganz, K. (2015, November). *Coaching orientation part 3 of 4: Roles and resources*. Retrieved from https://www.youtube.com/watch?v=RGkTIgU365M

Source: Washington Department of Early Learning. (n.d.). *ECEAP outcomes 2014-15*. Retrieved from http://www.del.wa.gov/publications/eceap/docs/ECEAP_Outcomes_2014-15.pdf; Washington Department of Early Learning. (2014, July). *2014-15 ECEAP performance standards*. Retrieved from http://www.del.wa.gov/publications/eceap/docs/ECEAP_PerformanceStandards.pdf

Figure 4.1. Washington's Preschool Enrollment Has Grown Over Time

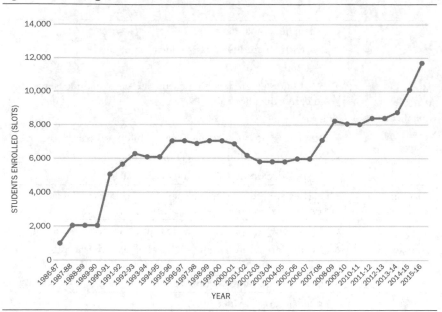

Source: Unpublished data from the Washington Department of Early Learning (personal communication, March 31, 2016).

Although the number of children enrolled is increasing (see Figure 4.1), the state still faces a significant unmet need. A recent report commissioned by the legislature concluded that an additional 26,929 eligible children were not enrolled in Head Start or preschool and that nearly 12,000 would likely participate if more slots were available.[10]

Most Programs Are Part-Day

The length of the program day is determined locally. About 80% of programs operate on a part-day basis (see Figure 4.A online). The state requires that these programs run for a minimum of 320 classroom hours each year, with at least 2.5 hours a day for 4 days a week. Full-day preschools operate on a schedule similar to K–12, meeting 5.5 to 6.5 hours per day, 4 or 5 days per week. Extended-day programs must be open at least 10 hours per day, 5 days per week. These programs run year-round. To be eligible for extended-day pre-K, a child's parents must be working or in a full-time education program.[11]

Figure 4.2. Washington Spends Over $7,000 Per Pupil for Part-Day Pre-K (2014)

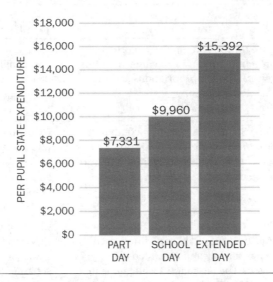

Source: Washington Department of Early Learning. (2014). *2014 ECEAP Models*. Retrieved from http://www.del.wa.gov/publications/eceap/docs/ECEAP%20Models.pdf

Spending Is Well Above the National Average

Total state funding for preschool was $76.7 million in 2014–2015, mainly coming from the state's general fund and the lottery (see Table 4.2).[12] Head Start funding was $137.6 million.[13] The National Institute for Early Education Research ranks Washington 8th in state spending and 6th in all reported spending for preschool.[14] The part-day program costs over $7,000 per child, about $2,500 more than the national average.[15] The higher cost is partly due to heavy investment in wraparound services. The tab for full-day programming is nearly $10,000 (see Figure 4.2), which is about the same as K–12.[16]

During its first 6 years, Washington's pre-K program grew steadily, eventually serving nearly 6,000 children, with a per pupil expenditure of around $6,000 (see Figure 4.B online). Funding, which was stable for the next decade, increased dramatically during Governor Christine Gregoire's first years in office, leaping from $33 million in 2005 to $62 million in 2008. This infusion of funds went to increasing both the number of students served and per-pupil spending; preschool enrollment jumped 38%, while average state spending per child rose from $6,604 to $7,580.[17]

Table 4.2. Washington's Pre-K Is Funded by a Variety of State, Federal, and Local
    Sources

Funding Source	Description	Funding Amount
State	State funds make up the majority of preschool funding, drawing from both general fund appropriations and the state lottery fund.	• State general fund: $36.7 million in 2013–2014 • State lottery fund: $40 million in 2013–2014[i]
Federal	Head Start funds are often combined, or braided, with state pre-K funds to serve additional children in the same program.[ii]	• Head Start: $137.6 million in overall funding in 2013–2014, a portion of which was combined with state preschool funds
	Child Care Development Block Grant (CCDBG) funds are sometimes used to pay for full- and extended-day classes. The amount set aside for state preschool has varied significantly over the past decade.[iii]	• Child Care Development Block Grant: $6.4 million set aside for state preschool in 2014–2015[iv]
	Title I and Individuals with Disabilities Education Act (IDEA), Part B, funding may also be used by school districts to fund state preschool, but the extent of this braiding is unclear.	
Local	State preschool programs may also receive substantial contributions from local sources such as local property tax revenue or transportation and facilities from local school districts. For example, Seattle has a property tax levy that will provide $58 million for the city's preschool program over four years.[v]	Amount varies

Though the Great Recession affected other social programs, early education was largely spared, and recently spending has increased again (see Figure 4.C online). The 2015 Early Start Act boosts the Department of Early Learning's budget by a third, and includes $24 million for an additional 2,400 preschool slots.[18] In addition to the state's investments, the federal government awarded Washington $60 million between 2012 and 2015 in Race to the Top grants. These funds went to quality improvement grants for providers, coaching, and the development of a kindergarten readiness assessment.

Table 4.2. Continued

	Foundation funding for non-programmatic costs, such as research, quality rating and improvement, and assessment development is substantial in Washington. Many foundations, including the Gates, Bezos, and Boeing Foundations, contribute through the state's public–private partnership, Thrive Washington.	Thrive Washington provided $10.8 million for all early learning programs in 2013–2014, a portion of which went to state preschool.[vi]
Public-private partnerships		

i. Unpublished data from the Washington Department of Early Learning (personal communication, March 31, 2016).

ii. Dropkin, E. (2013, July). *Partners for success: Case studies of collaboration between Head Start and pre-k.* Washington, DC: National Head Start Association.

iii. Washington Department of Early Learning. (2015, February). *2014 ECEAP Models.* Retrieved from www.del.wa.gov/publications/eceap/docs/ECEAP%20Models.pdf

iv. In 2014-2015, the state conducted a one-year pilot to extend the school day with Child Care Development Block Grant funds. This pilot has been suspended, and little to no funding was allocated from CCDBG in 2015–2016 at the state level (any braiding that occurred happened at the local level).

v. City of Seattle. (n.d.). *Seattle Public Preschool implementation plan.* Retrieved from www.seattle.gov/Documents/Departments/OFE/AboutTheLevy/EarlyLearning/SPP%20Implementation%20Plan.April%201.PostCommittee.pdf

vi. Thrive Washington. (2014, April). *2014 annual report.* Seattle, WA: Thrive Washington.

Child-Care Programs Also Serve Many Preschool-Aged Children

Although this case study focuses primarily on state preschool, Washington's subsidized child-care program, Working Connections, will also be discussed since it is increasingly viewed by policymakers as an important part of the state's early learning landscape. Working Connections Child Care provides subsidies to parents who have a household income up to 185% of the federal poverty level ($48,500 for a family of four) and are working or in school.[19]

Funding for Working Connections comes primarily from the federal government's Child Care Development Block Grant and state matching funds. In FY 2014 the state received over $300 million in block grant funds from the federal government.[20] Providers who serve children through Working Connections receive significantly less funding than preschool programs. Daily child-care reimbursement rates range from $23 to $32, depending on the region, which means about $6,000 to $8,500 per year when children are in the program 8 hours a day, 260 days per year.[21] (Full-day, full-year preschool costs over $15,000 per child on average.)[22]

Child-care subsidies are available to children from birth to age 12, with a funding cap of 50,000 children from a maximum of 30,000 families. During a typical month in 2015, 12,691 3- and 4-year-olds received child-care vouchers, slightly more children at any given time than enrolled in either preschool or Head Start. In 2015, more than 26,000 3- and 4-year-old children cycled through the subsidy program.[23]

While the state's Department of Social and Health Services runs the day-to-day operations of Working Connections, since 2007 the Department of Early Learning has set child-care policy. Children receiving child-care vouchers through Working Connections obtain care in a variety of settings. About two-thirds go to day care centers, and the rest are enrolled in home-based care, including family day care homes in which a caretaker, in some cases with an assistant or two, takes care of a small group of children.[24]

Combined, Washington's publicly funded programs serve more than 40,000 3- and 4-year-olds each year: 10,091 in state preschool, 26,195 in Working Connections Child Care, and 11,387 in Head Start.

Services for Children Under 3 Are Limited

The main publicly funded programs for infants and toddlers in Washington, other than subsidized child care, are Early Head Start and home visiting. These programs are relatively small, because, as in most states, preschool has received most of the attention and state dollars. Federally funded Early Head Start enrolled 6,461 children under age 3 in 2013.[25] Around 2,100 families were served by home visiting programs in 2015.[26]

Home visiting programs, in which trained professionals provide support in the home to new and expectant parents, are one of the earliest interventions the state offers. The Department of Early Learning and its public–private partner, Thrive Washington, jointly administer Washington's Home Visiting Services Account.[27] The majority of counties use nationally recognized programs, such as Nurse Family Partnerships, Parents as Teachers, and Early Head Start Home-Based.[28] But unlike other states in which each home visiting program is run and funded independently, Thrive oversees the myriad home visiting programs and funds them from federal, state, and private money blended into a single source. By focusing on families that may be experiencing the stress of poverty, community violence, or teen parenthood, the home visiting program promotes the healthy development of the state's most vulnerable children.

POLITICS OF EARLY EDUCATION

Leading politicians and a strong, diverse coalition of advocates have pushed significant investments in early education in Washington. Their efforts have been bolstered by glowing evaluations of the state's program and a willingness by the legislature to invest in improving the quality of child care as well as preschool.

Governors Push the Agenda

Governor Booth Gardner, a Democrat, was a proponent of Head Start. Recognizing that Head Start served only a small fraction of Washington's vulnerable children, he called for the creation of a state preschool program. During his tenure, from 1985 to 1993, the state program steadily grew from 1,000 children in its first year to around 6,000 students.[29] Of the governor's passion for early education, Joel Ryan, who heads the Washington State Association of Head Start and ECEAP, says:

> Governor Gardner was ahead of his time when it came to early childhood education. He was a trailblazer who started ECEAP [state pre-K], and, in turn, helped thousands of Washington's at-risk children start school ready to be successful and live up to their fullest potentials.[30]

For the next decade, the program remained essentially unchanged in the number of children it served, its funding levels, and its program structure. In 2005, when Christine Gregoire was elected, early education was not initially among her priorities. She says that quickly changed:

> I went in, frankly, with the attitude "What can we do with high school?" We began to hear everybody talk, and I thought, we need to go deeper. We said, "Okay, middle school, what do we do there?" Well, you know the rest. We went to grade school, and then we got to the real heart of it, which all begins in early learning. In the process of doing it, I really did develop a passion for it. I went around to early learning programs, saw them firsthand, saw the statistics, did the research, and all of it led to my firm conviction that this was an issue that was nonpartisan.

Governor Gregoire, together with key lawmakers, led the campaign to expand full-day kindergarten and boost the number of preschool slots. She also was committed to improving preschool quality. She recalls:

When I started, preschool was [widely viewed as] babysitting. And we really have fundamentally changed the culture in this state, to bring the respect, to bring the salaries, to bring all of the attention necessary for people to understand preschool is not babysitting.

Gregoire worked closely with lawmakers to substantially increase the preschool budget from $33 million in 2005 to $62 million in 2008.[31] Those added funds led to several improvements, including comprehensive early learning standards, more robust teacher professional development, and the reduction of class size from a maximum of 24 children to a maximum of 20. During Governor Gregoire's 8-year tenure, Washington went from meeting six of the quality benchmarks identified by the National Institute of Early Education Research to meeting nine of the benchmarks.[32]

Gregoire also addressed the state's fragmented early learning bureaucracy, promoting legislation that brought a host of programs under the roof of a cabinet-level agency, the Department of Early Learning. She helped launch a public–private partnership, Thrive by Five (now Thrive Washington), to coordinate government agencies, businesses, and nonprofits working on early learning across the state.[33]

Washington's current governor, Democrat Jay Inslee, has continued Gregoire's efforts, making expansion of the program a priority of his administration. In a speech at the signing of the 2015 Early Start Act, the Governor credited the passage of the legislation to the work of a handful of legislators—the same legislators who collaborated with Governor Gregoire:

> I thank the bipartisan group of members who have shown outstanding leadership on this bill. Representative Ruth Kagi has long been a champion for children and for early learning in particular. She has been instrumental in moving our state forward as the national leader in early learning. Senator Steve Litzow was his chamber's sponsor of the bill. I also recognize Representative Walsh and Senator Billig who have co-sponsored it over the past few sessions. And I appreciate the hard work of the budget team, Senators Hill and Hargrove, and Representatives Hunter and Chandler.[34]

Key Legislators Build Bipartisan Momentum

This handful of influential veteran lawmakers from both sides of the aisle worked together for years to expand and improve the state's early education program, and their efforts were essential to the adoption of the governor's proposals.Washington may be known for solidly liberal politics on the national stage—the state last voted for a Republican presidential candidate in 1984—but local politics present a much more complicated reality.While the Seattle-Tacoma area and state capital are strongly liberal, the eastern two-thirds of the state are Republican. Democrats have narrowly won recent gubernatorial races, and the legislature has been split since 2012, with the Senate controlled by Republicans and the House controlled by Democrats. Bipartisan support for early education has thus been critical.

Jon Gould, Deputy Director of the Children's Alliance, an early childhood advocacy coalition, describes the importance of bipartisanship in securing the most recent funding increases:

> We needed this combination of senators: Republicans, being willing to invest as long as there's accountability, and Democrats essentially seeing early learning as part of the education continuum.The only way we could get into the hundreds of millions [of state funding dollars] for child care was by giving each chamber something that they really wanted.

A handful of well-placed lawmakers led the effort. Republican Senator Steve Litzow says,"The core group has been bipartisan and bicameral from the get-go. [We have a] full team of eight on both sides of [the] aisle. That has been critical in getting this through."

His Democratic colleague, Representative Ruth Kagi, adds,"We hammer out legislation and our colleagues generally rely on us."

Bipartisan Momentum Hits the Recession

In 2009, these lawmakers introduced a measure that would have included preschool in the definition of "basic education." This would have protected funding for preschool from budget cuts, just as K–12 funding is protected. The bipartisan bill made it to Governor Gregoire's desk, but she vetoed it. Advocates felt blindsided, having assumed that the governor would support more stable investment in pre-K. She describes her decision as being motivated by a desire to keep early learning separate from K–12 bureaucracy:

> You bring the success that we were having with early childhood education, with the flexibility to innovate . . . think of all that.You can't do it in all the rules and the regulations and the boundaries set in the K–12 system. I had

legislators who asked me, who assumed I was going to do it [sign the legislation], but I said to them, "The day our K through 12 education functions as well as what we've been able to accomplish thus far in early education, I will be the first to sign that bill."

Some advocates believe that funding was the real motivation for the governor's veto, however. The change to include preschool in the definition of basic education, proposed at the height of the Great Recession, could have had significant budgetary consequences.

In a more successful endeavor in 2010, the lawmakers, concerned that many eligible children were on waiting lists for preschool because of a paucity of slots, mandated that by 2018 all poor and at-risk 3- and 4-year-olds have the opportunity to enroll in state preschool.[35] (This mandate was later pushed back to 2020.) Despite being an entitlement program, typically anathema to Republicans, this bill had strong bipartisan backing, an indication of the broad base of support that preschool has come to enjoy.

Two years later, in 2012, Representative Kagi, Senator Litzow, and a handful of other preschool advocates in the legislature proposed making pre-K available to every 3- and 4-year-old, a proposal that received substantial bipartisan support.[36] But the timing—the end of the recession—still was not right. As Governor Gregoire notes:

> If it was today, we'd have a heck of a lot better chance. . . . It was unfortunate because we came all together from a perfect point from a policy standpoint, but the economy was in the dumps. We were just hanging on, and we knew over the long haul we had to just maintain our investment. We just confronted a bad economic time.

Still, the debate surrounding these measures contributed to a sense of urgency among lawmakers regarding the state's obligation to serve its poorest children. The Department of Early Learning issued a report in 2014 stating that nearly 27,000 eligible 3- and 4-year-old children were not being served by either state preschool or Head Start.[37] Waiting lists were long, and the department estimated that 63% of eligible families would want their children to participate if offered the opportunity. That report catalyzed action, and the legislature dramatically expanded funding for early education in the Early Start Act.[38]

Relying on Home-Grown Research

Though copious literature exists on the benefits of early learning, during debates over expanding and improving preschool Washington's policymakers have relied heavily on research produced within the state, particularly research that focuses on the state's own programs. Philanthropic and business partners have played an important role in generating this research.

A 2014 report on the essentials of a good preschool education, written by former Microsoft executive James Minervino and issued by the Gates Foundation, focused the statewide policy conversation on increasing the amount of time a child spends in preschool. The report points to a full-day, two-year program as the key to improving children's educational outcomes.[39] Department of Early Learning Director Ross Hunter, a former legislator who was named to the post in 2015, has made the expansion of full-day programming a top priority, and Heather Moss, his deputy, described the subsequent shift in thinking as "the path of new adventure." The fact that the Gates Foundation sponsored the study added to its credibility, says former Director of the Department of Early Learning Bette Hyde. Hunter and Minervino had been colleagues at Microsoft, Hyde adds, noting, "I think because of that history, with Gates and Microsoft, it [Minervino's report] is like the Bible."

The strong positive findings and fortuitous timing of another Washington study, a 2014 evaluation of the state's preschool program conducted by the highly regarded Washington State Institute of Public Policy, and commissioned by the legislature, concluded that students enrolled in state preschool made impressive gains compared with their counterparts who were not enrolled.[40] This evaluation examined the test scores of 5,436 children who participated in state preschool between 2003 and 2008. Researchers retrospectively matched the background of preschoolers with nonparticipants who were similar in terms of family income, family composition, and home language.[41] Compared to their matched pairs who did not participate, preschool participants showed gains equivalent to a 7% boost in reading and a 6% increase in math scores in 5th grade.[42] These effects are almost twice as large as those found from other early childhood programs that have been deemed effective.[43] What is more, the effects of preschool persisted—there was no indication that the gains made in early education faded out over time.

These two studies profoundly affected the legislature's decision to invest more in early education, according to Representative Kagi:

[The Minervino report] was immensely helpful in pushing back against some of the arguments we were hearing from people: "Well, the Head Start study, it [shows preschool] doesn't really make a difference." It makes a huge difference! And then, our own preschool study came out in December. I mean, how can you argue with that? [The Washington Institute of Public Policy] is our own institute, which we have tremendous respect for and follow their recommendations. And they consistently said, "It's the best investment you can make."

Grassroots and Grasstops Champions

As part of the efforts to expand early learning opportunities in Washington, so-called "grasstops" associations such as the Gates Foundation teamed up with grassroots groups. Child advocacy organizations joined forces with more unlikely supporters, such as the Business Roundtable.

The Gates Foundation, the nation's largest philanthropic foundation and a powerful force in its home state, kick-started the public–private partnership, Thrive Washington, to fund and implement projects that serve young children across the state. Thrive received support from major companies like Boeing and other philanthropies, including the Bezos Foundation.[44] The fact that Bill Gates's father served along with Governor Gregoire as a founding co-chair added heft to the new venture. Mary Seaton, former Director of Early Learning for the Office of Superintendent of Public Instruction (K–12), notes that Thrive helped to persuade K–12 educators that early learning was important:

> It's hard to get people [in K–12] to start thinking about pre-K as part of their work. We started focusing policy conversations on pre-K to grade 3 for the definition of "early learning." The relationship with the Department of Early Learning and our private-public partnership, Thrive, was critical because it basically said we are showing that we believe this all connects and needs to be connected. We could have some common messaging around not only what was good for kids, what they needed, but what kind of systems needed to be attended to at all levels.

More recently, the Gates Foundation has funded initiatives that bring early education advocates together. The Early Learning Action Alliance, a coalition begun in 2005, has enabled sometimes- fractious advocates to speak with a unified voice. A "big-tent" enterprise, it includes more than 50 member organizations, including preschool and home-visiting providers, labor unions, and the Head Start and ECEAP trade group. Alliance Deputy Director Jon Gould explains the rationale for the Alliance:

> There was increasing recognition that the early learning advocacy field was divided and we were hurting ourselves. We couldn't get it together, was

sort of the rap. The Gates Foundation was instrumental, frankly. They essentially came to us and said, "We want you to be a convener, and we're willing to invest in the advocacy resources to do that." So funding was helpful. The prompting of key policymakers like Representative Ruth Kagi was helpful. Ruth would say to everybody, "We're not going to win in Olympia unless you have a unified agenda."

Building trust among these organizations with different priorities required a great deal of effort, but over time the Alliance members have learned to trust one another. During the legislative debate over expanding preschool, the Service Employees International Union (SEIU), which represents child-care workers, decided to oppose the measure that would ultimately become the Early Start Act due to leadership's concerns about the potential burden of a new quality rating system on poorly paid family home care providers. If the union had defected from the Alliance, it would have weakened the coalition significantly. Members of the Alliance worked hard to keep them at the table, however, and while the SEIU never backed the Early Start Act, it also did not leave the coalition. The continued involvement of the SEIU in the negotiations led lawmakers to incorporate substantial funding for child-care providers' supports.[45]

Widespread Backing Pays Off: The 2015 Early Start Act

The Early Start Act of 2015 added $158 million to the Department of Early Learning's operating budget—a 25% increase.[46] Of the total funds, $41 million were slated to expand preschool access: $24 million to pay for new part-day and full-day classes (about 2,400 slots), and the balance to maintain the current number of full- and expanded-day slots.[47] But the lion's share of the new funds—$98.5 million—was earmarked for efforts designed to improve the quality of subsidized child care for children from birth to 5 years of age.[48] The state's quality rating and improvement system (QRIS), Early Achievers, was strengthened, and providers were required to meet the new benchmarks within five years to continue receiving state child-care subsidies.

This unprecedented focus on child care as a way to improve early education, instead of directing all new funding to preschool, emerged as a political compromise. This deal was the product of state budgetary constraints, limited infrastructure for expanding preschool in its current form, the desire to preserve options for families, and concern for maintaining diversity in the early-care and education workforce.

Innovation Without Money. Washington's policymakers made a pragmatic choice by investing in child care in addition to preschool. The state's fiscal situation made a substantial expansion of preschool a heavy lift. Even though Washington ranks 10th in the nation in median household income, its budget has remained relatively small because of the lack of tax dollars.[49] The state has neither an income tax nor a capital gains tax. Since it depends heavily on the sales tax, which fluctuates in tandem with the state's economy, the budget is especially volatile. Former Budget Committee chairman and current head of the Department of Early Learning Ross Hunter puts it frankly:

> It's the nation's most regressive tax structure. The cost of state and local services gets balanced on the backs of low-income and middle-class families, while the wealthy pay only a tiny fraction of their income in taxes.[50]

The paucity of state revenue, combined with the high price tag of the preschool program, has made it hard for the state to deliver pre-K even to the narrowly targeted group of eligible children.

Child care carries a much lower price tag. Reimbursement rates vary, depending on the region's cost of living, between $23 and $32 for a full day, approximately $6,000 to $8,500 for a full year. That is about half as much as the state pays for extended-day preschool.[51] That differential makes increasing reliance on child care a tempting option for fiscally strapped lawmakers. However, the lawmakers recognized that the educational quality of child-care programs is not comparable to preschool. That is why the Early Start Act legislation commits two-thirds of the new state dollars to center- and home-based child care.[52]

Ryan Pricco, the Policy and Advocacy Manager at Child Care Aware, explains the rationale for the new focus on child care.

> We knew that we had a great state-funded preschool program. The conversation began, "How do we provide that level of care for everyone?" There was a pretty robust debate between universal preschool, which is actually something we made a run at several years ago in the legislative session and there wasn't the money and the political will to do it. So we came back around, and really all along we were working with the mind-frame that the best approach is to go where the kids are, wherever their families have already deemed that "this is where I want my child to be," and just make sure that environment is high quality.

This approach requires less money than expanding preschool, and it will likely improve care for thousands of children now enrolled in home- and center-based child care. Yet no one contends that improved child care will be comparable to quality preschool. Because the least advantaged families often choose family child-care homes over center-based preschool, the strategy risks missing the opportunity to provide the best early education to the very children who need it most.[53]

The Benefits and Risks of Focusing on Child Care. The idea to "go where the kids are" had political traction. Advocates were concerned that a focus on preschool, which requires that teachers have at least an AA degree in child development, would eliminate providers from underrepresented racial, ethnic, and linguistic backgrounds, particularly in the rural, sparsely settled eastern half of the state where higher education institutions are less accessible.[54] Bolstering child care could keep the diversity of providers and enable families to choose the caretakers that they saw as best meeting their needs. Somali families, for example, tend to put their children in family child-care homes run by providers who speak their language.[55] Because Somali children make up 18% of the eligible children in Seattle's King County, Department of Early Learning Director Ross Hunter asserts that "if you don't have a solution that addresses Somali kids, you don't have a solution."

What is more, Washington has a chronic shortage of space and qualified preschool teachers. The legislative requirement that all eligible students have access to state pre-K by 2020 means that the program will nearly double in size during the next four years and will require an estimated 640 new classrooms and as many new teachers.[56] The long-term goal is that child-care providers take advantage of a formal pathway to become ECEAP (preschool) teachers. Because child-care providers already offer care to more than 26,000 children a year, focusing on them avoids many of the problems that scaling up the state-run preschool program entails.[57]

PROGRAM ADMINISTRATION AND MANAGEMENT

The unification of early learning programs at the state level during the past decade through the creation of the Department of Early Learning has helped shift the policy mindset, enabling officials to see child care and preschool as components of a single early learning system. Strong department leadership coupled with effective coordination has been instrumental in improving the quality of early education—there is greater alignment of early learning programs, both fiscally in the management of complex funding streams and conceptually in the understanding of age-appropriate strategies for the developing child.

Organization Matters

When Governor Christine Gregoire took office in 2005, she asked which agency was responsible for early learning. What she discovered was a panoply of programs scattered across various agencies:

> I could go to Social Services and ask, "tell me about ECEAP [the state's pre-K program]" and they would talk to me about social services. I could go to another state agency and say, "OK, what are you doing?" and they would tell me they were doing something else. There really wasn't any coordination or focus.

The remedy, she decided, was to create a single entity. "Consolidating our efforts into one early learning department won't solve all the problems of early learning, but it will make solutions possible," she recalls thinking. A new department had not been established in decades, but departmental status would signal the importance that the state attached to early education. The Senate Republican Caucus, opposed to any expansion of the state's role, initially blocked the governor's initiative. She prevailed in 2007 after enlisting the support of the business leaders who had backed early education since the state launched the preschool program a generation earlier.[58]

The Department of Early Learning oversees most of the state's early childhood programs, including preschool, child care, and home visiting. It contracts out recruiting and training coaches to Child Care Aware, and overseeing the home visiting programs to Thrive Washington. It also shares responsibility for child care with the Department of Social and Health Services. The Department of Early Learning drafts the rules concerning program quality and health and safety standards; the Department of Social and Health Services handles day-to-day administration. This coordination has sometimes posed problems, explains Subsidy Policy Supervisor Matthew Judge.

> There's a lot of gray area between what is policy and what is implementation, and we're working in that gray area all the time. Naturally, we try to have

recognized fences around who does what, but the Department of Social and Health Services is advocating for positions that have policy implications, and it's just a natural outgrowth of the work that they do. At the same time, the stuff we state policy-wise [is] inseparable from implementation, and kind of gets into their territory. I think we've just been really good about recognizing that we're all oriented towards the same mission.... Maybe in the past there's been some butting of heads, but I feel like [now] we're in a way better place.

Interagency relationships have been purposefully cultivated in an effort to assure that the departments do not retreat to their silos. A state-level Early Learning Partnership, formed in 2009, is meant to institutionalize these relationships. The partnership, which initially included the Department of Early Learning, the Office of Superintendent of Public Instruction (representing K–12), and Thrive Washington (representing private and philanthropic partners), has been expanded to include the Department of Health and the Department of Social and Health Services, in recognition of the important role those agencies play in the lives of children and their families.[59]

Meetings of the Partnership have occasionally been contentious, however—so contentious that an outside facilitator became necessary. Robert Butts, Assistant Superintendent of Early Learning in the Office of Superintendent of Public Instruction, explains why:

The new people, they come in, they say, "what do we need to pay this facilitator for, everything is wonderful." Well, [for example] there have been conflicts between the Department of Early Learning and Thrive over home visiting. There are turf issues, there are things that you're just going to have. Having a third party that can set the agenda so they can say, "I think I heard you say . . . ."

Informal connections also promote the relationships needed to overcome bureaucratic distrust and the temptation to expand an agency's turf. Butts and Nicole Rose, the Assistant Director for Quality Practice and Professional Growth at the Department of Early Learning, live across the street from one another. They talk through their concerns during a regular Friday walk, and over the years they have become friends as well as colleagues. These formal and informal efforts at collaboration have yielded some positive results. For example, a multipronged approach to teaching numeracy was initiated by early education teachers when the state's kindergarten readiness assessment revealed that this was an area in which students showed the least growth.[60] Early Learning Partnership members coordinate their expenditures, which enables the agencies to avoid duplication, and the joint Early Learning Plan specifies strategies that the partners are using in tandem.

The Qualities of Effective Leadership

Strong leadership at the helm, in addition to relationships and facilitation, also matters. Since its inception in 2009, the Department of Early Learning has had two leaders with very different styles. Betty Hyde, a forceful advocate for early education, led by enthusiasm. Her successor, Ross Hunter, has emphasized efficient management.

Hyde is an insider in education circles. As superintendent in Bremerton, a city of 40,000, she tackled the task of integrating pre-K with K–3—a challenging assignment since K–12 and preschool have historically had little to do with one another. A passionate promoter of early education, she was among the few Gregoire-era agency heads whom Governor Inslee retained.[61]

Quality was her watchword:

> If it's not quality, don't bother. You'll feel good, you'll say, "Hey, we're saving 3% more!" but if it's not quality you know we are wasting their time, our money, and have a lot of false expectations. Legislators love giving out more slots. You know, because they feel good! They say, "I did that!" They can count it, it's a quantifiable kind of thing. The quality is a little more . . . what does that look like? . . . But it costs more. You get what you pay for.

As for Hyde's successor, Ross Hunter, management is his forte. Hunter began his career at Microsoft, where a premium is placed on efficiency. While in the legislature, his selection as chair of the House Appropriations Committee, which oversees the budget, was a testament to his administrative acumen. As a lawmaker, Hunter became interested in early education, and at his request Hyde provided him with reams of research.[62]

Cultivating champions in positions of power was one of Hyde's strong suits. She recounts,

> [It was] relentless, constant reeducating, over and over, about brain science, about research . . . so it's kind of like one-on-one combat. Each legislator, each governor at a time. . . . Hunter and I, one summer, every Friday morning we'd have a one- or two-hour call about new research. He wanted to look

at only peer-reviewed research—not opinion papers. I'd send him things, he'd read it, we'd talk about it. We'd talk about our quality rating and improvement system, critique it, he'd say that's bullshit (because that's how he talks!) and we'd have a great conversation.

As a result, Hunter now has a solid understanding of the research that complements his command of the intricacies of management and budgeting. As Republican Senator Steve Litzow, a central player during the 2014 preschool negotiations and a Thrive Washington board member, points out:

> The biggest concern is making sure Ross Hunter is successful in implementing [the Early Start Act]. He has a huge task in front of him—coming back to the legislature in 2017 and needing to say "the program [the quality rating system] is working, we spent the money well." If he's unable to do that the program will fail.

The Complexities of Early Education Funding

One aspect of the administrative challenge is navigating a convoluted web of funding streams and varying program standards. As in other states, Washington pays for its early care and education programs with a host of funding streams. State-run preschool, administered by the Department of Early Learning, is underwritten mainly by the state's general fund and lottery revenue. Head Start centers, which serve even more children than state-funded preschool programs, contract directly with the federal government. Subsidized child care, paid for by the federal Child Care and Development Fund, is administered by the Department of Health and Social Services, with standards set by the Department of Early Learning. These programs receive varying, and sometimes substantial, support from local governments and nonprofits.[63]

Combining Funds at the Local Level. The line that separates preschool, Head Start, and child care at the local level has grown increasingly blurred. State and federal programs have not kept up, however; each program is governed by its own rules that can make local administrators' heads spin. Many administrators combine—"blend" and "braid" are the commonly used terms—funding streams to maximize the number of students they can serve and the amount of time these children can receive services.

When implemented well, this blending and braiding results in a user-friendly experience for families, who have no reason to know that their child is in a classroom that is funded by more than one program. One parent described the seamless experience that her son had at Valley View Early Learning School in Highline School District:

> To me, as a parent, preschool has been the most important thing [for my son] so far. We would be lost without it, especially for a student with special needs. His time at Valley View has been better than speech therapy or any of the other services we've gotten.

As a 3-year-old, her son was enrolled in a special needs preschool classroom at Valley View that was paid for by federal special-education dollars. The following year, he participated in a blended classroom with state preschool as well as special education students in the same classroom. His mother noticed a tremendous growth in her son's social skills.

The most common form of braiding links Head Start with state-funded preschool. The fit makes good educational sense, since both programs are premised on the same values—individualized education, parental engagement, and the provision of health and nutritional support—but the seamless experience described at Valley View is not always achieved. In Seattle, for example, Head Start providers tend to operate separately, rather than participate in a blended preschool–Head Start model. Leilani Dela Cruz, Early Learning and Child Development Manager for the City of Seattle, says:

> Head Start in the city kind of operates like every grantee is their own. It's kind of like they're the Vatican. The Vatican's in Italy, but they don't follow Italian law. They follow their own law. That's kind of how I feel about some of the Head Start folks. They operate unto themselves. They're pretty much independent entities.

Despite these administrative silos, an estimated two-thirds of the state's prekindergarteners are enrolled in centers that receive both Head Start and state preschool funding.[64] For the most part, these programs have one class that is entirely paid for with Head Start dollars and another that is underwritten by state pre-K. When there are not enough students to warrant two full classes, some programs blend Head Start and preschool dollars in a single classroom.

Many preschool providers also braid preschool and child-care dollars to offer a longer day. A provider might run a pre-K classroom in the morning, for instance, but use child-care support to keep the same classroom open in the afternoon. To do so, however, requires that distinct, and sometimes inconsistent, data-reporting requirements and program standards be met. Providers must walk a labyrinth of regulations and paperwork to get funded. The preschool standards run 35 pages; Head Start's rules are four times longer. The paperwork burden, often borne by the teacher, is substantial, and so is the loss of time that would otherwise be spent preparing for classes. Sandy Nelson, Assistant Superintendent of Early Learning for Educational Service District 113 in western Washington, has unhappy firsthand experience with this issue:

> [We usually keep] the classrooms funded completely by one source—you're either a Head Start teacher or a state preschool teacher—but if you walked into one or the other you wouldn't know the difference. For two years we had a blended classroom—that poor teacher had to report her time and effort separately, not a fun thing to do.

Katy Warren, Deputy Director of the Washington State Association of Head Start and ECEAP, gives an illustration of the hoops a provider must jump through:

> When you do the six-hour version [of state preschool], you suddenly have to be licensed as child care, and so there are a lot more requirements, both structurally and in terms of your furniture and your blinds. . . . To get licensed, you suddenly have to get sprinklers! We're also doing some work with aligned standards, . . . but what I keep bringing up in meetings is please, for the love of God, align the building codes too!

Program directors routinely deal with conflicts between licensing and standards. Kristi Baker, who runs the Southwest Washington Child Care Consortium, describes the difficulty of working in such a system. Her staff received contradictory messages from the preschool quality raters, who follow the Environmental Rating Standards for quality of the classroom, and state licensing officers, whose focus is health and safety:

> In one of my pre-K classrooms they set up the environment with the Environmental Rating Standards, and licensing [auditors] came in and put everything against the wall and said that teacher couldn't see kids across the room. But if we were to be rated [by the quality rating and improvement system], we'd get a poor rating even though we were following what Environmental Rating

Standards are. That's the kind of thing—it creates a discrepancy when they're not on the same page.

State officials are responding to these concerns in an ongoing project intended to streamline and reconcile the rules.

Combining Funds at the State Level. In 2014, the Department of Early Learning tried to take some of the burden off local providers by braiding funding streams for preschool and Working Connections Child Care at the state level. This strategy would have enabled a limited number of children in preschool to attend a full-day program. The proposal called for the state to pay for part of the school day, with child-care money covering the rest. Some preschool programs already do this at the local level, and the plan would have reduced the paperwork for these providers. Ross Hunter explains the reasoning behind this initiative:

> If you're trying to make a program that meets all these rules, it's crazy. We're not hiring day care center operators with that set of financial skills. A better strategy would be to blend funding at the state level. Can we combine them into one payment and one set of rules for the providers? Yes.

But this effort soon ran aground. These two programs have different missions, different pots of money, and different eligibility requirements. As its name, Working Connections, indicates, federally funded child care is aimed at the working poor, defined as those earning less than 185% of the poverty level (parents who are enrolled in school may also receive subsidies). In contrast, preschool is directed at the state's poorest families, defined as those earning no more than 110% of the poverty level, and many of these households have no working adult.

When the Department of Early Learning initially proposed that all full-day preschool programs receive Working Connections Child Care subsidies, federal program officers and the Department of Health and Social Services rejected the idea on the grounds that the children of nonworking parents are not eligible for subsidized care. But a lack of funds may have been the real sticking point. A report projected that offering child-care subsidies to many children in part-day pre-K would exhaust the available child-care funds. Ross Hunter, who backs full-day preschool, explains:

> I stepped back from it as the budget chair because the plan the Department had last year would have resulted in consuming all of the Child Care Devel-

opment Fund money for the state's 4-year-olds in a relatively short period of time. They would have spent all of it on kids below 110% of the federal poverty level and none of it would have been available for low-income working moms. And that doesn't seem like a good outcome.

The Department of Early Learning received permission to pilot the plan, but that experiment lasted only one year. However, the departments have not abandoned the proposal, and Ross Hunter believes that a modified version can be implemented.

GETTING TO QUALITY

Research has shown that Washington's preschool program is of high quality.[65] Washington has worked to achieve this result by (1) defining quality in terms of multiple domains of a child's development; (2) aligning expectations across grade levels; (3) using both incentives and sanctions to improve both pre-K and child care; and (4) investing in teacher and provider coaching.

What Does Quality Mean?

A defining feature of Washington's early learning programs is that they were designed to address the needs of the whole child, rather than merely to boost reading or math scores. The state's developmental guidelines, as well as its investment in wraparound services and teacher coaching, make this plain. The state preschool program provides a gateway to services that take place off-site, such as nutrition counseling and referrals for housing or legal services. Katy Warren, Deputy Director of the Washington State Association of Head Start and ECEAP, expresses the commonly held belief that wraparound services are key to ECEAP's success:

> It's always hard to separate out the parts of a program that you think are working. We do think that the fact that ECEAP is running kind of a Head Start model where they're working very closely with families has a lot to do with that, particularly in the population that we're looking at; [most are] below 85% of the federal poverty level. That family piece is really important.

The Department of Early Learning lays out its expectations for healthy cultural, social-emotional, physical, and cognitive development in the *Child Developmental Guidelines for Early Learning*. These guidelines are a roadmap for caregivers and families of children from birth to age 8. Unlike many K–12 standards, the goals are much broader than promoting academic preparedness. Social and physical development are given the same weight as traditional cognitive measures of success, and play is emphasized. For example, one developmental benchmark for ages 3-4 states that children may:

- Explore, practice, and understand social roles through play. Adopt a variety of roles and feelings during pretend play.
- Plan play by identifying different roles needed and who will fill these roles. Consider changing roles to fit the interests of children playing.
- Tell stories and give other children the chance to tell theirs.[66]

These benchmarks are meant for everyone in the early learning field, part of the Department of Early Learning's efforts to align student standards from pre-K to 3rd grade.[67]

Another foundational document, *The Core Competencies for Early Care and Education Professionals,* describes the expectations for adults who teach children from birth to 3rd grade. These guidelines focus on teachers' "process" competencies, the quality of the interactions between teachers and children. The core competencies stress the importance of teachers having real conversations with students, for example, as well as encouraging children to work on projects in small groups.[68]

The state further defines quality in the prekindergarten setting by the *Program Performance Standards for State Preschool.* Similar to the National Institute for Early Education Research benchmarks, these standards focus on the structural elements of a good program. They specify everything from the minimum level of teacher education (an AA degree with 30 credits in early childhood education or a teaching degree) to the maximum class size (20 children) and child-teacher ratio (10:1). These standards also include measures of adequate health, nutrition, and family engagement, as well as measures of instruction that incorporate children's home language.[69]

A holistic curriculum complements these standards. Rather than require a particular course of study, the preschool standards simply call for a "developmentally appropriate and culturally relevant curriculum" that is play based and child centered. However, the Department of Early Learning offers free or low-cost training and support for only two research-based curricula: Creative Curriculum, which aligns with the state

A Closer Look at State Preschool Wraparound Services

Like Head Start, Washington's state preschool focuses on making sure that children's basic needs are met so that they can arrive at school ready to learn. The state requires that programs provide a minimum of 6 hours of family contact each year, although many programs offer much more.

Physical health

Health advocates provide both well-child and dental exams for preschool students, sometimes in the classroom, and connect them to medical and dental providers for comprehensive, ongoing coverage. The program serves as a gateway to medical services for families, many of whom previously lacked access, says Sandy Nelson, Assistant Superintendent of Early Learning for Educational Service District 113. Across the state, in the beginning of their preschool year, only 55% of children were up-to-date on their dental services, compared to 92% of children by the end of the preschool year. These services are critical for early prevention. A parent in Skagit County, for example, credits a preschool screening for referring her son to a pediatrician for a hearing assessment. Had she waited much longer, the pediatrician said, her son would have permanently lost hearing in that ear.

Family engagement

Teachers meet with families multiple times per year to discuss their child's development and school readiness. They also work with families to make sure family needs are met—not just those of the child. They set family goals, discuss progress toward meeting those goals, and connect families to community resources. Many programs run parent education classes, too. End-of-year surveys suggest that these services make families more familiar with community resources and strategies to support their child behaviorally and academically at home. Further, parents feel like full partners in making educational decisions for their children.

Source: Washington State Department of Early Learning. (2012). *Early childhood education and assistance program, Head Start and Early Head Start in Washington State: 2012 Profile.* Olympia, WA.

WHAT DOES HIGH-QUALITY PRESCHOOL INSTRUCTION LOOK LIKE?

Every year at Valley View Early Learning School, all of the preschool classes engage in a unit studying animals, culminating with a fieldtrip to the zoo. By connecting lessons to a broader unit of study, students gain rich content knowledge. Students spend much of their time working in small group or independent center-based activities, but whole group instruction is used as well. The lessons are fast paced and offer children many opportunities to interact with each other and the teachers, and also connect the content of the lessons to their own lives.

During one lesson, the teacher reads aloud about different animals with bright colors. A blue peacock! A purple walrus! Her students are arranged on the carpet, some sitting "criss-cross applesauce" and others leaning in to see the book better.

Together, they count the peacock feathers and discuss the walrus— What color is he? Had any of the students seen or heard of a walrus before? One boy exclaims, "A walrus? Let me see! A purple walrus . . . I've never seen a purple walrus before." The teacher and students discuss the real and imaginary colors for the animals in the story. Several volunteers are interspersed with students on the carpet, keeping them focused and engaged. One volunteer sits in the back, quietly translating the conversation for two Spanish-speaking students.

After a few minutes, circle time ends and the students leave the carpet, moving to the next activity. Some play zoologist in the dress-up center with binoculars and a lab coat, while others count, sort, and match animals. Later in the day the class will make animal hats for a parade, one of the school-wide activities that concludes the animal unit.

Source: Site visit to Valley View Early Learning School.

---

kindergarten readiness assessment, and HighScope. In 2013–2014, 87% of state preschool sites used Creative Curriculum and the remaining providers used HighScope.[70]

A Shared Definition of Quality: Birth-to-Age-8 Alignment

The view among K–12 educators that preschool is little more than babysitting has largely receded into history. Now officials are working together to make sure that teachers' and administrators' expectations for young children are aligned. Katy Warren, Deputy Director of the Washington State Association of Head Start and ECEAP, is enthusiastic about this alignment:

> Pre-K to grade 3 is great. There have been a lot of places in Washington that have done some work around that, really early work. They have to adjust their K–12 curriculum, they've brought in their child-care providers, and the [families].

The Department of Early Learning and the Office of Superintendent of Public Instruction (K–12) have recently worked together to develop a shared kindergarten readiness assessment with private funding from the Gates Foundation and Thrive WA.[71] The assessment, WaKIDS (the Washington Kindergarten Inventory of Developing Skills), specifies developmental markers that all children should reach before starting kindergarten. It is based mainly on Teaching Strategies GOLD, an assessment that was developed by Creative Curriculum, publisher of the most widely used curriculum in the state. Educators supplement Teaching Strategies GOLD with a parent-child inventory that the Department of Early Learning developed using federal Race to the Top funding.

To conduct the assessment, teachers observe each child individually, during everyday classroom activities and in a one-on-one setting. They record the child's ability to regulate his or her own emotions and behaviors, for example, or to use language to express thoughts and needs.[72]

WaKIDS is "a way to see whether preschool is working," says Ross Hunter. But it is more than a one-shot evaluation; it is a tool that preschool and kindergarten teachers can use as a bridge to collaborate. WaKIDS is also a mechanism for parental engagement, requiring a one-on-one meeting between parents and their child's teacher before kindergarten starts.[73] Sandy Nelson, Assistant Superintendent of Early Learning at State Educational Service District 113, says:

> It provides a common language around kids' skills. [For decades, the objectives of preschool] depended on what the kindergarten teacher or principal I talked to said they expected. Now we actually say this is what we are hoping and expecting that kids come in with. Preschool providers have been knocking on the door for years, asking for guidance—now the information is there for them. It's an amazing step.

Assessments consume a lot of teachers' time, and for that reason sometimes evoke resentment, but advocates believe that having the assessment

WHAT DOES PRESCHOOL TO 5TH GRADE ALIGNMENT LOOK LIKE?

A hundred yards up the hill from Dearborn Park International School, an elementary school in Seattle, Causey's Learning Center serves 40 preschoolers in a small stand-alone facility. Although Causey's has its own classroom space and play yard, the learning taking place in the pre-K classrooms is closely linked to the academic instruction at the elementary school. Dearborn Principal Angela Sheffey Bogan views high-quality preschool as an integral part of a "pre-K to grade 5" educational program. Whenever possible, Causey's students are enrolled at Dearborn Park for kindergarten, easing their transition to elementary school. To help lay the groundwork for that transition, preschool students regularly receive library and physical education instruction at the elementary school.

Teachers in both programs work together closely. Causey's employees attend Dearborn Park staff meetings after school, and Causey teachers get substitutes so they can have common planning time with the elementary teachers. One preschool teacher says the joint planning time gave her an opportunity to understand what arithmetic skills students were expected to develop in the early elementary grades. Based on that deepened understanding, she was able to incorporate new math activities in her play-based curriculum to better prepare her preschool students for the demands of kindergarten and beyond.

Other collaborative structures are in place as well. A Family Educational Rights and Privacy Act (FERPA) release allows Causey staff to share student information with Dearborn's staff members. The school-based health clinic at Dearborn Park serves Causey's students and families. This tight communication and collaboration results in a well-designed experience for students and families who participate in the preschool-to-5th grade continuum.

Note: Beginning in the 2016–2017 school year, Causey's Learning Center will be relocating to another site.

Source: Site visit to Causey's Learning Center and Dearborn Park International School.

results will improve classroom practice in both preschool and kindergarten. The Department of Early Learning and K–12 administrators have already started to use the data; after tests revealed that incoming kindergarteners were weakest in math readiness, professional development for prekindergarten teachers focused on that subject.[74]

Measuring Quality:
Washington's Quality Rating and Improvement System

With the standards clearly defined, Washington's quality rating and improvement system (QRIS) serves as the tool for measuring their implementation. Starting in 2017, state preschool and subsidized child-care providers will be assessed using the state's new QRIS, called Early Achievers. While preschools have been required to use this system since 2013, participation for child-care providers has been voluntary. Beginning in 2017, however, only those providers who rate highly on the QRIS will be eligible for state subsidies. That makes participating in the enterprise a "voluntary mandate."

The Early Achievers system has five tiers. The first two tiers can be met by simply enrolling in the QRIS, getting licensed in basic health and safety, and participating in trainings and professional development. Tiers three to five are reached through an assessment by an outside observer in which the provider receives a certain number of points on a rating scale that measures student-teacher interactions and the physical classroom environment.[75]

While the QRIS applies to both preschool and child-care, requirements for the two programs are different (see Table 4.3). A pilot study showed a significant overlap in the preschool accreditation requirements and first two levels of the QRIS. A validation study further showed a high level of consistency in quality among pre-K providers. To streamline the QRIS rating process, then, preschool programs are automatically assigned a level 3 until they receive their first rating.[76]

Child-care providers, on the other hand, must go through the rating process and receive at least a level 3 rating to retain their state subsidies. The introduction of a minimum quality standard for child care marks a substantial, and controversial, change in expectations. Until recently, these programs only needed to satisfy basic health and safety standards, and there was no measure of instructional quality.[77] The Early Start Act takes a carrot-and-stick approach: Providers must meet the minimum quality threshold, but they also receive a subsidy increase for meeting higher standards (see Table 4.4). As Senator Steve Litzow notes, "The state will not pay for bad quality early learning. That was a big thing."

Early Achievers rates programs based on various factors, with a major focus on the nature of the interactions between staff and children. The quality of child-teacher interactions is assessed using the nationally recognized Classroom Assessment Scoring System (CLASS), while the

Table 4.3. Washington's QRIS Differs for Pre-K and Child Care

State Preschool Providers	Child Care Providers
• Facilities are automatically rated a level 3 upon receiving a state preschool license.	• Facilities are required to receive a level 3 rating to receive subsidies.
• Enrollment is mandatory for providers.	• Enrollment is "optional," but providers must be enrolled in Early Achievers to receive state subsidies.
• Coaching is provided to programs through the Department of Early Learning.	• Coaching is provided to programs by Child Care Aware, a statewide nonprofit, through the Department of Early Learning.
• The reimbursement rate for providers is fixed.	• The reimbursement rate for providers varies by quality level.

Source: Washington Department of Early Learning (2016, January). *Early Achievers: Participant operating guidelines.* Retrieved from www.del.wa.gov/publications/elac-qris/docs/EA_operating_guidelines.pdf

Table 4.4. Higher Rated Programs Receive Larger Subsidies and Grants in Washington

QRIS Level	Subsidy Rate Increase	Quality Improvement Award[i]	Professional Development Grants[i]
1	0%	None	None
2	2%	None[ii]	None
3	4%	$5,000 (center) $2,000 (home)	• $4,000–$6,000 tuition for training • $1,000 books for training
4	10%	$7,500 (center) $2,250 (home)	
5	15%	$9,000 (center) $2,750 (home)	

i. Awards and grants are for one-time funding only.

ii. Home-based providers reaching level 2 were eligible to receive $750 through June 30, 2015.

Source: Washington Department of Early Learning. (2016, January). *Early Achievers: Participant operating guidelines.* Retrieved from http://www.del.wa.gov/publications/elac-qris/docs/EA_operating_guidelines.pdf

physical classroom environment is measured using the Environmental Rating Scale. Together these two ratings account for 70 of the 100 points that providers can receive.[78] An additional 10 points each are awarded for "child outcomes" (which means using assessments and sharing data with families), professional development and training, and family engagement and partnership. A family child-care operator describes the progress she has made on one element of CLASS, asking open-ended questions:

> Before I used to say things like, "oh look, you have a red block. Let's put it over here. Can you put it over here?" And now it's more of, "What do you have? What are you going to do with it?"[79]

Being held accountable for a particular learning environment and style of student-teacher interactions is a major change for many caregivers, according to Stacie Marez, Early Learning ECEAP Coordinator in Yakima County:

> Centers typically work kind of on a skeleton crew . . . they're used to just acting according to those ratios. . . . So the mindset of the model is different. Working with providers to get them to change that mindset and get them to staff beyond just ratios is a challenge.

The Service Employees International Union was particularly vocal about the need to support child-care providers as expectations for the quality of their care increased.[80] The Early Start Act includes more money for programs reaching higher quality levels, grants for purchasing classroom materials, scholarships for teachers to pursue additional education, and in-class coaching (see Table 4.4). Thrive's Community Momentum Director Dan Torres notes that by the time the Act was hammered out, "advocates in the state were in agreement. The supports were enough to make the mandates worth it." Even more importantly, these supports were written into law as ongoing funding, guaranteed by the legislature. Children's Alliance Deputy Director Jon Gould explains:

> The scholarships, grants, tiered reimbursements to low-income communities are not onetime bits of funding. They get calculated by the Governor's office as needed, and folded into maintenance-level funding. We never used the word "entitlement" with the legislature, but that's exactly what we did when we wrote: The state SHALL fund.

Improving Quality Through Coaching

Of the supports funded by the Early Start Act, the one that is viewed as especially promising is coaching. Indeed, the state has made coaching the engine that drives improvement for all early learning, especially child care. Although state pre-K programs have deployed coaches for a long time, coaching for child-care providers is a massive new effort. Any program that reaches level two of Early Achievers receives a coach who works with teachers in the classroom. The hope is that by investing in coaching, the state can close the quality gap between child care and preschool.[81]

This focus on coaching came from a Washington study, the Seeds to Success pilots financed by the Department of Early Learning and the Gates Foundation. In 2009, children in two counties were randomly assigned to one of 66 providers. Half of the providers received coaching, quality improvement grants, and funds for professional development. The others got only funds for professional development.[82] According to Ryan Pricco of Child Care Aware:

> The biggest takeaway is that using a coaching approach—where programs have a coach on site with them, working hand in hand with them to make daily improvements to their interactions with kids or simple improvements to their environment—very quickly and very efficiently improved the quality of care.[83]

The state has extended the coaching model statewide. Caroline Shelton, program director at Child Care Aware, estimates that since the Early Start Act passed in 2014, Washington has recruited more than 100 coaches. All of them have experience in the early education field and have (or are acquiring) a BA in child development. They receive two days of formal training, run jointly by the University of Washington and Child Care Aware, augmented by webinars and meetings with fellow coaches and trainers. The Department of Early Learning is currently developing a regional support model, with coaches conducting their own professional development locally.[84] Shelton asserts:

> You can only sustain quality from a centralized university or state organization to a point. What we're trying to do is to build [continuous improvement] oversight in the regional offices.

The coaches' job is to help preschool teachers improve the structure of the classroom and, more importantly, the way they relate to children, using the core competencies framework as a guide. A coaching session can focus on anything from developing engaging lesson plans to coaxing a provider to talk more to infants. An early learning teacher describes a session with her coach:

> We had a conference about how to get science into the room because that's what I struggled with. She told me just to take regular day things and try to find out how they work. And that's science—the little bits. The rain coming down is now a science activity. We're learning about evaporation just from a cup of water being there on the counter and watching how low it gets. She did a lot to open my eyes and show me how I can improve it. It's worked very well. [The kids are] very into every little thing they do now.[85]

The coaches' training, based on a model developed by the University of Washington, is "relationship based," building trust between coach and child-care staff. Some providers initially distrusted the coaches, but Shelton explains that this attitude is changing:

> Most [child-care staff] have been in a regulatory environment, with a licenser telling them what they're doing wrong. Now there's a coach telling them what they are doing well. After receiving coaching, most programs say it's what they value most in their whole experience [with the quality rating and improvement system].

Most child-care workers lack a college degree and have not taken early education courses, making coaching more challenging than in a preschool setting.[86] Coaches must introduce fundamental pedagogical concepts familiar to traditionally trained teachers, like "scaffolding," a technique that provides students with the tools they need to gradually increase their understanding. That is not an easy concept for child-care workers to absorb, says Stacie Marez, Early Learning Coordinator of Educational Service District 105 in Yakima County:

> What we're specifically working on, for four years, is moving someone from a child-care mindset to a high-quality mindset. They're hard conversations, lots of back and forth having standards conversations. We're starting over with a new child-care partner, owned by a couple, from square one. What we're working on is not only do we need curriculum in place, but daily schedule and lesson planning.

Trained coaches are scarce, especially in rural areas. The demand for bilingual coaches in particular has outstripped the supply. There is not a large base of experienced teachers to choose from, and the Department of Early Learning competes with preschool program administrators for these experienced professionals.[87] The University of Washington adapted Head Start's virtual coaching program, Coaching Companion, to fill the gap, but Internet connections are spotty in many child-care settings, and there is little evidence yet of the effectiveness of online coaching.[88] To compound the problem, Child Care Aware anticipates a sizable influx of providers who need to be enrolled in the QRIS and receive coaching as the 2017 deadline for Early Achievers enrollment approaches.[89] For Washington's strategy to work, the state must make sure sufficient coaching is available to all, but at this point it is unclear how that can be accomplished.

Seattle's Experiment with High-Quality Preschool

While the state continues to focus on its poorest 4-year-olds, Seattle has decided that quality and universal access go hand in hand. The city's voters opted to make full-day preschool available to all 4-year-olds and many 3-year-olds.[90] The city provides the program free for families who earn less than 300% of the federal poverty level, and higher-income parents pay on a sliding fee scale. The program will reach a far greater portion of children in need than the state-funded one with its stringent income eligibility rules.

Quality is Seattle's goal. In devising its model, it looked to Boston, Washington, DC, and New Jersey, all of which have strong reputations for the caliber of their early education efforts.[91] Leilani Dela Cruz, Early Learning and Child Development Manager for Seattle, explains how its program was designed:

> We hired consultants to survey high-quality preschool programs across the country.... It's been a combination of working with consultants and researchers and Jim [Minervino]'s documents, looking at the quality elements we wanted to have. There was a real intense conversation about quality vs. quantity ... [but since] we have a high ECEAP and Head Start saturation rate, we were really focused on quality.

The Seattle program stresses teacher support. Educators receive individual and group coaching for everything from teaching strategies to classroom management. The salary scale is comparable to K–12—a major difference from state-funded preschool—and that encourages veteran teachers to stay.[92] And unlike the state pre-K program, in Seattle teachers must hold a BA.[93]

Rather than scaling up quickly to meet the pent-up demand, the city started by funding only 14 sites that already offered state preschool and scored well on the QRIS.[94] Nevertheless, the program has suffered its share of growing pains. As in many cities, space is a problem. The decision to blend funding streams, including locally raised dollars, within classrooms has led to familiar confusion in budgeting and reporting.[95]

University of Michigan professor Christina Weiland, the co-evaluator of the Boston program who has worked closely with Seattle officials, praises the program for being "unusually thoughtful" in its approach. However, many questions remain. Can quality be maintained among multiple community-based organizations? How will Seattle's decision to devise its own curriculum, rather than rely on an evidence-based curriculum already on the market, affect children's experience? In a geographically large city without an adequate public transit system, how will logistics issues be solved? Seattle has scant time to demonstrate progress, since the 4-year pilot ends in 2019, when voters will have an opportunity to maintain or abandon it.[96]

Challenges to Quality: A Shortage of Teachers and Space

Ask early education administrators in Washington to identify their biggest problems and the same issues invariably top the list—finding and keeping teachers and locating space. The good news that pre-K and kindergarten are enrolling more children has unfortunately made the situation worse.

Requirements to make kindergarten a full-day, rather than part-day, program have exacerbated these shortages. By 2017, all 5-year-olds were entitled to attend full-day kindergarten because of a Washington Supreme Court ruling that access to kindergarten falls under the state's constitutionally protected right to a "basic education." An estimated 23,000 students became eligible starting in 2016–2017, and for preschool providers this meant trouble.[97]

The main reason teachers move from preschool to kindergarten is to receive a higher salary.[98] Kindergarten teachers belong to the K–12 union, and the average salary of an elementary school teacher is $45,370. Compared to the preschool average of $32,500, it makes financial sense for a teacher with a credential to move to K–12.[99] The expansion of kindergarten has created new teaching positions, and preschool teachers as well as coaches are migrating there. This leakage of veteran preschool teachers into kindergarten is particularly concerning because research shows that teachers get better with experience.[100] Lani Todd of the Service Employees International Union puts it this way:

> The giant elephant in the room is that it's going to cost a huge amount to make high-quality affordable child care . . . any solutions have to involve compensation. If we're expecting these providers and teachers to have degrees, and give the best, evidence-based curriculum, and be 100% up on all of their classes, then we should be paying them professional wages.

The expansion of state-funded preschool adds to the shortage. Between 2016 and 2020, when all eligible children are entitled to enroll in preschool, an estimated additional 9,627 youngsters will enroll.[101] Roughly 500 lead and assistant teachers will be needed to meet the coming demand, far more than are entering the pipeline.[102]

Lack of classroom space is another major problem caused by the expansion of kindergarten and preschool. Elementary schools, which need additional classrooms to accommodate the influx of 5-year-olds, are in some cases evicting preschools that had used those classrooms.[103] Finding suitable and affordable alternatives can be a challenging task, with few resources available to build new preschool facilities. The Office of Superintendent of Public Instruction's facility advisory committee estimates that the state will need thousands of additional pre-K and kindergarten classrooms by 2020. The governor's proposed $10 million infrastructure budget would barely make a dent in the cost of supplying these facilities.[104]

The pressing need for new teachers and additional space partly explains why Washington opted to put more focus on child care, rather than simply expanding state preschool. As Representative Ruth Kagi points out, to fill the gap more child-care providers must become licensed as preschool teachers. "We can't expand preschool unless we have quality child-care providers who are willing to take that on—we just can't serve the number of kids we have to serve."

Challenges to Quality: Resources in Rural Washington

The teacher shortage problem is particularly acute in the rural areas of the state. The Cascade Mountains divide Washington into two regions, east and west, and the contrast is far more than a matter of geography.

KEEPING TEACHERS IN PRESCHOOL

The Southwest Washington Child Care Consortium (SWCCC) has found some innovative ways to keep teachers in preschool classrooms. Like preschool centers elsewhere, SWCCC struggled to maintain its 160 teachers. It has responded with a two-pronged strategy: intensive training and better pay.

The training consists of a short "Career Academy" before new teachers begin the school year, as well as a longer-term apprentice program that gets child-care workers a degree. The six-week academy covers the basics of child development. Child-care workers, some of whom teach pre-K at the consortium, are paid to attend; they learn about the elements of good curriculum and effective pedagogy, and then apply what they have learned in one of the consortium's classrooms. In the apprenticeship program, child-care workers complete college modules while staying on the job. SWCCC's executive director, Kristi Baker, says:

> They leave the six-week session understanding the importance of where we connect to the children and what their individual needs are, and that is a huge part of their job. They are able to work out in the consortium, come back and talk about what they have learned, and experiences they have had with families and kids. These were teachable moments. . . . We still have a lot of staff from the Career Academy working for us today.

The staff are also paid better than at neighboring child-care centers and receive health care benefits, an additional incentive to remain. The consortium can be more generous because it keeps costs relatively low through economies of scale and generates revenue from fees paid by parents whose income exceeds the state-funded preschool maximum.

Baker points to another, less tangible factor in explaining why her program has been able to retain its staff—the culture of the organization. Unlike child-care homes or smaller centers, it has a human resources system with the capacity to consistently select staff who have demonstrated a commitment to young children. Expectations are made clear and coaching is individualized to address the needs of each teacher. And the staff have a voice in the organization. "You need to make sure that the staff members are heard and have a part in the process," Baker explains.

Source: Interview with Kristi Baker, Executive Director, Southwest Washington Child Care Consortium (2015, November 9); Southwest Washington Child Care Consortium. SWCCC overview. Retrieved from web3.esd112.org/swccc

Western Washington is relatively densely populated, generally well-off, well-educated, and liberal. Conversely, eastern Washington is much poorer, rural, less educated, and conservative.[105] These differences have had a profound impact on the character of early education in each area.

The most basic problem in eastern Washington is the lack of providers. As Dan Torres, Director of Community Momentum at Child Care Aware, notes, "The availability of quality care is more of an issue in this region of the state. Just having licensed child care [let alone a state-funded center or pre-K] is sometimes challenging."

To avoid the new QRIS requirements, Department of Social and Health Services officials say that some early education providers may shift their focus from preschoolers to school-age children because the quality standards do not apply for older students. Other child-care homes and centers may simply shut down. If this happens, families will need to rely on family members or unlicensed child-care homes. Susan Cavanaugh, who directs the Frontiers of Innovation program at the Department of Social and Health Services, states this concern: "No one is interested in that happening, but it would be the outlet if family child-care providers stopped being licensed."

Child-care providers are particularly scarce in eastern Washington because education levels are low. Because only 19% of the adult population has a college degree, two-thirds the level elsewhere in the state, centers and preschool programs have a hard time recruiting early education teachers with a BA.[106] Providers interested in furthering their education have few colleges and universities within commuting distance. Child-care workers in rural areas may also receive less coaching, since the coaches must spend a greater portion of their time driving from site to site.

Regional differences in language and culture also make it harder for the state to deliver the support that providers need. In Yakima County, in western Washington, more than half of the population is Latino and 40% speak a language other than English at home.[107] Many of the child-care workers who serve this population speak only Spanish, which makes coaching difficult because most coaches are monolingual.

One pilot program has attempted to address the challenges of language and low QRIS ratings. When the Department of Early Learning found that Latino providers in Yakima County were the least able, statewide, to meet the minimum standard required for licensing, it contracted on a trial basis with Child Care Aware to offer Spanish-language coaching to those who failed to meet the quality standards. The Department of Early Learning typically only provides coaches to providers receiving a rating level of 2 or higher. The pilot was a success, and providers managed to meet the state standards with coaching.[108] However, the Department cannot readily expand the model if it lacks bilingual coaches.

Geography makes it difficult for providers in eastern Washington to build relationships in the state capital, Olympia. Torres explains, "If we have statewide [meetings] in Olympia or Seattle, there is just a basic logistics issue. Unless someone from Spokane [280 miles away] is flying in, they are out of the loop." The emergence of regional early learning coalitions, backed by Thrive Washington, is intended to address these problems in the regions and in Olympia. These coalitions convene local child care, Head Start, and preschool providers to build a common agenda. In 2013–2014, Thrive Washington spent $850,000 to underwrite the coalitions.[109] CEO Sam Whiting explains:

> We convene the coalitions, support cross-pollination, and help them stay connected to the state through participating on the Early Learning Advisory Council. We also build local and regional voices to be loud and bossy in state policy making. We've adopted a community organizing model over the years. We want a provider in Walla Walla [in central Washington] to have the confidence and knowledge to speak up when they encounter their representative, Maureen Walsh, the ranking Republican on the House Early Learning and Human Services Committee, in the cereal aisle of the grocery store.

But Torres sounds a cautionary note. The success of the coalitions has been uneven, he notes, and some have been unable to garner local support. "[Child Care Aware] really should focus there, since these are the people we need to convince that early learning matters." Meanwhile, the Department of Early Learning continues to look for ways to overcome the barriers of distance, education, and language.

NEXT STEPS FOR WASHINGTON

Washington has successfully provided its most vulnerable children with extensive wraparound services. Moving forward, the state plans to increase access to its preschool program, improve the quality of child care by encouraging providers' participation in the quality rating and improvement system, and determine how to braid funds to boost the availability of full-day preschool.

Meeting the Mandate: Expanding State Preschool by 2020

Washington's preschool program must, by law, have enough space to enroll all eligible children by 2020, which means it will nearly double in size. This deadline will be hard to meet. The program grew by 1,350 slots in 2014; the growth plan now requires it to grow nearly twice as much—by 2,400 slots a year—through the deadline of 2020.[110]

The Department of Early Learning plans to establish new programs where the need is greatest. The department's expansion plan, published in 2013, explains that growth should be prioritized in places with full-day kindergarten that have the greatest "opportunity gap," that is, places with low take-up of Head Start or state preschool. The department also notes that despite the cost, it will "continue the comprehensive service approach [wraparound services], which is essential to supporting improved child outcomes."[111]

Officials believe that existing preschool providers can serve about 60% of the anticipated demand, but the Department of Early Learning will have to find new agencies to serve the rest. To find these new contractors, it intends to focus on improving career pathways for child-care workers to become certified preschool teachers by partnering with local colleges.[112] This option offers the advantage of maintaining both the state's diverse provider base and mixed delivery system.[113] Most of these new teachers will likely come from child-care centers. Some may come from family child-care homes—the Service Employees International Union and Child Care Aware are each piloting a child care-to-preschool pathway in Spokane that would allow home care providers to offer certified preschool from their homes.[114] That strategy requires strengthening the skills of current child-care staff.

By investing heavily in child care in the Early Start Act, legislators implicitly chose a slow road to expanding the preschool program. They recognized that a rapid expansion of preschool might be stymied by a lack of capacity and could lead to a less diverse workforce.[115] Another important factor legislators must consider is whether there is enough money to support a major expansion, since the state's Supreme Court has commanded that K–12 funding be raised dramatically, and that will adversely affect the resources available to early education.[116] The legislature will need to appropriate an additional $73 million annually to fund all eligible preschool children—again, more than doubling program costs.[117]

PREPARING CHILD-CARE PROVIDERS
TO OFFER STATE PRESCHOOL PROGRAMS

Educators in child-care centers and family child-care homes will be key in expanding the state preschool teaching force. But what do they need to successfully provide joint child-care and preschool services? A two-year pilot program, run by Child Care Aware and the Department of Early Learning, delved into this question with six family child-care providers and eight child-care center providers in eastern and southwest Washington. The providers' educational backgrounds ranged from a high school diploma to a bachelor's degree. All were passionate about serving low-income communities, had stable businesses, and were interested in offering state preschool classes.

The child-care providers received training, a toolkit that introduced them to ECEAP, and individualized coaching. They also received financial coaching, since focus groups conducted before the pilot showed that providers were concerned about how to make ends meet, how to recruit families on a tight timeline, and what business model to adopt. Participants regularly conducted self-assessments, and coaches adapted training to their needs. For example, providers wanted more help in strategies to work with dual-language learners and children with special needs, and more information about how to provide comprehensive services such as medical and dental exams.

According to a 2016 evaluation, participating providers made great progress toward preparedness for becoming state preschool providers, although there was work they needed to do before offering state preschool programs on their own. Finding facilities to expand their enrollment was noted as the biggest challenge. Identifying ways for these programs to financially support expansion into state preschool will be an important next step for the state to make the child care-to-state preschool pathway a reality.

Source: Washington State Department of Early Learning. (2016). *Early Childhood and Assistance Program (ECEAP). Pathway Pilot: Year 1 report—Helping child care providers offer comprehensive preschool services.* Retrieved from https://del.wa.gov/sites/default/files/public/ECEAP/Pathway%20Pilot%20Year%201%20Helping%20child%20care%20providers%20offer%20ECEAP.pdf

Increasing Participation in the Quality Rating and Improvement System

With the Early Start Act, Washington has embarked on an ambitious effort to support its child-care providers. The aim is to improve the experience of the thousands of children currently in child care and, eventually, to increase the number of qualified preschool teachers. The state needs to persuade providers to enroll in the QRIS to improve those providers' skills, so that they can meet at least the minimum quality threshold. It also needs to rethink the strategy in parts of the state where there are not enough potential child-care providers.

Increasing enrollment in the state's QRIS is the key to developing child-care quality, since QRIS is the mechanism by which providers get coaching support. As of December 2015, the state had exceeded its Race to the Top goal for preschool centers, with 932 centers enrolled. However, it has only enrolled 70% of its target for home care providers, with 1,000 fewer than anticipated having signed up. Unless those providers enter the system by 2017, they stand to lose the subsidies they depend upon.[118]

One reason these providers have not yet signed up may be a lack of familiarity with the new system. Cindy Morris, Early Learning Coordinator for Chelan and Douglas Counties, in eastern Washington, observes that many rural home providers did not know about the requirement until recently:

> People are sitting in meetings and having conversations about this, and about how it impacts the child-care providers, but child-care providers are just now starting to understand what that means to them, here. So I definitely think more will happen!

The Department plans to renew its efforts to inform family home care providers. Some will need to be convinced that participating in the QRIS is worth the investment of time and resources. Lani Todd of the Service Employees International Union notes:

> The average age of the family child-care provider is like 52. So a lot of providers are just saying, "It's not worth my time." I would say a large portion of them will sign up and do the first few steps, and be done until they're forced to do more.

For providers who are signed up, the next step is supporting them in reaching the required quality threshold on Early Achievers. Once a child-care provider is enrolled in Early Achievers, it has two and a half years to achieve that threshold.[119] Because coaching is the state's strategy for achieving this goal, the state must recruit an expanded cadre of coaches.

Current providers who do not meet the minimum quality standards may well shut their doors or enroll only children whose families do not depend on child-care subsidies. This would make it challenging for low-income families that depend on these providers to find licensed care.[120]

Governor Inslee is aware that raising standards while maintaining an adequate supply of child-care providers will be challenging. Upon signing the Early Start Act into law, he said:

> I have heard concerns from providers and parents about the mandatory requirements of the bill, which have the potential to reduce the number of licensed child-care providers in the state. I share those worries—and we will do what we can to make sure it doesn't happen. That is why I am directing my staff to work to preserve our wonderful child care and early learning facilities and to take the steps necessary to ensure that we are growing the licensed care in our state, not shrinking it.[121]

If the state is going to improve quality, it must maintain its investments. The 2015 legislation was a major step, and funds earmarked for low-income providers to improve their credentials are described in the statute as "ongoing" programs.[122] However, the Department of Early Learning depends upon the legislature to continue to pay for these programs.

Braiding Funds to Allow for Full-Day Pre-K

Expanding full-day preschool remains a priority for Department of Early Learning Director Ross Hunter. The department will conduct an evaluation that compares the impact of full- versus part-day preschool, testing the hypothesis that "full-day matters." He explains:

> It's hard to imagine that it doesn't, but we want to look at that evaluation and make sure. From that we will generate a prescription for future expansion. My goal, as we roll out that expansion, is to move to full-day for everybody. The places that have had significant kindergarten readiness improvements—Maryland, New Jersey, Boston—are full-day programs for 2 years. I think it's unlikely that we can move the dial with two and a half hours a day for four to five days a week.

An earlier experiment in braiding child-care and preschool funding to extend the school day failed after a year. Hunter remains confident that federal funds from the Child Care Development Block Grant can be blended with state preschool funding, but fiscal and technical difficulties make this a tall order. On the technical side, many questions need to be

answered. Who will do the screening for eligibility—individual providers, or the Department of Social and Health Services? What happens to
children in preschool programs during school vacations if their parents
are working full-time? The failure of the braiding experiment in 2014
showed Ryan Pricco, at Child Care Aware, that "the devil is in the details."

Hunter understands, too, that there is a tradeoff between spending limited child-care dollars on children who are already enrolled in a pre-K
and expanding access for the children of working families. Many Department of Early Learning officials believe it is important to align Working
Connections Child Care with state preschool for eligible children who
cannot attend part-day programs, but in 2014 the legislature decided such
a strategy makes child-care subsidies unavailable for too many working
parents.[123] With limited funding, the way forward is not clear.

KEY TAKEAWAYS

Washington's state preschool, the Early Childhood Education and Assistance Program, is high quality and focuses on children's academic,
social-emotional, and physical needs through thoughtful instruction,
coaching, and intensive wraparound services. Research on the program
found that participants exhibited academic gains that persisted at least
through the 5th grade. The program is very small, however, and serves
just a fraction of the children in need in the state. This may change soon
with an impending preschool expansion. Key takeaways from Washington that might be of interest to other states include the following:

The model that the state initially chose remains largely intact. When
Washington initiated a preschool program in 1985 the state borrowed
the Head Start model, with its emphasis on the "whole child," and made
quality its byword. Like Head Start, it targeted the poorest children. This
stability is partly attributable to the fact that the model has strong defend-
ers who are unwilling to tolerate major changes, including program staff
who believe that wraparound services are a critical part of their work
with children. These services have endured even though its high price tag
makes it difficult to expand in a state with limited fiscal resources.

*Bipartisanship, homegrown research, and a united coalition have creat-
ed the political will to expand preschool funding.* While Washington's preschool program has not grown substantially, it has weathered economic
downturns. Political champions, buttressed by grassroots and grasstops

advocates, have carried the day, and local leaders have made their voices heard in Olympia. A public–private partnership has helped coordinate business, philanthropic, and government leaders and fund early learning initiatives. Coalition members relied on research demonstrating the positive impact of the state program to make a case for early learning that helped persuade lawmakers to expand the program.

Short-term funding from the federal government and foundations has catalyzed long-term investment. Early Achievers, the state quality rating and improvement system, and birth-to-age-8 alignment are prime examples. The Gates Foundation helped fund the initial Early Achievers pilot, which led to a statewide experiment with coaching for child-care workers. The Foundation also invested in promoting programmatic alignment from birth to age 8, a strategy that has been adopted by the Department of Early Learning. Similarly, Race to the Top funds fueled the development of the quality rating and improvement system and the kindergarten readiness assessment, which links pre-K with kindergarten. The quality rating and improvement system and the assessments are now integral parts of preschool teachers' work in the classroom, despite the grants' termination.

Administration at the state level has been streamlined by consolidating early education programs in a cabinet-level department. The decision to create a cabinet-level Department of Early Learning put early education on the same administrative plane as K–12, signaling the importance the state attaches to early learning. Other departments continue to provide child-related services, but turf wars have faded as a working group has fostered cooperation among the departments. Washington, like other states, has been able to combine Head Start and state funding within individual programs; however, overlapping rules and reporting requirements are a burden for program directors and teachers. The state must address this through the establishment of a coherent early education system that effectively merges funding streams.

The simultaneous expansion of full-day kindergarten and preschool has exacerbated two chronic problems in early education—lack of space and a teacher shortage. The pressing need for additional kindergarten classrooms to accommodate the influx of 5-year-olds is forcing preschool classes out of public schools, and suitable space elsewhere is hard to find. Too few teachers with early-education credentials are graduating from state colleges and universities to meet the demand. Preschool teachers are migrating to the better-paying kindergarten jobs, and coaches are also in short supply. This situation creates opportunities for preschool teachers looking to enter the profession, but headaches for program providers looking for staff.

The state has addressed the tension between quality and access by investing in the workforce for child care, as well as preschool. Lawmakers lack the resources to substantially expand the high-cost, high-quality state-funded preschool. Instead, they have chosen to focus on improving the quality of child care to narrow the quality gap between these programs. The state's recently developed quality rating and improvement system, which places a heavy emphasis on classroom environment and student-teacher interactions, focuses on teaching quality, allowing more child-care providers to get coaching and earn bonuses for improving their classrooms. To maintain its diverse early-learning workforce while raising educator standards, the state is investing in scholarships and increasing reimbursement rates. Coaching is seen as the way that educators will improve. It is hoped that some child-care providers will, over time, acquire the credentials needed to be preschool teachers.

Washington currently confronts challenges that relate to both the quality of, and access to, early education. The response has been increased collaboration, among government agencies and also among government, nonprofits, and foundations, as well as experimentation with novel ways to deliver cost-effective early education. There is much to be gleaned from its experience.

NOTES

1. Washington State Legislature (2012). *Report on the pre-kindergarten programs: An overview and comparison with other states.* Retrieved from leg. wa.gov/Senate/Committees/EDU/Documents/UniversalVoluntaryPreschool.pdf

2. Bania, N., Kay, N., Aos, S., & Pennucci, A. (2014). *Outcome evaluation of Washington State's Early Childhood Education and Assistance Program* (Document No. 14-12-2201). Olympia, WA: Washington State Institute for Public Policy.

3. Washington Department of Early Learning (2014, July). *2014–15 ECEAP performance standards.* Retrieved from del.wa.gov/sites/default/files/imported/publications/eceap/docs/ECEAP_PerformanceStandards.pdf

4. U.S. Department of Health and Human Services (2016, January 25). *Poverty guidelines.* Retrieved from aspe.hhs.gov/poverty-guidelines

5. Students with an individualized education plan (IEP) are entitled to special education services, which may (but need not) include state preschool. Students can also qualify for state preschool based on a mix of locally determined factors

that are "shown by research to affect educational progress." Washington Department of Early Learning (2014, July).

6. Washington Department of Early Learning (n.d.1). *ECEAP outcomes 2014–2015*. Retrieved from del.wa.gov/sites/default/files/public/ECEAP_Outcomes_2014-15.pdf

7. Office of Head Start (2015). *Program information report (PIR): Enrollment statistics report—2015—state level*. Washington, D.C.: Administration for Children and Families.

8. Barnett, W. S., Friedman-Krauss, A. H., Gomez, R., Horowitz, M., Weisenfeld, G. G., Clarke Brown, K., & Squires, J. H. (2016). *The state of preschool 2015*. Retrieved from nieer.org/wp-content/uploads/2016/05/Yearbook_2015_rev1.pdf

9. Washington Department of Early Learning (n.d.1).

10. Washington Department of Early Learning (2014, December). *Report to the legislature: Early Childhood Education and Assistance Program (ECEAP) caseload forecast*. Retrieved from del.wa.gov/sites/default/files/imported/publications/research/docs/2014PreKCaseloadForecast.pdf

11. Washington Department of Early Learning (2014, July).

12. Unpublished data from the Washington Department of Early Learning (personal communication, March 31, 2016).

13. Data for FY 2014. Includes general Head Start funds as well as programs for American Indian and Alaskan Natives (AIAN), which totaled $14 million in FY 2014. Office of the Administration for Children and Families. (2014). *Head Start program facts fiscal year 2014*. Retrieved from eclkc.ohs.acf.hhs.gov/hslc/data/factsheets/docs/hs-program-fact-sheet-2014.pdf

14. Barnett et al. (2016).

15. Washington's preschool costs from Washington Department of Early Learning. (2015). *Report to the legislature, Early learning compensation rates comparison*. Retrieved from app.leg.wa.gov/ReportsToTheLegislature/Home/GetPDF?fileName=Early%20Learning%20Compensation%20Rates%20Comparison_7f6cd0b3-83dc-483b-a112-570f74e79bb9.pdf; National average preschool cost from Barnett et al. (2016).

16. U.S. Census Bureau (2015). *Public education finances: 2013, G13-ASPEF*. Washington, DC: U.S. Government Printing Office.

17. Reported in 2015 dollars. Unpublished data from the Washington Department of Early Learning (personal communication, March 31, 2016). Average spending includes part-, full-, and extended-day slots.

18. Washington Department of Early Learning (2013, September). *Report to the legislature: Serving all eligible children by 2018–2019*. Retrieved from del.wa.gov/sites/default/files/imported/publications/research/docs/ECEAP_expansion_plan.pdf

19. Washington Department of Early Learning. *Working connections child care*. Retrieved from www.del.wa.gov/care/help/connections.aspx

20. U.S. Administration for Children and Families (2016, February 3). *FY 2014 CCDF table 3a—all expenditures by state—detailed summary*. Retrieved from www.acf.hhs.gov/programs/occ/resource/fy-2014-ccdf-table-3a.

21. Yearly rate based on author's calculations. Reimbursement rates from the Washington State Legislature. (2015). *Daily child care rates-licensed or certified family home child-care providers*. Retrieved from apps.leg.wa.gov/wac/default. aspx?cite=170-290-0205

22. Washington Department of Early Learning (2014).

23. The discrepancy between the monthly average and the yearly total may be due to churn, with children leaving the program and new children taking their place. Unpublished data from the Washington Department of Early Learning (personal communication, January 28, 2016).

24. Unpublished data from the Washington Department of Early Learning (personal communication, January 11, 2016).

25. National Kids Count Database (2014). *Head Start enrollment by age group*. Annie E. Casey Foundation. Retrieved from datacenter.kidscount.org/data/ta-bles/5938-head-start-enrollment-by-age-group?loc=1&loct=1#detailed/2/49/false/36,868,867,133,38/1830,558,559,1831,122/12570.

26. Washington Department of Early Learning (2015, May). Home visiting service account. Retrieved from del.wa.gov/helpful-resources/home-visiting/home-visiting-services-account

27. Roderick Stark, D., Gebhard, B., & DiLauro, E. (2014). *The maternal, infant, and early childhood home visiting program: Smart investments build strong systems for young children*. Washington, DC: Zero to Three Policy Center.

28. Thrive Washington (2012). *Home visiting services account grantees*. Retrieved from thrivewa.org/wp-content/uploads/cohort_chart.pdf.

29. Unpublished data from the Washington Department of Early Learning (personal communication, March 31, 2016).

30. Quoted in Wyrwich, H. (2013, March 20). *Remembering Governor Booth Gardner's contribution to early learning*. Retrieved from thrivewa.org/remembering-gov-gardners-contributions-to-early-learning/

31. Reported in 2015 dollars. Unpublished data from the Washington Department of Early Learning (personal communication, March 31, 2016).

32. The only benchmark it has yet to meet is teacher degrees. Washington requires preschool teachers to have an AA; the NIEER benchmark is a BA or higher. Barnett, W. S., Hustedt, J. T., Hawkinson, L. E., & Robin, K. B. (2006). *The state of preschool 2006*. Retrieved from nieer.org/wp-content/uploads/2016/10/2006yearbook.pdf; compare with Barnett, W.S., Hustedt, J.T., Friedman, A.H., Stevenson Boyd, J., & Ainsworth, P. (2007). *The state of preschool 2007*. Retrieved from nieer.org/wp-content/uploads/2016/10/2007yearbook.pdf

33. Interview with Governor Christine Gregoire (2015, October 27).

34. Washington Department of Early Learning (2015, July 6). *Historic Early Start Act passes: Governor Inslee's speech*. Retrieved from delconnect.blogspot.com/2015/07/historic-early-start-act-passes_7.html

35. Washington State Legislature. HB2731: *2009-10 final bill report*. Retrieved from app.leg.wa.gov/billsummary?BillNumber=2731&Year=2009

36. See S. 6449, 62d Leg., Reg. Sess. (Wash. 2012) and H.R. 2448-S2, 62d Leg., Reg. Sess. (Wash. 2012). Neither passed out of committee.

37. Washington Department of Early Learning (2014, December).

38. The Early Start Act, Wash. Rev. Code § 43.215.100(8)(a) (2015).

39. Minervino, J. (2014, September). *Lessons from research and the classroom: Implementing high-quality pre-k that makes a difference for young children.* Seattle, WA: Bill and Melinda Gates Foundation.

40. Bania et al. (2014).

41. To address the possibility of selection bias, the researchers applied an "instrumental variable" approach.

42. The control group may have participated in another early education program, such as Head Start.

43. Bania et al. (2014).

44. Thrive by Five Washington. (2011) *Annual report: July 2010–June 2011.* Seattle, WA: Thrive Washington.

45. Interview with Jon Gould, Deputy Director, Early Learning Alliance (2015, September 22).

46. Department of Early Learning historical budget data received from personal correspondence with Christopher Stanley, Budget Director, Washington Department of Early Learning (2016, April 11).

47. These slots had been temporarily paid for by federal Child Care Development Block Grant funds in 2014–2015, but the legislature chose not to continue braiding child care and preschool funds. Washington Department of Early Learning (n.d.). *2013–2015 expenditure authority.* Retrieved from del.wa.gov/sites/default/files/imported/publications/communications/docs/DEL%202015-17.pdf

48. Mongeau, L. (2015, July 6). Washington State to spend more on Early Learning than it ever has. *Edweek.* Retrieved from blogs.edweek.org/edweek/early_years/2015/07/washington_state_to_spend_more_on_early_learning_than_it_ever_has.html

49. State median income from 2011–13 data. United States Census Bureau. (2014). *Income of household by state: Ranked from highest to lowest using 3-year-average medians.* Retrieved from www2.census.gov/programs-surveys/demo/tables/p60/249/stateonline_13.xls

50. Tax experts' calculations back up Hunter's assertion that the tax structure is the nation's most regressive. Institute on Taxation and Economic Policy. (2015). *Who Pays? Washington: State and local taxes in 2015.* Retrieved from www.itep.org/whopays/states/washington.php

51. Rate based on author's calculations. Assumes 260 days per year of care and an average of $15,392 for extended day preschool. Reimbursement rates from the Washington State Legislature. (2015). *Daily child- care rates-licensed or certified family home child-care providers.* Retrieved from apps.leg.wa.gov/wac/default.aspx?cite=170-290-0205

52. Interview with Representative Ruth Kagi (2015, September 23).

53. Nelson, C., Porter, T., & Reiman, K. (2015, October). *Examining quality in a family child-care network: An evaluation of All Our Kin.* New Haven, CT: All Our Kin.

54. Interview with Dan Torres, Director of Community Momentum, Child Care Aware (2015, November 12).

55. Interview with Ross Hunter, Director, Washington Department of Early Learning (2015, November 20).

56. Washington Office of Superintendent of Public Instruction. (2015, April 3). *K-3 class size reduction and preschool and full-day kindergarten expansion: Capital facility needs for classrooms*. Presented to the School Facilities Citizen Advisory Panel.

57. Unpublished data from the Department of Early Learning (personal correspondence, January 28, 2016).

58. Gregoire interview (2015, September 22).

59. O'Connor, M. (2015, August 4). *Washington Early Learning Partnership recommits to working together*. Retrieved from thrivewa.org/washington-early-learning-partnership-recommits-to-working-together/

60. In addition to preschool, the partnership's priorities include infant and toddler services, parent support, and social-emotional development. Washington Department of Early Learning. (2014). *Early Learning Partnership: 2013 key accomplishments and 2014 priority strategies—Early Learning Plan*. Olympia, WA: Department of Early Learning, Superintendent of Public Instruction, Washington, & Thrive by Five Washington.

61. Interview with Marty Loesch, Governor Gregoire's former Chief of Staff (2015, September 28).

62. Kagi interview (2015, September 23); interview with Sen. Steve Litzow (2015, October 1).

63. There exists no reliable measure of how much funding local governments and nonprofits provide.

64. Interview with Katy Warren, Deputy Director, Washington State Association of Head Start and ECEAP (2015, September 23).

65. Bania et al. (2014)

66. Washington Department of Early Learning. (2012). *Washington State early learning and development guidelines: Birth through third grade*. Olympia, WA: Washington Department of Early Learning.

67. Washington Department of Early Learning (2012).

68. Washington Department of Early Learning (n.d.2). *Core competencies for early care and education professionals*. Retrieved from del.wa.gov/sites/default/files/imported/publications/partnerships/docs/CoreCompetencies.pdf

69. Washington Department of Early Learning (2014, July).

70. Washington Department of Early Learning (n.d.3). *Preschool essential elements: Supporting strong curricula*. Retrieved from del.wa.gov/sites/default/files/imported/publications/eceap/docs/curriculum.pdf

71. Washington Department of Early Learning (n.d.) *Washington Kindergarten Inventory of Developing Skills*. Retrieved from www.del.wa.gov/development/kindergarten/pilot.aspx

72. Teaching Strategies, LLC. (2015). *Teaching Strategies GOLD Objectives and Dimensions* (WaKids). Retrieved from www.k12.wa.us/WaKIDS/pubdocs/

GOLD_HNDT_Objectives.pdf

73. Washington Office of Superintendent of Public Instruction (2015, December 17). *WAKids: Family Connection.* Retrieved from www.k12.wa.us/WaKIDS/Family/default.aspx.

74. Interview with Robert Butts, Assistant Superintendent of Early Learning in the Office of Superintendent of Public Instruction (2015, September 22).

75. Washington Department of Early Learning (2016, January). *Early Achievers: Participant operating guidelines.* Olympia, WA: Washington Department of Early Learning.

76. Washington Department of Early Learning (2013, July). *Pilot project report and reciprocity plan.* Retrieved from depts.washington.edu/cqel/PDFs/CQELReports/Early_Achievers_pilot_summary_HS_ECEAP.pdf; see also Washington Department of Early Learning (2016, January).

77. Interview with Nicole Rose, Assistant Director for Quality Practice and Professional Growth, Department of Early Learning (2015, September 22); Kagi interview (2015, September 23).

78. Washington Department of Early Learning (2016, January).

79. Testimony of Debra Simmerson. Department of Early Learning (2013, January 30). *Early Achievers provider video.* Retrieved from www.youtube.com/watch?v=-e_V1bamxIs

80. Gould interview (2015, September 22).

81. All programs, regardless of rating, may receive coaching until mid-2016 after receiving their first ratings. Washington Department of Early Learning (2016, January). Information about the intent of the bill from interview with Rep. Ruth Kagi (2015, September 23).

82. Boller, K. et al. (2010). *Seeds to success modified field test: Findings from the outcomes and implementation studies.* Princeton, NJ: Mathematica Policy Research.

83. The evaluation showed that the teachers who were coached were able to design significantly better classrooms—that is, to make structural improvements—and were less likely to leave the field. The study did not, however, find a significant improvement in teacher–child interactions, a key factor in defining quality.

84. Interview with Caroline Shelton, Program Director, Child Care Aware (2015, November 12).

85. Testimony of Ashley Shrewsbury. Department of Early Learning (2013, January 30). Early Achievers provider video. Retrieved from www.youtube.com/watch?v=-e_V1bamxIs

86. Bureau of Labor Statistics (2014). *Child-care workers.* Retrieved from www.bls.gov/ooh/personal-care-and-service/childcare-workers.htm; Shelton interview (2015, November 12); interview with Stacie Marez, Early Learning Coordinator, Educational Service District 105, Yakima County (2015, December 15).

87. Shelton interview (2015, November 12).

88. National Center on Early Childhood Development. *Coaching companion.* Retrieved from eclkc.ohs.acf.hhs.gov/sites/default/files/pdf/coaching-companion.pdf

89. Shelton interview (2015, November 12).

90. City of Seattle (n.d.). *Seattle Public Preschool implementation plan*. Retrieved from www.seattle.gov/Documents/Departments/OFE/AboutTheLevy/EarlyLearning/SPP%20Implementation%20Plan.April%201.PostCommittee.pdf

91. Weiland, C., & Yoshikowa, H. (2013, November). Impacts of a prekindergarten program on children's mathematics, language, literacy, executive function, and emotional skills. *Child Development, 84*(6), 2112–2130; Wong, V., Cook, T., Barnett, W. S., & Jung, K. (2008). An effectiveness-based evaluation of five state pre-kindergarten programs. *Journal of Policy Analysis and Management, 27*, 122–154; Weiland, C., & Yoshikawa, H. (2013, September 5). Want great preschools for all? Look to Boston. *Seattle Times*. Retrieved from www.seattletimes.com/opinion/ guest-want-great-preschools-for-all-look-to-boston/.

92. City of Seattle (n.d.).

93. City of Seattle (n.d.).

94. This number is to be increased gradually until 2018–2019, when the city is projected to serve 2,000 children. City of Seattle, Office of Education (n.d.). *Frequently asked questions*. Retrieved from www.seattle.gov/Documents/Departments/OFE/AboutTheLevy/EarlyLearning/SPP_FAQs.pdf

95. Interview with Leilani Dela Cruz, Early Learning and Child Development Manager, City of Seattle (2015, September 23).

96. City of Seattle (n.d.).

97. Washington Office of Superintendent of Public Instruction (n.d.). *State funded full-day kindergarten in Washington*. Retrieved from www.k12.wa.us/EarlyLearning/ FullDayKindergartenResearch.aspx

98. Whitebook, M., & Sakai, L. (2003). Turnover begets turnover: An examination of jobs and occupational instability among child-care center staff. *Early Childhood Research Quarterly, 18*(3), 273–293.

99. Bureau of Labor Statistics (2015, May). *May 2014 state occupational employment and wage estimates*. Retrieved from www.bls.gov/oes/2014/may/oes252011.htm

100. Kini, T., & Podolsky, A. (2016, June). *Does teaching experience increase teacher effectiveness? A review of the research.* Palo Alto, CA: Learning Policy Institute. See also Ladd, H., & Sorenson, D. (2014, March). *Returns to teacher experience: Student achievement and motivation in middle school* (Working Paper No. 112). Retrieved from /www.caldercenter.org/sites/default/files/WP%20112%20Update_0.pdf

101. Author's calculation: the difference between the total projected enrollment in 2020 (22,897) and the enrollment in 2015–2016 (13,270). Washington Department of Early Learning (2014, December).

102. Author's calculation based on an increased enrollment of 9,627, a class size maximum of 20, and a staff-to-student ratio of 1:10, assuming that teachers offer two part-day classes per day.

103. Dela Cruz interview (2015, September 23).

104. Washington Office of Superintendent of Public Instruction (2015, April 3).

105. This region is often divided into "central" and "eastern" Washington. This study will refer to the eastern two-thirds of the state as "eastern Washington." Demographic data from Kids Count Data Center. Retrieved from datacenter.kidscount.org/data#WA/5/2/3,6,5,4/char/0 .

106. Percentage of adults with a college degree is the author's calculation based on county-level education and population data from National Kids Count Data Center.

107. United States Census Bureau (2014). *QuickFacts: Yakima County, Washington*. Retrieved from http://www.census.gov/quickfacts/table/PST040214/53077

108. Information about the Yakima pilot from interview with Ruth Kagi (2015, September 23).

109. Thrive by Five Washington (2011). Annual report: July 2010–June 2011. Seattle, WA: Thrive Washington.

110. Washington Department of Early Learning (2013).

111. Washington Department of Early Learning (2013).

112. Washington Department of Early Learning (2013).

113. Kagi interview (2015, September 23).

114. Interview with Lani Todd, Legislative and Public Policy Coordinator, the Service Employees International Union (2015, September 24).

115. Kagi interview (2015, September 23); Litzow interview (2015, October 1).

116. O'Sullivan, J., & Brunner, J. (2015, August 13). State funding back on table as court fines state $100,000 a day. *Seattle Times*. Retrieved from www.seattletimes.com/seattle-news/education/supreme-court-orders-100000-per-day-fines-in-mccleary-case/

117. Washington Department of Early Learning (2013).

118. The Department of Early Learning notes that this goal may have been too ambitious, as it didn't take into account the churn in family child-care providers, many of whom have exited the field since the goal was set. Washington Department of Early Learning. (2015, May). *Early Achievers participation: Progress on implementing a quality rating and improvement system in WA state*. Olympia, WA: Washington Department of Early Learning.

119. Washington Department of Early Learning (2016, January).

120. Interview with Susan Cavanaugh, Director of Frontiers of Innovation, and Shane Riddle, Program and Policy Administrator, Department of Social and Health Services (2015, November 9).

121. Washington Department of Early Learning (2015, July 30). *Join DEL's professional development community*. Retrieved from delconnect.blogspot.com/2015/07/historic-early-start-act-passes_7.html

122. The *Early Start Act*, Wash. Rev. Code § 43.215.100(8)(a) (2015).

123. Hunter interview (2015, November 20).

CHAPTER 5

North Carolina

Birth-to-Age-3 Leads the Way

North Carolina has long been a trailblazer in early education. The state was the first to offer free, full-day kindergarten, and it is still one of only a handful of states to do so.[1] In addition, North Carolina was one of the first of two states to adopt a quality rating and improvement system for child-care providers.[2] More recently, the state had the top-scoring application for the first cohort of the Race to the Top–Early Learning Challenge grant.[3] North Carolina also is home to the Frank Porter Graham Child Development Institute, which has garnered national acclaim for its longitudinal Abecedarian Early Intervention Project (one of the oldest and most often cited early childhood education programs) and the development of the Early Childhood Environment Rating Scale (ECERS) to assess early childhood classrooms.

North Carolina developed Smart Start, a groundbreaking public–private partnership, to assess community needs and coordinate early education services. Smart Start began in 1993, and by 1997 had reached all 100 counties in the state.[4] As a result, in 2001 when the state introduced public preschool—then known as More at Four and later renamed NC Pre-K—the program was smoothly integrated with existing early childhood services in counties across the state. More at Four soon grew to serve around 30,000 at-risk students. Since then, North Carolina has maintained the quality and reach of both initiatives in the face of significant challenges due to the Great Recession of 2008 and a change in political control to a General Assembly that prioritized cutting taxes. Two decades of program evaluation results from the Frank Porter Graham Child Development Institute reveal an increase in highly rated child-care programs and improvement in early childhood teacher education levels. NC Pre-K student gains outpaced expected developmental benchmarks in language and literacy, math, general knowledge, and behavior skills, particularly for dual language learners and low-income students.

North Carolina's innovative and high-quality programming offers important lessons on how to:

- capitalize on visionary gubernatorial leadership to advance early childhood programming;
- harness local support to increase engagement with early education initiatives and to protect against funding reductions when political priorities change;
- construct a "one-stop shop" experience for families with children birth to age 5 that benefits from strong leadership at the local level; and
- develop a strong quality rating and improvement system as well as effective workforce supports to raise teacher education levels, drive structural change, and promote quality in early childhood services.

North Carolina also offers precautionary lessons about how early learning may become destabilized when it gets caught up in partisan politics.

This case study begins with an overview of North Carolina's Smart Start birth-to-age-5 services network and NC Pre-K state-funded preschool program. It then explores four dimensions of the North Carolina story: political context, state administration and management, program quality, and next steps for the state.

STATE-FUNDED EARLY EDUCATION IN A NUTSHELL

North Carolina has two major state-funded early education initiatives, Smart Start and NC Pre-K. Smart Start is a network of 75 nonprofit agencies that offer "one-stop shop" coordination of services for families and children birth to age 5 in each of North Carolina's 100 counties. In addition to offering services such as parenting classes, child-care program consulting, and case management or referral services for families, Smart Start provides administrative oversight and strategic planning for early childhood programs. As one member of North Carolina's early childhood community explains:

> Smart Start is not a pre-k program in the sense that we understand: classrooms and buildings with pre-k students. It was created to be a system to support early care and education, rather than direct service—the oil that works in between the cogs of the machine. One important part of the mission is to make determinations about where service gaps are and what resources or strategies might help fill the gap on a case-by-case basis at the local level. For

example, if a community has a high incidence of lead poisoning in children birth to age 5, Smart Start would emphasize resources to combat this.

Each county (or group of counties in rural areas) has its own local Smart Start partnership agency, and the North Carolina Partnership for Children—a state-level nonprofit agency primarily funded by the Department of Health and Human Services—draws upon public and private resources to offer coordination, support, and oversight of local Smart Start partnerships. This structure allows for a balance between offering consistent services statewide and allowing flexibility to respond to the strengths and needs of each community.

North Carolina Pre-Kindergarten (NC Pre-K) is North Carolina's state-funded preschool program for 4-year-old children at risk of educational failure (see Table 5.1 for NC Pre-K Program highlights). NC Pre-K began with a pilot serving 1,244 children in 2001 (see Figure 5.A online). The program ramped up quickly, adding 9,000 students in just 2 years. Year three represented a milestone when NC Pre-K was provided in all 100 counties. The program continued to grow over the following years with a major 10,000-slot expansion in fiscal year 2008, bringing the total enrollment to over 30,000. Enrollment has decreased slightly since then due to state budget cuts, with 26,781 slots available in 2015–2016.

A local committee comprising representatives from the school district, Smart Start, child care, Head Start, Department of Social Services, and the parent community determines whether NC Pre-K is administered by Smart Start, the school district, or a nonprofit agency. In 2014–2015, 56 of 100 counties selected Smart Start to administer their programs.[5] The local NC Pre-K Committee also develops operational policies and procedures and provides fiscal and programmatic oversight. The contracting agency subcontracts NC Pre-K classrooms. In 2014–2015, 53% of NC Pre-K classrooms were located in public schools; the remainder were run by child-care and Head Start providers.[6]

Smart Start for All and NC Pre-K for At-Risk 4-Year-Olds

Smart Start is not just for low-income families. Smart Start partnerships offer services that target at-risk children and families, such as partnering with Medicaid providers to offer developmental and health screenings, as well as services that benefit the broader community, such as providing technical assistance to improve the quality of child care.

NC Pre-K, in contrast, is designed to target North Carolina's most vulnerable children. Enrollment is open to 4-year-old children from households at 75% or less of the state median income ($51,000 for a family of four), with priority given to children with no prior formal educational or child-care experiences. Up to 20% of children may qualify based on risk factors other than family income, including having a family member on active military duty, limited English proficiency, or the presence of a disability or chronic health condition (see Table 5.1).

Overall, NC Pre-K serves approximately 27,000 students, which represents 22% of all North Carolina's 124,000 4-year-old children, and 35% of those who have been identified as at-risk (see Figure 5.1). In addition, Title I preschool serves approximately 5,000 low-income 4-year-olds and Head Start serves another 4,000. Federally funded special education preschool services serve another nearly 4,000 children.[7] Still, approximately 68% of 4-year-olds overall do not receive public preschool services in North Carolina.[8]

Services

Each local Smart Start partnership determines the services it will offer. Partnerships often provide funding and technical assistance to programs they support, and sometimes administer programs directly. Smart Start services typically fall into the following areas:[9]

- *NC Pre-K.* Partnerships frequently administer the program directly and/or provide supplemental funding.
- *Child-care quality and access.* Partnerships frequently offer technical assistance such as coaching to local child-care providers, subsidize teacher wages, and/or administer federal child-care subsidies.
- *Health and nutrition.* Partnerships frequently develop high-quality outdoor early learning environments and/or partner with Medicaid providers to offer developmental and health screenings.
- *Parent and family support.* Partnerships frequently offer parenting classes, home visiting services, and/or referral to local resources for other family needs (e.g., housing or food).
- *Early literacy.* Partnerships frequently support early literacy programs that offer free books at well-child check-ups and/or facilitate book lending in early learning classrooms.

NC Pre-K offers a full-day (6.5 hours, 5 days per week) program that follows the 10-month public school calendar.[10] The emphasis on full-day classes is an important design element of the program; it is based on research showing the increased benefit that children receive when they spend more time in preschool.[11]

Table 5.1. Key Facts About North Carolina Prekindergarten

Element	
Number of children served	26,781 children in 2015-16[i]
Age	4-year-old children
Eligibility	Targeted for children in greatest need. • Family earns 75% of state median income or less ($51,000 for a family of four). • Up to 20% of students may qualify based on other risk factors (e.g., special education status, family on active military duty, limited English proficiency). • Priority is given to children with no prior formal educational or child care experiences.
Length of program day	Full-day (100% of children)
Maximum class size	18
Teacher-child ratio	1:9 or better
Administration	• Department of Health and Human Services, Division of Child Development and Early Education, administers the program at the state level. • Smart Start partnerships or school districts, as determined by a NC Pre-K Committee, administer the program locally.
Setting	Classrooms were located in a variety of settings in 2014–2015[ii] • Public schools (53%) • Private for-profit child care centers (25%) • Head Start centers (14%) • Private nonprofit child care centers (8%)
Curriculum	Over 25 state-approved options • Creative Curriculum is the most prevalent (used in 78% of classrooms in 2014–15)[ii]

i. Unpublished data from the North Carolina Department of Health and Human Services, Division of Child Development and Early Education (personal communication, February 25, 2016).

ii. Unpublished data from the North Carolina Department of Health and Human Services, Division of Child Development and Early Education (personal communication, November 6, 2015).

Source: North Carolina Department of Health and Human Services, Division of Child Development and Early Education. (2016). *North Carolina Pre-Kindergarten Program (NC Pre-K) Requirements and Guidance: Effective State Fiscal Year 2015-2016.*

Table 5.1. Continued

Minimum teacher qualifications	Lead teachers must have: • B.A. in early childhood education, child development, or a related field and • Birth-through-kindergarten teaching license or • Preschool add-on teaching license Assistant teachers must have: • High school diploma or GED and • A.A. in Early Childhood Education or Child Development or • Child Development Associate credential
Coaching for teachers	Coaching, observational assessments, and support for first three years in classroom as part of licensure process, followed by annual observational assessments and professional development thereafter
Wraparound services	Children receive a variety of wraparound services, including: • Universal developmental screenings • Health assessment upon program entry, with referrals for additional services as needed
Family engagement	Providers must: • Develop a family engagement plan in conjunction with their local NC Pre-K committee that includes elements such as home visits, formal and informal parent-teacher conferences, and parent education opportunities • Keep a log of activities, opportunities, or communications made for family engagement on file at the NC Pre-K site

Funding for Smart Start and NC Pre-K Has Declined in Recent Years

Smart Start began as a $32 million pilot in 1993 serving families in 12 geographically diverse congressional districts and 18 counties.[12] The initiative grew steadily through 1997, at which point all remaining counties were brought in. Funding peaked in 2000 at $310 million and remained above $200 million for nearly the next decade (see Figure 5.B online). Following the Great Recession of 2008 and the ascension of a newly elected Republican supermajority in the General Assembly, the North Carolina Department of Health and Human Services applied required budget reductions across the agency, reducing Smart Start funding each year. In addition, the legislature imposed a 20% budget cut to Smart Start in 2011.[13] This cutback brought annual funding levels below $150 million, the lowest since

Figure 5.1. Only a Fraction of 4-Year-Olds Receive State-Funded Preschool
    in North Carolina[i]

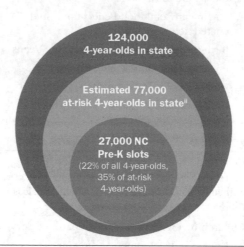

i. All 4-year-old children enrolled in NC Pre-K attend full-day preschool programs.

ii. We derived this number mathematically knowing that (1) there are 27,000 NC Pre-K slots and
    (2) NC Pre-K serves 35% of the state's "at-risk" 4-year-olds according to the state's Preschool
    Development Expansion Grant application. While the grant narrative does not define "at-risk,"
    we assume it equates to the risk factors that qualify students for NC Pre-K. The grant narrative
    also does not explain the state's methodology for determining this percentage, so this number
    should be viewed as a rough estimate.

Note: All numbers rounded to the nearest thousand.

Source: State of North Carolina. *Preschool Development Expansion Grant: Application for
    Initial Funding* (2014).

the 1998 fiscal year. Funding has not been restored, despite the improving
economy.

Historically, NC Pre-K has been funded through the state general fund
and lottery revenue (see Figure 5.C online). The program began with
an $8.5 million pilot in 2001; funding peaked in fiscal year 2009 at $188
million.[14] As with Smart Start, the legislature began decreasing the general fund investment after the recession hit; in some years, it also shifted
Temporary Assistance for Needy Families (TANF) federal funds to partially cover the shortfall. In the 2011–2013 biennial budget, NC Pre-K, like
Smart Start, suffered a 20% cut. Although there have been slight fluctuations since then, program funding has not been restored to pre-recession
levels.

Almost all NC Pre-K contractors—local Smart Start organizations,
school districts, or other nonprofit agencies—subcontract at the child

---

PROMOTING HOME LITERACY IN EDGECOMBE COUNTY

In all counties, Smart Start investments extend beyond the pre-K classroom to include other investments that promote early learning. In Edgecombe County, for example, the local Smart Start—the Down East Partnership for Children—has invested extensively in supporting print-rich home environments. There, local families receive books from their pediatricians or other medical care providers, who distribute them at well-child check-ups to encourage families to read together as part of the national Reach Out and Read initiative. During these visits, the providers take time to discuss the importance of reading and model reading out loud and discussing the book with the child. Likewise, the Partnership supports Raising a Reader, a program that provides weekly book exchanges and read-alouds for children through a local library, as well as training for parents and teachers on children's literacy development. Child care centers with a mid- to high-quality rating (three to five stars according to the quality rating and improvement system) and a high percentage of low-income children are targeted for participation. One mother, whose child attends NC Pre-K and receives a weekly book bag through the initiative, reported that her daughter is always excited to read the books she receives and often asks to visit their local library as a result.

Source: Interview with anonymous parent; The Down East Partnership for Children. (n.d.)
Funded programs. depc.org/about-depc/funded-programs/

---

level rather than the classroom level, meaning that they purchase space for individual NC Pre-K students within a class rather than paying for an entire NC Pre-K classroom.[15] This arrangement creates "blended" classrooms that may include children funded by state preschool sitting beside children funded by other programs, such as Head Start or Title I, or beside fee-paying children. The state intentionally made this design choice to spread public preschool funds across the public, private, and not-for-profit sectors. In addition to increasing socioeconomic integration, all blended classrooms benefit from NC Pre-K quality-improvement efforts.

NC Pre-K per-child funding peaked in fiscal year 2003, at $7,256 per child (see Figure 5.D online). Since then, it has hovered between $4,500 and $5,500 per child.[16] The state purposefully allocates an amount less than the true program cost, which is at least $7,000 per child or more, supplementing the state contribution with federal and local funds (see Table 5.2).[17] The Department of Health and Human Services offers tiered

Table 5.2. NC Pre-K Is Funded by a Variety of State, Federal, and Local Sources

Funding Source	Description	Funding Amount
State	State funds make up the majority of preschool funding, drawing from both general fund appropriations and lottery receipts.	• State general fund: $48 million in 2014–2015 • Lottery receipts: $75.5 million in 2014–2015[i]
Federal	Temporary Assistance for Needy Families (TANF) funds sometimes supplement state funding for NC Pre-K.	• TANF: $19.8 million allocated to NC Pre-K in 2014–2015[i]
	Head Start funds are combined, or braided, with state funds when NC Pre-K slots are offered in Head Start classrooms.	• Head Start: $191 million in overall funding in 2014–2015, a portion of which was combined with NC Pre-K funds[ii]
	Title I preschool funds are also used in some NC Pre-K classes that are offered in public schools.	• Title I: $50 million estimated annual set-aside for NC Pre-K[iii]
	Individuals with Disabilities Education Act (IDEA), Part B, is sometimes braided with NC Pre-K, but the extent of this braiding is unclear.	
Local	NC Pre-K programs may also receive contributions such as local property tax revenue or transportation and facilities from local school districts.	• Amount varies

per-student reimbursement rates according to how much access provid-ers have to additional funding sources. Head Start providers currently receive $400 per NC Pre-K student each month, while public schools receive $473 per student and private child-care providers receive $550 to $650 per student, depending on the licensure status of the lead teacher.[18]

North Carolina also benefited from a Race to the Top–Early Learning Challenge grant, which brought in $70 million from 2012 to 2015.[19] The grant has supported systemic improvement efforts, such as redesigning the state's quality rating and improvement system, offering enhanced pro-fessional development opportunities for child-care consultants and pro-viders, implementing a new K–3 assessment, and creating an integrated early childhood data system.[20]

Table 5.2. Continued

	Local Smart Start agencies are required to match state funds with a combination of private grants and cash or in-kind donations. Many agencies use a portion of this funding to supplement the state reimbursement rate for private NC Pre-K providers who lack access to other funding sources. In 2014–15, the local match requirement was 15%.[iv]	• Smart Start local match: $29 million in 2014–2015 for all Smart Start programs ($20.5 million cash and $8.5 million in-kind contributions).[iv] The amount spent on NC Pre-K varied locally.
Public–private partnerships		

i. Unpublished data from the North Carolina Department of Health and Human Services, Division of Child Development and Early Education (personal communication, February 3, 2016).

ii. Administration for Children and Families Early Childhood Learning & Knowledge Center, Office of Head Start. (2015). *Head Start program facts fiscal year 2015*. Retrieved from https://eclkc. ohs.acf.hhs.gov/hslc/data/factsheets/docs/head-start-fact-sheet-fy-2015.pdf.

iii. Unpublished data from the North Carolina Department of Public Instruction, Office of Early Learning (personal communication, May 10, 2016).

iv. North Carolina Partnership for Children. (2015); North Carolina Fiscal Research Division. (2016, January 28). *Smart Start*.

POLITICS OF EARLY EDUCATION

North Carolina has had a long history of bipartisan support for its early education programs, but in recent years that support has eroded as political priorities have changed. The state stands out for its visionary gubernatorial leadership. The accomplishments of Governor James Hunt provide material for a master class in how to take advantage of an opportunity to build an innovative early education program. However, because Smart Start and NC Pre-K are viewed as signature Democratic initiatives, early education has become politicized. Recent funding reductions to both initiatives—the result of a restructured tax code and the recent economic recession—are jeopardizing access to and quality of services, particularly for Smart Start.

Champions with an Innovative Vision

North Carolina's governors have a strong track record of focusing attention and resources on early education. Governor James Holshouser (Republican, 1973–1977) led the charge by implementing state-funded full-day kindergarten. Governor James Hunt (Democrat, 1977–1985 and

1993–2001) developed Smart Start during his second double term. Governor Michael Easley (Democrat, 2001–2009) started NC Pre-K.

Governor Hunt was a particularly effective champion, gaining national prominence for his efforts for early education. He ran as the "education governor" in his first two terms, but his focus at that time was primarily on K–12 issues. While he was out of office for the next 8 years, he realized that he had neglected a very important part of education—early education. He had witnessed the early childhood development of his own grandchildren and heard from many educators about how important it was for children to arrive at school prepared.[21] When he ran for office again, he made early childhood education the top item on his agenda, and once he returned to office, the governor acted on this campaign promise. Richard Clifford, a researcher from the Frank Porter Graham Child Development Institute who worked with Governor Hunt, recalls:

> We worked very long days. The Governor would like to call me at ten o'clock at night. This was his number one priority. He talked about it in every single speech he made for four years.

The governor developed Smart Start, his signature initiative, after bringing together a broad coalition of leaders in health, early intervention, and education to help flesh out a framework for supporting early education at the state level. Smart Start was designed as a comprehensive system that would be implemented by a public–private partnership. High-quality early childhood services would be available to all children, and families would be engaged in making decisions about what services to prioritize within their community. Smart Start employed a multi-tiered approach, with a statewide agency providing support and oversight and local nonprofits making decisions about service delivery in each county. This would not be an initiative run by the state—it would belong to the whole community.

To foster this sense of communal ownership, Governor Hunt insisted that each participating county create a brand new nonprofit rather than relying upon an existing agency. As he explained:

> I had in mind trying to ensure we kept things going, and also that we got those local people thinking that it's theirs, like their schools, not just some services that are provided and paid for by bureaucrats they don't love.

Governor Hunt cites Stanley County as an example of how local decision-making increases buy-in from communities. Many residents of Stanley

County thought that mothers should be able to stay at home with their children. However, child-care subsidies were only available for working mothers. Consequently, the local Smart Start partnership used flexible funding to provide formula and diapers to mothers who chose to stay home during their child's first year of life, if they agreed to attend parent education classes. This flexibility met the needs of that county and improved outcomes for participating families. The resulting program, highly popular with Stanley County residents, broadened the constituency that supported Smart Start. While Stanley County maintained a focus on caring for children in the earliest year of life, other counties employed their local flexibility to support a range of initiatives spanning a child's early years, including coaching for child-care providers, parenting classes, early childhood literacy programs, and standardized preschool enrollment processes.[22]

Governor Hunt used a variety of tactics to build support for implementing Smart Start. He traveled throughout the state, drumming up excitement for this new early childhood initiative. He also encouraged local supporters to contact their legislators, hold town hall meetings, and talk to editorial boards and reporters—basically, to generate buzz and to lobby on behalf of the initiative.

Governor Hunt took the private element of the public–private partnership very seriously, and invested great effort in winning support from the business community as well. He recounts:

> The way I explained [Smart Start] to the state was, I put it in the context of economic growth and jobs. That connects with everybody—liberal, conservative, in between. Everybody. Everybody wants a good economy and good jobs. They should, and they do. Business wants that. And I'm sure that, as we established this effort here . . . we had more business support than any state has ever had in America in establishing an early childhood program.

Indeed, the first chair of the state Smart Start board was Republican businessman Jim Goodmon. The CEO of Capitol Broadcasting Company and owner of WRAL-TV, Goodmon developed a Smart Start documentary and created a weekly television show called Smart Start Kids.[23] When Governor Hunt struggled to convince the legislature to expand the Smart Start pilot, another businessman, J. Walter McDowell, President of North Carolina Banking for Wachovia, commissioned a report arguing that the initiative should encompass all 100 counties in the state; he hand-delivered copies of that report to every member of the House and Senate.[24] Businesses also donated millions of dollars to local Smart Start organizations during this period.

The conservative religious community, a powerful force in the state, was initially troubled by the increased involvement of government in areas traditionally considered to be the role of parents. Karen Ponder, who worked closely with Governor Hunt in getting Smart Start off the ground, recalls being flooded with letters from pastors and parishioners who were concerned that the Governor was trying to take children out of their homes. Hunt responded by holding a luncheon at his mansion with the state's religious leaders. As Ponder remembers it:

> The Governor started saying, "Not only is this God's work, I need you to help me do it." We never got another letter from people about it. It was like suddenly he took all the arguments away. "We're not trying to tell families what to do, we're supporting families. They choose where their children are every day, but we want every single one of those to be the highest quality possible." . . . It was like magic. But it's part of believing in the mission and being able to sell it, and then politically knowing how to manage those things that are going awry.

After Governor Hunt secured funding for the 12-county Smart Start pilot in 1993, he and his team held a conference for counties interested in applying. The event drew 96 of the state's 100 counties, and all 96 subsequently submitted applications for the first round of funding.[25] Smart Start was off to an auspicious start. Ponder reflects:

> It took somebody with [Governor Hunt's] political savvy to do what we did in 1993, because you could believe with all your heart that early education matters, but if you can't sell it in a way that gets public opinion completely bought into it, in the way he did, it would have never—I mean, the rest of us worked for years and years and felt like we were making tiny little increments of progress.

Hunt's skillful political leadership created a window of opportunity—a political opening for public investment in early childhood programs—of which he took full advantage. He courted business and religious leaders, parents, and educators, who in turn pressured their representatives to support the program. Those skills were also needed to push through the expansion of Smart Start and the introduction of state-funded preschool. As Governor Hunt describes:

> I know how you get this done politically. . . . You get the business people behind it, you get the church people behind it, you get the education people

behind it, you get the parent people behind it. If you can't win with those groups, you ought not be in politics. But you have to work at it.

Building the System Through Carefully Managed Growth

It took 4 years to fully implement Smart Start in all of North Carolina's 100 counties. From that point, the statewide system was able to grow and mature. In 2001, a new opportunity arose to introduce a state-funded preschool program that capitalized on Smart Start's support system. However, this later development would not have been possible without maintaining momentum during the early years of Smart Start.

Once the Smart Start pilot was underway, Governor Hunt and his team immediately began to consider how to effectively expand the initiative. Hunt invited all county teams that were not selected for the first round of pilot funding to attend a luncheon in the Governor's mansion. He talked to the group about the importance of letting their legislators know that more funding was needed so that all counties could participate—again, enlisting a broad base of community members to lobby for Smart Start. The enthusiasm level was so high that some counties even raised private funding to start their own partnerships.[26] These efforts helped keep momentum going to expand the pilot.

The Smart Start administrative team went to work shoring up the commitment of leaders in participating counties in order to increase buy-in. Ponder, recalling the demands made on the local teams implementing Smart Start, says:

> We required them to come to Raleigh or to come to some central point in the state for three different three- or four-day periods in the first year. I mean, can you believe we did that? These were like the head of the health department—it was everybody with power in the community. And we were saying, "You're going to leave the community, and you're going to come to this meeting, and you're going to learn all about young children." And we did that, and they came. . . . We taught them everything from the basics of how child-care subsidy works to what is quality. So we really immersed them.

As the initiative grew, Smart Start was confronted by various challenges. Early on, the legislature initiated an outside performance audit of the services network, an effort largely driven by opponents of the program who anticipated negative audit results.[27] But that attempt to kill the program backfired. Even though the initiative was still not fully implemented, the results of the audit were largely positive; the report called for expanding the services network statewide. In the end, the audit helped prod legislators into fully funding the program.[28] Smart Start was implemented statewide by 1997, and until the political climate changed, it continued to flourish.

With Smart Start fully in place, the next step was to introduce high-quality public preschool. Governor Easley established NC Pre-K (then called More at Four) when he took office in 2001. An enthusiastic supporter of early education, Governor Easley wanted to develop his own signature early education initiative just as Governor Hunt had done.[29] Three years later, an updated ruling in a long-running school finance case helped to strengthen the case for state-funded preschool. The North Carolina Supreme Court found that every child in the state had a constitutional right to the opportunity to obtain a sound basic education, a finding that later specifically included at-risk preschool-age children.[30] Although the court refrained from ordering the state to adopt preschool as the remedy, the ruling nevertheless gave advocates new ammunition in their campaign for preschool.

Because Smart Start had created a strong infrastructure to support early education services in each county, it was possible to roll out state preschool fairly quickly and smoothly. For example, the existing needs assessment process carried out by local Smart Start partnerships allowed state leaders to determine where additional capacity to serve at-risk children was most needed.[31]

NC Pre-K was initially housed in Governor Easley's office, signaling his strong commitment to the program, but it was later moved to the Department of Public Instruction. This move had the benefit of linking preschool with the K–12 system, although one informant described it as a politically motivated decision to place the program under the control of the State Superintendent of Public Instruction, an office long controlled by the Democratic party. Regardless, the initial design decisions made while building the early education system—emphasizing local control for Smart Start, and elevating the importance of state-funded preschool through strategic administrative placement—would prove to be vital in helping both initiatives to weather tough times.

Protecting Early Education in Tough Times Through Committed Administrators and Local Engagement

In 2010, a series of challenges confronted North Carolina's early education effort. The Great Recession was still acutely affecting the state, and control of both the House and Senate switched to a Republican superma-jority for the first time since 1896.[32] The Republican leadership saw early education as a "Democratic issue," and so Smart Start and NC Pre-K be-came political targets. Matt Gross, Policy Director for the North Carolina Partnership for Children, explains:

> Politically speaking, although I think you're seeing a lot of states—and this one included—where early childhood education really cuts across party lines, the folks who built the early education system here were Democrats, which made sense because that's who was in power at the time that this was becoming an emerging field. So there was that political aspect to it, where it's always been associated with Jim Hunt, or with Mike Easley, or with the Democratic leadership. So there's this feeling of, "Who's going to own this work now that there are different people in charge?"

In 2011, the Republican leadership released spending targets that called for the Health and Human Services and Education Subcommittees in the House and Senate to consider consolidating or eliminating Smart Start and NC Pre-K (then called More at Four).[33] Ultimately, funding for both programs was cut by 20%.[34] The 2011 state budget also capped More at Four/NC Pre-K enrollment for at-risk children at 20% of available slots, stipulating that the remaining 80% of slots could go to fee-paying families whose children are not at-risk. The lawmakers also shifted administration of the program from the Department of Public Instruction to the Depart-ment of Health and Human Services. These attempts to limit the reach of the program for at-risk students mostly failed. The North Carolina Su-perior Court, assigned to monitor compliance with the North Carolina Supreme Court's earlier finding that at-risk students have a right to early education, issued a ruling striking down the copayment for fee-paying families and 20% enrollment cap for at-risk students as unreasonable bar-riers to a sound basic education.[35] The Superior Court allowed the state to shift More at Four to the Department of Health and Human Services, at which time the program was renamed NC Pre-K.

The Republican Party's control was strengthened when Pat McCrory was elected governor in 2012, the first Republican to win that office in 20 years. One of the first initiatives that GOP leaders undertook was a com-prehensive tax reform effort establishing a modified flat tax system. It was projected that the new tax structure would result in a $2.4 billion revenue loss over a five-year period, and the reduction of tax revenue prompted drastic cuts to programs that depended on public funding.[36] Smart Start was among those programs.

Smart Start is a popular program, and many North Carolinians opposed these cuts. Since 1996, there has been an annual Smart Start rally in Raleigh that brings local advocates to meet with their legislators, tell their stories, and remind policymakers that this is an initiative that voters care about. These events draw busloads of small children and adults to the state capitol.[37] A "Tuesdays for Tots" initiative brought delegates from local partnerships to the state capitol to meet with their representatives on a weekly basis during the legislative session.[38] These activities are the culmination of Governor Hunt's decision to focus on local control. More recently, the North Carolina Early Childhood Foundation introduced the "First 2000 Days" campaign (referring to the amount of time between a baby's birth and when he or she starts kindergarten) to educate legislators about the benefits that can accrue from supporting children and families during this key developmental period.[39] Gross asserts:

> The First 2000 Days finally articulated the value of early education in a way that made it much more accessible to legislators and everyday people. I remember being in meetings with legislators where they were giving me the First 2000 Days message, which is great. We've actually gotten to a place now where I'm fairly confident in saying that we no longer have the discussions around whether this is the role of government. I think it's widely accepted that is an important role to play. I think the question we're facing now is "What is the most effective way to meet the goals of the First 2000 Days?"

Yet despite the successful messaging of the First 2000 Days campaign and other Smart Start advocacy efforts, legislators have not restored early education funding to pre-recession levels. North Carolina, which was among the most innovative states in early education, is now falling behind other states in funding and quality. Laura Benson, Executive Director of Durham's Partnership for Children, explains that "Quality is getting chipped away at the edges as we're serving more children without more infrastructure and capacity to continue providing robust professional development."

Further funding reductions could reduce program quality; however, according to State Senator Louis Pate (Republican, 2011–present), the most recent budget negotiations resulted in a proposal to boost early childhood spending in fiscal year 2017.[40]

PROGRAM ADMINISTRATION AND MANAGEMENT

North Carolina has developed a complex system to oversee early care and education. Smart Start coordinates and funds services locally, making programs, including NC Pre-K, more easily accessible for families. However, administrative inefficiencies and duplication of services may still occur. Attempts to streamline state administration of early childhood programs have yielded mixed results.

Strong local leadership is an important piece of the puzzle, originating from both Smart Start partnerships and school districts. Increasing fiscal constraints are a problem for local leaders, who find themselves making do with diminishing resources.

Administrative Complexity at the State Level

The relationship between the various agencies administering NC Pre-K and other early childhood programs is complex (see Figure 5.2). The Department of Health and Human Services oversees NC Pre-K, regulates child-care licensing and subsidies, and supports NC Pre-K teachers working in private child-care settings. Funding for Smart Start flows from the Department of Health and Human Services to the North Carolina Partnership for Children, a state-level nonprofit agency that administers local Smart Start partnerships. Smart Start partnerships directly supervise and/or provide supplemental funding to NC Pre-K providers, and coordinate other early childhood services at the county level. The Department of Public Instruction oversees K–12 public education in the state, including local school districts that provide NC Pre-K. It also administers federal early education programs, including special education and Title I preschool programs, as well as Head Start, manages kindergarten readiness assessment efforts, and supports NC Pre-K teachers working in public school settings.

This closely intertwined system, which includes both public and nonprofit agencies, has generated a broad commitment to early education. Further, there has also been a lot of cross pollination among the leaders of these closely related organizations, as many administrators from state agencies, academic institutions, and nonprofit organizations end up working in more than one setting over the course of their careers. This leadership pipeline reinforces a shared understanding of the early education and care system.

Figure 5.2. Multiple Agencies Administer Early Childhood Services in North Carolina

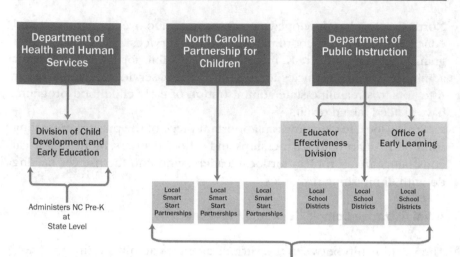

The complexity of this system can make it hard to explain its workings. Cindy Watkins, President of the North Carolina Partnership for Children, wonders:

> How do we hold the complexity and the richness of this work—to find a way to simplify some of the processes and the way we talk about this work, so it doesn't come across as this big, convoluted, non-integrated, unaligned system? It seems that way when we talk about it. But when you see it on the ground, it works. How do we hold onto that?

Local Smart Start and NC Pre-K administrators concur, noting the inherent challenge of this complexity. As one local administrator said, "The system has a lot of players, there are so many pieces of the whole child." Another local administrator likewise remarked, "There's no magic bullet. You need the whole package [of early childhood services]."

If administrators and advocates cannot effectively convey to legislators the important role that each agency and program plays, early childhood services may be affected. North Carolina policymakers have responded to concerns about systemic complexity by attempting to streamline the administration of early childhood programs, most notably by moving More at Four/NC Pre-K from the Department of Public Instruction to the Department of Health and Human Services. Some members of the early childhood community perceived this move to be politically motivated, an attempt to wrestle control of the program away from the State Superintendent of Public Instruction, an elected office that has been held by Democrat June Atkinson since 2005.[41] Others viewed it as a result of private child-care providers lobbying to get a bigger portion of state preschool dollars. However, former Representative Rick Glazier (Democrat, 2003–2015) asserts that there were also valid programmatic reasons for the move:

> There were at least, I think, reasonable goals as to why [the move] happened, outside of the ideological context—administrative efficiencies, transition capacity, and some recognition that birth-to-5 ought to be sort of seamless in itself.

Although the goal may have been to move toward a more seamless system of services for children from birth to age 5, the results have been mixed. On one hand, oversight of child care, NC Pre-K, and Smart Start (indirectly via the North Carolina Partnership for Children) was consolidated under one roof. Program quality was also preserved. Deborah Cassidy, former Director of the Division of Child Development and Early Education at the Department of Health and Human Services and professor at the University of North Carolina at Greensboro, recalls:

> We weren't going to change what we knew was a good thing. . . . I absolutely knew that we could run state preschool as well. It was going to look a little different in terms of administration, but we weren't going to touch the curriculum, we were going to keep all the same topics.

The data bear out her claim. The National Institute for Early Education Research, which conducts an annual assessment of state preschool programs using 10 benchmarks of quality, found that NC Pre-K continued to satisfy 10 out of 10 benchmarks after the move, as it had since 2005.[42] Researchers from the state's Frank Porter Graham Child Development Institute, which has conducted annual program evaluations of NC Pre-K since its inception, also found that the quality of the program and outcomes for children did not change significantly.[43]

On the other hand, what was gained in efficiency may have been lost in staffing and coordination with K–12. During the transition, the legislature eliminated around 25 positions at the Department of Public Instruction, many of which were focused on coaching preschool teachers and supporting classroom instruction.[44] It has taken time to rebuild that capacity at the Department of Health and Human Services. Furthermore, NC Pre-K is now separated from the federally funded early childhood programs that are housed at the Department of Public Instruction, as well as kindergarten readiness and K–3 formative assessment efforts. Local NC Pre-K administrators report that the move brought restrictive limits on administrative overhead, coupled with an increased focus on compliance and paperwork, making it difficult to fully support teachers and focus on educational quality, while overseeing NC Pre-K classrooms. Despite the best efforts of officials on both sides, the reality is that the Department of Health and Human Services operates separately from the K–12 public school system, and local NC Pre-K providers did experience some discontinuity in state support when the program moved.

Balancing the Tension of State and Local Interests Through Smart Start

Smart Start has also experienced administrative turbulence. Balancing local innovation with statewide strategic guidance is a difficult task. Deborah Cassidy reflects:

> One of the struggles with Smart Start has been that there's North Carolina Partnership for Children, and then there's all these local partnerships. There's a fair amount of wrestling for control. . . . There are some locals that resist any control, and they'll just run to their local legislator and say, "The North Carolina Partnership for Children is trying to boss me around." And the legislator, they think those are their dollars, and they're going to stick up for their local [Smart Start] executive director. So, it gets messy on that level.

State leaders sometimes find it difficult to administer programs efficiently when local Smart Start partnerships have different preferences. Anna Carter, President of the Child Care Services Association, explains that some partnerships opt to forego the statewide WAGE$ initiative, which supplements the income of poorly paid child-care providers. Instead, they use discretionary funding to offer a homegrown wage supplement program. Smart Start partnerships may choose this option if they disagree with the state's eligibility criteria, but in doing so the local partnerships lose out on federal funds that cover administrative costs for WAGE$, and ultimately send less money directly to providers.

Another challenge with administering Smart Start locally is the potential for duplication of services to providers, which can lead to disparate advice based on conflicting program requirements. For example, some

local Smart Start partnerships employ child-care consultants, while resource and referral agencies offer this service as part of their core mission. There may be a formal relationship between the two at the local
level (e.g., jointly funding a consultant), but this is not always the case.
Furthermore, technical assistance coaches may not always give consistent
advice to providers. Carter explains:

> What you have to do is make sure you coordinate those services so that it's
> not—why is it that in this one center they're having six different people
> come into this one classroom, and they don't know about each other, and
> one is telling the teacher, "Move this here, move that there," and the next
> says, "Oh no, you want to move that [here] . . . " So, coordination is what
> is key. I think sometimes providers, they just know the technical assistance
> person, they don't know necessarily who the funding is from. So, it can be
> confusing and they may feel like it's duplicative. But for the most part, if
> you really break it down and look at it, it's not duplicative. It's just multiple
> funding streams with different goals and purposes.

Still, Smart Start has had a powerful impact on the lives of many children. While it cannot untangle the web of state administration, it can
sustain local programs and make it easier for families to access services.
A parent in Edgecomb County describes visiting the pediatrician with
her 4-year-old daughter, who received a book bag at each visit through
the Smart Start-funded Raising a Reader program, and who often asks to
visit the library now. Her daughter also attends a private child-care center
supported by the Down East Smart Start Partnership, and has progressed
from the toddler classroom to NC Pre-K. The mother reports that her
daughter is "learning a lot" and "loves school."

The Importance of Strong Local Leadership

State policy is essential for designing sound early childhood programs,
setting high-quality standards, and offering funding and support to providers, but it also takes strong leadership at the local level to deliver services that change children's lives. In North Carolina, this leadership can
originate from Smart Start, the public school system, or other organizations that make up the intricate tapestry of the early childhood system.
Despite strong leadership in many local communities, statewide variation
in capacity may result in uneven service access or quality. Recent funding constraints are placing an increasing demand on local leaders to of-

BRINGING PRESCHOOL PROGRAMS TOGETHER IN DURHAM

Durham's Partnership for Children is the county's Smart Start agency. Administering NC Pre-K is just one of the many roles it plays in the community. To help families enroll their 4-year-old children in public preschool, the partnership has developed a shared application process that encompasses NC Pre-K in private child-care centers, Head Start, and Title I preschool programs. Families fill out a single application, which they can turn in to any of the agencies. Executive Director Laura Benson says there is "no wrong door" for families accessing preschool services. The agencies together review the applications and assign children to program sites based on eligibility, location, family need, and program capacity. Multiple agencies collect parents' applications, including the local Department of Social Services, Child Care Services Association, Smart Start, Head Start and Early Head Start, East Durham Children's Initiative, and Durham Public Schools. NC Pre-K Program Manager Danielle Johnson explains that participating agencies benefit from reduced recruitment demands, and gain access to technical assistance offered by the partnership.

Benson describes this application process as reducing duplication, offering a user-friendly experience to families, and ensuring the wise use of public preschool dollars. The system seems to be working—preschool applications have increased since it was put into place. Benson observes:

> Sometimes in our work we get so invested in "Oh, well that's Head Start," "That's Durham Public Schools Title I," "That's NC Pre-K." In the broader community, even in our messaging about how to grow community awareness and momentum and buy-in about publicly funded access to high-quality early education, we've learned people's eyes glaze over about the funding streams, and they don't really care which dollar pays for which classroom seat. What they want to know is that as many children as possible are being served in settings that are most appropriate and are highest quality, so that we enhance and increase school readiness, and are providing the strongest foundation for our kids to succeed.

Source: Site visit to Durham's Partnership for Children.

fer strong and creative stewardship in both the fiscal and programmatic realms. Transportation needs, which are substantial in rural parts of the state, must also be addressed with dwindling resources.

Leadership Across Different Early Childhood Settings. The local Smart Start infrastructure offers a promising source for strong early childhood leadership in different communities. Yet while both Smart Start and NC Pre-K benefit from a remarkably talented and dedicated cadre of administrators and staff, it is difficult to maintain the same level of experience and training among all 75 partnerships. The North Carolina Partnership for Children does step in to offer support services to local directors and staff as needed, but it cannot be everywhere at all times.

The reality is that some partnerships have pulled ahead of others in terms of depth and innovation of programming. Cindy Watkins, President of the North Carolina Partnership for Children, reflects:

> It goes back to local leadership. In communities where the executive director is really good at relationship building, and able to inspire the vision of how we serve the most children in the best, highest quality environments possible under limited resources, and how we keep that as our goal, it's amazing how communities will come together and really make good decisions. And it's not, "Do I have the money, or do you have the money?" It's "How can we serve the most children?" And they usually get to a better place.

Smart Start is not the only source of strong local leadership; local school district superintendents and community leaders can play an important role as well. While Smart Start administers NC Pre-K in over half of North Carolina counties, the public school system runs the program in many others, including in Hoke and Mecklenburg counties. Elizabeth Mitchell, NC Pre-K Director for Hoke County Schools, received strong support from her superintendent:

> He said to me, "I want you to make this the best program possible. I'm not going to micromanage. If you need my help, I'm here for you. All you've got to do is let me know what you need." And I've been doing it ever since. That's where it all starts, that leadership coming from the top down.

Julie Babb, Director of Pre-K Programs for the Charlotte-Mecklenburg Public Schools, also received strong support from the superintendent who founded the program, and his two successors. However, when a new superintendent came in who was less supportive of preschool, the tides turned. Babb recalls:

A DAY IN THE LIFE OF THE DOWN EAST PARTNERSHIP FOR CHILDREN

The Down East Partnership for Children spans two rural, low-income counties in North Carolina, Nash and Edgecomb. Executive Director Henrietta Zalkind and her team have administered and coordinated early childhood services in both communities since the partnership's inception in 1993. Upon entering the colorful headquarters, an abandoned building in a rough neighborhood that the partnership reclaimed, families are welcomed by a Family First specialist, who guides them through an intake process connecting them to relevant services. Resources in the building range from weekly parenting classes and play groups to a supply of children's books for doctors to give out at well-child check-ups. There is also a workroom stocked with free supplies for early childhood teachers, and a lending library full of developmentally appropriate toys for child-care providers to borrow. Across the street is a brand new playground, open to the entire community, which serves as a model outdoor learning environment for child care providers and families. The partnership's reach extends far beyond the immediate vicinity of the headquarters. Consultants visit local child care providers to help improve quality, and the partnership also administers NC Pre-K and child care subsidies in the community, working closely with the public school system and other partners.

It takes an expansive vision and strong leadership to put together this comprehensive set of resources. Zalkind notes that the partnership has diversified its funding sources, with Smart Start and NC Pre-K accounting for about 80% of funding. Private donations and grants make up the remainder of the budget, with local businesses and statewide foundations often stepping up to the plate. No doubt Zalkind herself deserves credit for forging connections with funders of all sizes in her quest to strengthen the partnership's funding base. Administrative costs also require creative problem solving, since state funds and grants often restrict the amount of money that can be used for those purposes. Partnership staff carefully track their time across different projects and are often paid from a blend of funding sources.

A Day in the Life, continued

Zalkind and her team also creatively blend available resources to solve local problems. For example, with support from the Blue Cross/Blue Shield of North Carolina Foundation and the North Carolina Partnership for Children, the Down East Partnership has transformed five elementary school playgrounds into outdoor learning environments that are open for community use during non-school daylight hours. Having access to these settings allows families to engage in healthy play and helps children feel comfortable when they start school in a familiar setting. Down East led a community planning process for the playgrounds and helped negotiate joint-use agreements that ensured the schools would not be held liable for public safety.

The Down East Partnership is not immune to the financial squeeze of recent years. However, Zalkind's determination to secure additional funding and build strong partnerships within the community has paid off in the form of a robust support system for young children and families.

Source: Site visit to the Down East Partnership for Children.

He tried to cut 105 of the [preschool] classes. That was announced January 11 [about five years ago], and people came out in droves—early childhood advocates, parents, some other agencies rallied around and got a lot of support. They campaigned to keep pre-k going. It was an amazing six months. Everybody wore buttons and shirts, and went to every school board meeting and every county commission meeting. They actually went to the county commission and asked for more money. It was an outpouring of support from many children's agencies and individuals who were significant leaders in our community.

At the end of the school year, the superintendent announced his resignation and the school board restored all pre-K funding. However, the turmoil damaged the program. More than 70 pre-K teachers and 90 assistant teachers quit during the six-month period when their jobs were threatened. Babb and her team also spent significant time packing, and then unpacking, classrooms—time that could have been spent on supporting teachers. These experiences in Hoke and Charlotte-Mecklenburg underscore the benefit of a supportive local superintendent as well as the harm caused by a superintendent who does not view preschool as part of a public school education. In Charlotte, as was the case for Smart Start, a groundswell of local support protected NC Pre-K. However, as state funding has decreased, local leaders increasingly find themselves scrambling to keep programs running.

Funding Challenges Intensify the Burden on Local Smart Start Partner-
ships. As state Smart Start funding has decreased, local leaders are experiencing ever greater fundraising demands in an increasingly restrictive
fiscal environment. These pressures negatively affect NC Pre-K and all the
other early childhood programs that receive support from Smart Start.
As part of their administrative role, Smart Start partnerships have always
been responsible for raising funds and supporting the integration of early childhood services within their communities. To provide families with
easy access to early childhood services, Smart Start partnerships undertake an intensive effort to combine different funding opportunities and
programs. In addition to the state funds that are passed from the North
Carolina Department of Health and Human Services to the North Carolina Partnership for Children and then on to local partnerships, Smart
Start directors at the county level must also apply for grant opportunities
and seek financial and in-kind donations from local community members.
State law currently requires that a minimum threshold of 17% of the local
partnership's budget be from sources other than the state.

Indeed, the fundraising capacity of local partnerships has become more
important as state funding decreases. During the 2014 legislative session,
the General Assembly directed the North Carolina Partnership for Children to increase local capacity to raise private funds. In response, the state
partnership provided fundraising training and approved modifications allowing local partnerships more flexibility to recruit board members with
business and fundraising expertise. Smart Start directors themselves increasingly need to develop business and fundraising skills in addition to
early childhood expertise and nonprofit leadership experience.

Another financial challenge for directors of local partnerships is the
state mandate to spend almost half of their budgets on child-care subsidies. This obligation has risen over the years, from 30% of the local partnership budget when Smart Start was created to the current 45% threshold.[45]
The original intention was for local partnerships to find creative ways to
use child-care subsidy funds, such as maintaining a soft requirement that
parents who receive a Smart Start voucher attend parenting classes or volunteer in their child's program. As the economic recession hit and state
funding was cut, the state Department of Health and Human Services as
a whole began to rely more heavily on federal funds, such as the Child
Care and Development Block Grant or Temporary Assistance for Needy
Families (TANF) funding, to cover its budget. The local Smart Start child-
care subsidy funds also began to count toward federal grant requirements,
which restricted the use of the funds. Local directors found their hands

tied in terms of how they could spend a large chunk of their budget. Stephanie Fanjul, former President of the North Carolina Partnership for Children, observes:

> It takes all the juice out of innovation because half of the money looks just like TANF money. . . . The requirements for that are so intense that the level of innovation at the local level has dramatically decreased and the number of kids that we can serve for anything else has also dramatically decreased.

Given these fiscal challenges, it takes initiative and ingenuity to continue supporting a high-quality early childhood system.

GETTING TO QUALITY

North Carolina has relied on two primary mechanisms for driving quality improvements in the state's early childhood system: program evaluation and child-care licensing. Partnerships with university-based researchers have proved invaluable in tracking progress over time for both Smart Start and NC Pre-K. In addition, the star-rated child-care licensing system has been a strong mechanism for driving structural change. Over the years, gradual and thoughtful implementation has allowed the quality rating and improvement system to mature and flourish, with strong program standards and financial incentives increasing the supply of high-quality programs, and parent education efforts driving demand for top-rated child care.

Using Evaluation to Drive Quality

North Carolina is home to a number of top-tier academic institutions, including the public University of North Carolina system and Duke University, both of which have helped drive investments in and improvements to Smart Start and NC Pre-K. The University of North Carolina at Chapel Hill's Frank Porter Graham Child Development Institute has played a particularly important role as a long-standing evaluation partner for the state. John Wilson, former Executive Director of the North Carolina Association of Educators, says:

> The Child Development Institute has been a key player as far as providing a research impetus, and has been a lighthouse. . . . It was probably a stimulus for politicians to move forward.

TRANSPORTATION: A FISCAL CHALLENGE FOR RURAL AREAS

While all local Smart Start partnerships and school leaders are encountering fiscal challenges, those in rural areas face the added expenditure of transporting young children to child-care and preschool programs. Families may live far away from the programs that offer the services they seek, and public transit options are few and far between, or even nonexistent. Lack of access to a reliable vehicle, or inflexible schedules for working parents, can compound the problem. This is a major issue in rural areas of North Carolina, and one that local leaders work hard to address.

Hoke County lies near the South Carolina border. As of the 2010 U.S. Census, the population was 47,000, with 43% of residents living in rural areas. Elizabeth Mitchell, NC Pre-K Director for Hoke County Schools, says: "If we did not provide transportation for our students, especially at our public sites, our families would not be able to provide transportation." Hoke County Schools draw upon federal funds, as well as state Smart Start funds, to help pay for these transportation services.

In Nash and Edgecomb Counties, closer to the Virginia border, the 2010 U.S. Census places the combined population at just over 153,000, with an average of 46% of residents living in rural areas. Here, local providers sometimes take matters into their own hands. For example, a provider who offers infant/toddler care and state preschool in her child-care center has enlisted her husband to drive a daily route for school pick-ups and drop-offs. He sets out in a van for pick-up at 6:00 AM every weekday, and begins dropping children off at 2:30 PM. One child who lives particularly far away is driven to a half-way point where his parents meet the van. The provider notes that there is very little financial support available to help offset these costs. However, she knows that without her husband's van route, children living "in the country" would not have access to her program. The Down East Partnership for Children, the local Smart Start Agency, does provide a small subsidy for some child-care providers who offer transit services. Also, Edgecomb County Public Schools provide free transportation for preschool students who live near existing bus routes with additional capacity. However, these sources of support do not meet the needs of all families. As state funding has declined in recent years, transportation is yet another necessity that local early-care and education leaders must address with dwindling resources.

Sources: AccessNC (2017). *North Carolina Economic Data and Site Information County Profiles.* Raleigh, NC: North Carolina Department of Commerce; Interview with Elizabeth Mitchell, NC Pre-K Director for Hoke County Schools (2016, January 14); Site visit to the Down East Partnership for Children.

The partnership between Frank Porter Graham and the state began at the inception of Smart Start. For the first decade of the initiative (1993–2003), an interdisciplinary team of researchers from the Schools of Education, Public Health, and Social Work conducted a statewide program evaluation.[46] Projects ranged from measuring changes in child-care quality and school success for participating children, to developing an evaluation resource to help local partnerships collect and use data on program improvement efforts.[47] These evaluations documented changes over time, such as improvements in child-care quality or children's receipt of health services within a community, demonstrating Smart Start's positive impact in North Carolina. For example, in the first cohort of participating counties, the percent of child-care classrooms scoring "high" on the measure of child-care quality known as the Early Childhood Environment Rating Scale, or ECERS, increased from 13% in 1994 to 41% in 2002.[48]

Frank Porter Graham researchers have conducted a statewide evaluation of NC Pre-K every year since the program began in 2001. Researchers have examined program services, classroom quality, and child outcomes. These evaluations, which have mainly looked at child and program outcomes over time, have shown consistency in classroom quality at the "medium" to "good" level on the Early Childhood Environment Rating Scale while the program scaled up to serve 30,000 children. Children participating in NC Pre-K also made greater gains than would be expected for normal developmental growth according to standardized outcome measures such as the Woodcock Johnson III Tests of Achievement, with particular benefits for dual-language learners and low-income students.[49] A report using statewide data found that participation in NC Pre-K (then called More at Four) reduced the gap in average 3rd grade test scores between low-income children and their peers who did not qualify for free or reduced price meals—in reading by 37% and 24% respectively in the 2006–2007 and 2007–2008 school years, and in math by 31% for 2006–2008.[50] Also, for the poorest children, approximately 3% of NC Pre-K students were identified as having a learning disability in 3rd grade, as compared to 6% of low-income children who did not attend NC Pre-K.[51] Researchers from Duke University likewise found that Smart Start and NC Pre-K together reduced the odds of 3rd grade special education placement by 39%.[52]

The Frank Porter Graham evaluations have also enabled state administrators to identify promising practices to drive quality improvement. For NC Pre-K, John Pruette, Executive Director of the Office of Early Learning at the Department of Public Instruction, recalls:

> I think one of the keys to our success [in administering state preschool] was
> through our external evaluations, the work that Frank Porter Graham did on
> an annual basis—to really look through that data, particularly the program
> quality data, and look to see where the gaps were and how we could better
> support programs. For instance, one of the evaluations talked about the high
> quality of literacy opportunities in the environment but the low quality of
> literacy instruction that was occurring. So I redirected the resources that we
> had supporting professional development opportunities to focus specifically
> on, not literacy per se, but the quality of instructional practices and interac-
> tions between teacher and child.

Overall, the breadth of research and consistency of findings show that
North Carolina has made impressive progress in building and maintaining
high-quality early childhood services and positively affecting the lives of
young children and families in the state. Information gleaned from these
evaluations has been helpful in doing this; the next section addresses the
other key mechanism for improving the quality of early childhood services in the state: child-care licensing.

Strong Quality Standards for Preschool and Child Care

In North Carolina, all licensed early education programs are required to
participate in the state's quality rating and improvement system. The state
has also established specific program standards for local Smart Start partnerships and NC Pre-K providers.

A Mandatory Quality Rating and Improvement System. In North Carolina, the child-care licensing system and the quality rating and improvement system (QRIS) are one and the same. North Carolina is one of just
a handful of states to adopt this approach, which requires that all legally
operating early childhood programs (including child care, state-funded
preschool, and Head Start) receive a program quality rating, rather than
simply allowing providers to "opt in" to the QRIS system.[53] On a scale from
one to five, a one-star rating indicates that a provider meets minimum
safety and compliance requirements. Beyond that, providers can choose
to meet higher quality standards by applying for a two- through five-star
license. In return, the state offers financial incentives and technical assistance for program improvement activities. This Star Rated License system
has proven to be a powerful mechanism for driving structural change.
Points are awarded in the following areas:[54]

- **Program standards.** These include environmental factors, such as adult-child ratio, sufficient space for activities or variety of toys, and quality of adult–child and peer interactions. A trained observer using the revised Early Childhood Environment Rating Scale (ECERS-R), a tool that examines different elements of program quality, assesses programs seeking a higher rated license. A classroom receiving a "good" or "excellent" rating offers children the choice of a variety of learning centers, ranging from dramatic play props, art materials, and musical instruments to sand or water tables. Teachers encourage communication and use language to support children's conceptual development, while maintaining a positive classroom culture and overseeing health and safety routines.[55]
- **Education standards.** A lead teacher in a child-care center must obtain a North Carolina Early Childhood Credential through a community college course. At the highest level of the education standards, 75% of lead teachers in a center have at least an AA degree in early childhood education, and 50% of assistant teachers have an AA or Child Development Associate credential, along with additional coursework in early childhood education and two years of full-time early childhood work experience. NC Pre-K lead teachers must have a BA degree and birth-through-kindergarten teaching license.
- **Quality bonus.** An additional point can be earned for going "above and beyond" expectations. For example, a point may be awarded when a lead teacher of a child-care classroom earns a B.A. degree, or a family child-care program uses an approved curriculum.

This QRIS, which dates back to 1999, is one of the oldest in the nation.[56] Soon after its introduction, Frank Porter Graham researchers conducted a validation study confirming that the system accurately reflected the quality of child-care centers.[57] In 2005, the Department of Health and Human Services changed the way facilities earned stars: Instead of awarding points for compliance with baseline health and safety standards, the focus shifted solely to program standards and staff education.[58] The addition of the observational Early Childhood Environment Rating Scale to measure classroom quality, as well as reductions in the allowable staff-child ratio, reflect attempts to strengthen quality standards over the years.[59] Now that the Star Rated License has been in place for over 15 years, North Carolina is further refining its QRIS to better differentiate between star rating levels, and to increase consistency among programs with the same star rating level.

Tying funding to licensing requirements has been a powerful lever for raising quality. For example, in 2016, a child-care center in Mecklenburg County offering care to 4-year-olds at the highest quality tier (five stars) would receive a 63% higher reimbursement rate than a provider offering one-star care.[60] This higher rate helps to offset the cost of paying better-educated teachers or purchasing additional classroom materials, although overall reimbursement rates fall short of the federally recommended 75th percentile of current market rates. After a provider has been operating for six months, it must maintain at least a three-star license to continue receiving state child-care subsidies.[61] NC Pre-K providers must maintain a four- or five-star license after a 6-month grace period to receive state funds.[62] Michele Rivest, Executive Director of the North Carolina Child Care Coalition, notes:

> All of these pieces are embedded in our law in North Carolina. That was always important to us, that we didn't just build the administrative structure. We wanted to build it into the infrastructure of our state statutes.

Parent education also has boosted demand for top-quality programs. Smart Start, the Department of Health and Human services, and non-profit child-care resource and referral agencies formed a three-way partnership to run a statewide campaign that asked the question, "Is my child care as good as my child?" Another television campaign used pediatricians and kindergarten teachers to inform parents about the importance of high-quality child care.[63] These parent education efforts gave child-care providers an added incentive to pursue a higher star rating.

Smart Start funding has played an important role in getting local child-care providers to pursue quality improvement activities through the licensing system. Prior to state funding mandates taking effect, local partnerships had already begun to gradually shift child-care subsidy funding and other forms of support to favor four- and five-star centers. Anna Carter, President of the Child Care Services Association, explains:

> When we started the rated license -one to five stars—you could be a one star, if that's all you want. Then as more and more got the higher stars, then there were things that [local] partnerships would say, "You can only participate in this project, this activity, if you have a four- or five-star license." Or, "We will only use our Smart Start [child-care] subsidy dollars in programs

that have four or five stars." So, you don't have to have a four-star license, but if you want to participate, then you'll do that.

Over time, this commitment has paid off with impressive growth in both access to highly rated child care as well as the education level of teachers. From 2003 to 2015, the percentage of child-care centers with a four- or five-star rating rose from 30% to 66% (see Figure 5.E online). The percentage of children served by four- and five-star programs has increased from 33% in 2003 to 73% in 2015, with 50% of children attending licensed child-care centers in five-star care (see Figure 5.F online).

A key component of the Star Rated License is staff education; accordingly, teacher education levels have also increased. From 2003 to 2015, the proportion of child-care teachers with an AA degree in early childhood education increased from 11% to 21%; the proportion of child-care teachers with a BA degree in early childhood education increased from 5% to 15%; and the proportion of child-care teachers with a birth-through-kindergarten teaching license increased from 3% to 12%. In NC Pre-K classrooms, all lead teachers are required to have a BA degree in early childhood education with a birth-through-kindergarten teaching license. During this period, there was also a 6% reduction in the turnover rate for full-time lead and assistant child-care teachers—in 2003, 24% of teachers left their positions during the previous year; by 2015, that number fell to 18%.[64]

Overall, the evidence points to substantial improvements in the availability of highly rated child-care programs staffed by well-trained teachers.

Evidence-Based Smart Start Standards. Smart Start has its own quality standards, which complement the rated license system. The *Smart Start Resource Guide of Evidence-Based and Evidence-Informed Programs and Practices* provides research evidence for programs and practices commonly funded by Smart Start partnerships, such as the Reach Out and Read program, which distributes free books through pediatricians' offices, or the coaching of early care and education professionals.[65] This guide was developed in response to a 2011 legislative mandate that programs operating with Smart Start funds must use evidence-based or evidence-informed practices. Although the Smart Start standards do not directly apply to preschool or child-care providers, they help local partnerships determine which support services to invest in, thereby shaping the early childhood landscape in each community.

NC Pre-K Has the Highest Standards. In addition to the Star Rated License quality standards, North Carolina's state-funded preschool provid-

A FIVE-STAR CLASSROOM

Brown's Early Learning School in Durham offers child care and NC Pre-K in a five-star-rated private center located on a quiet residential street. With one class of 18 children and three teachers, Brown's maintains an exceptionally low adult-child ratio that allows for ample attention to each student. The classroom itself offers an array of language-rich and hands-on activities within a 4-year-old's reach, and children get to choose how to spend their hands-on learning time. At the water table, budding scientists can see whether objects float or sink, while in another part of the room a teacher helps children label drawings about their homes and families for a class book. A small desk in the corner holds three little pig figurines. The class recently read the classic fairy tale, and the children have been practicing together how to retell the story. Now, students can quietly practice retelling the story on their own, using the pigs as props. To enhance the classroom experience, quiet and noisy activities are spaced apart. Teachers circulate between all the centers, asking questions and introducing new vocabulary.

Soon it is circle time. Although children spend most of the day at learning centers, whole group lessons are also important, and are kept short and engaging. As a soothing song plays, students begin to put their activities away and wander over to the carpet. They move at different rates, but they all know where they are going and what they need to do by the end of the song. The teachers have established a clear routine to transition from one activity to another, and have left ample time for students to prepare for the next activity. As the students settle on the carpet, they are ready to continue learning.

Source: Site visit to Brown's Early Learning School.

ers must adhere to the even more rigorous *NC Pre-K Requirements and Guidance*. From the start, these preschools were designed to provide the highest quality education in the state. John Pruette, Executive Director of the Office of Early Learning at the Department of Public Instruction, points out, "First and foremost, it was about establishing program standards that were rigorous and informed by the research. And those are still in place."

A local NC Pre-K provider agrees, noting that the certification process can be "tedious," but "that's part of how they maintain quality." Indeed, the NC Pre-K standards have satisfied all 10 of the program quality benchmarks established by the National Institute for Early Education Research since

Table 5.3. NC Pre-K and Five-Star Child Care Program Standards

	Five-Star Child Care	NC Pre-K
Teacher qualifications	AA in Early Childhood Education	BA plus Birth-to-Kindergarten License
Adult-child ratio	1:12	1:9
Class size	24	18
Minimum environment rating scale score	Average of 5 out of 7 across all classrooms	5 out of 7 in the NC Pre-K classrooms
Developmental screenings	No	Yes
Approved curriculum	Yes	Yes
Early learning standards	No	Yes

Source: North Carolina Department of Health and Human Services, Division of Child Development and Early Education (2016). *North Carolina Pre-Kindergarten Program (NC Pre-K) Requirements and Guidance: Effective State Fiscal Year 2015–2016*; North Carolina Department of Health and Human Services, Division of Child Development and Early Education (2016). *North Carolina Child Care Rules and Law.*

2005. As of the 2014–2015 school year, North Carolina was one of just six states to meet this high bar.[66] The NC Pre-K standards are more rigorous than those for a five-star child-care center in the areas of teacher education, adult-child ratio, class size, and curriculum/instruction (see Table 5.3).[67]

The recently revised *North Carolina Foundations for Early Learning and Development,* a set of goals and developmental indicators for children from birth to age 5, are intended to serve as a shared vision of kindergarten readiness for parents, educators, administrators, and policy makers.[68] NC Pre-K providers are required to use these early learning standards, while child-care providers are not.

In contrast, both preschool and child-care providers seeking a four- or five-star license are required to select from a list of preapproved curricula. The current list contains more than 25 options, although 78% of preschool classrooms chose the Creative Curriculum in 2014–2015.[69] In recent years, the process by which curricula are chosen to be on the pre-approved list has become politicized—and potentially less rigorous—as the requirement to use a preapproved curriculum has expanded to apply to child-care providers seeking a higher program quality rating, as well as state-funded preschool providers. Catherine Scott-Little, Associate Professor of Human Development and Family Studies at the University of North Carolina at Greensboro, explains:

> As the process reached out past NC Pre-K, there was strong opposition from [child-care] providers. . . . The recommendations became quite contentious about what curriculum would or would not be approved. My understanding is that it's easier to get on the list now and I'm not sure there is a lot of selectivity around what's on the list.

Although the curriculum selection process may be a cause of concern, in general North Carolina has succeeded in setting a high bar for both child-care and preschool quality.

Building a Strong Early Childhood Workforce

North Carolina invests substantial resources to build a strong early childhood workforce. The gradual introduction of more rigorous teacher education standards has been accompanied by financial supports and training opportunities for child-care workers and preschool teachers.

In 1990, North Carolina's nonprofit Child Care Services Association created the Teacher Education and Compensation Helps (T.E.A.C.H.) Early Childhood Project to address the issues of under-education, poor compensation, and high turnover in the early childhood workforce. T.E.A.C.H. provides scholarships to help early care professionals pursue AA or BA degrees in early childhood education. Articulation agreements with North Carolina universities enable educators with an AA degree in early childhood education to transfer those credits toward the first 2 years of coursework for a BA degree in the same field. There are also scholarships available for an online MA degree focused on early childhood leadership, management, and policy, as well as a specialized birth-through-kindergarten teaching license. The employer and the individual are each responsible for a portion of tuition and book costs, ranging from 10% to 50% depending on the degree and scholarship program.[70]

After completing a T.E.A.C.H.-sponsored program, each participant receives a predetermined raise or bonus paid for by his or her employer. In return, participants agree to stay at their current jobs or in the early care field for 6 months to a year, depending on the scholarship program. T.E.A.C.H. has spread to 25 states in addition to North Carolina. With 2,500 to 3,500 teachers participating each year, North Carolina is the largest participant.[71] There was a jump in participation following the 2005 revisions to the rated license system, which allocated more points to staff education. However, there have been no big systemic changes to teacher education requirements in the past 10 years, and accordingly, demand has decreased.[72]

T.E.A.C.H. has been a game-changer in improving the caliber of early educators. When the North Carolina Early Childhood Credential was introduced in the 1990s—the equivalent of 4 semester hours (1 course) of community college training—participating teachers received tuition assistance and a bonus through the T.E.A.C.H. program. In 1997, after most teachers had completed their Early Childhood Credential, every lead child-care teacher was required to hold the credential.[73] Stephanie Fanjul, Director of the Department of Health and Human Services, Division of Child Development when the Star Rated License was introduced in 1999, reflects:

> What a lot of people don't get, the only reason I could go forward with a five-star license was because, as the Director of the Division, I made huge investments in T.E.A.C.H. And so I could see my workforce moving up into a place where I could actually expect them to average, to handle five stars. People forget that you can't build an industry and expect it to be fine without investing in the people who work in it.

When NC Pre-K was introduced in 2001, the critical missing piece, once again, was teacher education. The requirement that all NC Pre-K teachers hold a BA and birth-through-kindergarten teaching license was a huge leap from the prior Early Childhood Credential requirement for child care.[74] This license qualifies early educators to teach in preschool or kindergarten classrooms, and requires the same amount of training as any other K–12 teaching license. The key to implementing this ambitious requirement lies in gradual implementation and flexibility. For the first decade lead teachers were allowed to study for a BA and birth-through-kindergarten licensure while remaining in the classroom. At that point the requirement changed—lead teachers must earn a BA before they are hired; they can continue to work on birth-through-kindergarten licensure while teaching if they have not attended a traditional preparation program beforehand.[75] This flexibility has been key in developing the pre-K teacher workforce as a whole, and has been particularly important in the private sector, where there were initially no licensed teachers, and few held a BA.[76]

Through gradual improvement and strong support structures, North Carolina has steadily increased the qualifications of its early childhood workforce.

HIGH-QUALITY PRESCHOOL INSTRUCTION IN ACTION

At Brown's Early Learning School in Durham, 18 students gather "criss-cross applesauce" on the carpet with the lead teacher in front and the two assistant teachers sitting with the youngsters. The lead teacher holds up a bucket of small plastic bears. She tells the students, "We're going to build a bridge," as she places a folded piece of paper on top of two wooden blocks. "How many bears do you think this bridge can hold? Thumbs up if you think five. Ten? More?" Already, the students are engaged in the lesson as they make predictions. Next, the teacher begins to place one bear on the bridge at a time as the class counts together, practicing their math skills. With each bear, she asks the students to give a thumbs up if they think the bridge can hold one more bear. When it finally falls down, the students shriek in laughter. Next comes a twist in the lesson—what happens if the paper bridge is crinkled up instead of smooth? Will it hold more or fewer bears? Again, the students practice their prediction and counting skills as they wiggle in anticipation of the dramatic collapse.

The learning taking place is rich, but no more than 10 minutes have passed. The teacher concludes the whole-group lesson by telling students that they will get to take the materials outside to build their own bridges. She reminds them that there are many ways to build a bridge, and the two ways she showed them are just to get them started. She wants them to know that, just like any scientist, they should test a variety of ideas and gather the evidence for themselves. The students cannot wait to test their newfound bridge-building skills. The opportunity to apply the concepts they just observed in a hands-on activity will help solidify the counting, prediction, and engineering skills that were just demonstrated. And who knows—maybe tomorrow, a budding scientist will choose to apply her bridge-building skills to the building blocks center during free choice time. In this classroom, the learning opportunities abound.

Source: Site visit to Brown's Early Learning School.

NC PRE-K EARLY EDUCATOR SUPPORT, LICENSURE, AND PROFESSIONAL DEVELOPMENT UNIT

North Carolina maintains high standards for NC Pre-K teachers, and offers robust support through the state Early Educator Support, Licensure and Professional Development Unit, housed in the Department of Health and Human Services, Division of Child Development and Early Education. It supports:

Fully licensed teachers in public and private settings

All state preschool teachers, regardless of where they work, are required to hold a birth-through-kindergarten (B-K) license. This also qualifies them to teach kindergarten in North Carolina public schools, and requires the same training as any other K–12 teaching license.

Mentoring for all teachers

All teachers who hold a B-K license receive mentoring and evaluation on a regular basis, with especially intensive support during their first 3 years in the classroom. The induction process for teachers working toward their full B-K license involves an annual cycle of self-assessment and goal-setting, as well as both formal and informal observation and coaching. Teachers at public school sites receive support from their local school district, while teachers at private child-care and Head Start sites receive support directly from the state.

Multiple pathways to licensure

Teachers can earn a provisional B-K license by completing their BA and attending a state-approved teacher preparation program, or they can earn a lateral entry B-K license by completing their BA and then taking the necessary higher education classes while working as a lead teacher in a preschool classroom. Either way, they will receive mentoring and support while working toward full B-K licensure. This flexibility has been key in developing the teacher workforce in the private sector, where there were initially no licensed teachers and few held a BA.

NC Pre-K Early Educator Support, continued

Experienced mentors

There are approximately 165 experienced early childhood educators currently serving as both mentors and formal evaluators—but not for the same teachers. Mentors often work in pairs to switch off the two roles. There are two sources for these experts. The Early Educator Support, Licensure and Professional Development Unit contracts with both the University of North Carolina at Charlotte and East Carolina University, paying 35 licensed education experts to serve as mentors and evaluators. Collaborating partners (e.g., Smart Start, Head Start, private child-care centers, public schools and universities) employ an additional 130 mentors/evaluators. All mentors/evaluators go through a series of training sessions developed by the state, regardless of setting.

Building local capacity and investing in the state preschool workforce

The goal is to continue building capacity at the local level, rather than just focusing on the state level. Race to the Top funds have been used for this purpose to support collaborating partners. Nonetheless, out of approximately 1,000 teachers in need of this induction support, only about 700 are currently being fully served. Lack of qualified mentors poses a challenge, as does lack of funding.

Source: North Carolina Division of Child Development and Early Education, Department of Health and Human Services. (n.d.). Early Educator Support, Licensure, and Professional Development (EESLPD) unit. Retrieved from www.ncchildcare.nc.gov//general/mb_eeslpd.asp; interview with Cynthia Wheeler, Senior Manager at the Department of Health and Human Services, Division of Child Development and Early Education (2015, November 4).

NEXT STEPS FOR NORTH CAROLINA

North Carolina has been a leader in early care and education. Still, no one is declaring victory, for there is always more to be done. Efforts to update the Star Rated License system, forge stronger connections between early education and K–12, and address inadequate teacher compensation and child-care reimbursement rates are on the horizon. At the same time, providers are struggling to adjust to the state's new funding and political realities.

Updating the Quality Rating and Improvement System

When a quality rating and improvement system is effective, the quality of providers will be raised and the early education system will evolve. With 65% of child-care centers now offering four- or five-star care, state Department of Health and Human Services officials recognize that there is too much variation in quality among programs with the same star rating level, and that many providers at the top end of the system are ready for a greater challenge. Deborah Cassidy points out that "no one believed that five stars was the ultimate in quality, but they knew they had to start somewhere. There was great consensus around that point."

Cassidy started an advisory group that generated more than 300 recommendations regarding how to improve the star system criteria.[77] This group helped North Carolina to develop the highest scoring application in the first round of Race to the Top–Early Learning Challenge funding, one aspect of which was a federally required QRIS validation study. Rather than studying the existing system, the state is validating the next generation of its QRIS with 300 child-care centers and family child-care homes across the state. The new Star Rated License seeks to improve consistency within the rating levels, allow for more growth at the top end of the scale, and place a greater emphasis on measuring the quality of teacher-child interactions.[78]

Another Race to the Top–funded project may offer a better alternative to assessing the overall quality of early childhood programs. The University of North Carolina at Greensboro is collaborating with the University of Delaware and the University of Kentucky to develop a new observational measure of program quality known as the Early Childhood Quality Improvement Pathway System, or EQuIPS.[79] This rating tool has been specifically designed for use with a state's QRIS, and all three collaborating states are currently piloting it. EQuIPS measures the quality of children's classroom experiences, focusing on where and how they spend their time over a continuous time frame rather than just one day, unlike the ECERS-R rating scale currently used by North Carolina that captures a snapshot of program quality over a few hours. The tool combines classroom observations with document review and interviews of parents, teachers, and administrators to assess the quality and consistency of practice across the program as a whole. As the state that originated the Early Childhood Environment Rating Scale in its University of North Carolina system, it is fitting that North Carolina is at the next frontier of quality-rating measures.

IMPLEMENTING A LOCAL COACHING PROGRAM

Charlotte-Mecklenburg Schools, headquartered in Charlotte, NC, operates 180 Bright Beginnings Title I preschool classrooms and 56 NC Pre-K classrooms in elementary schools and community partner sites. Coaching offers a key professional learning opportunity to all 236 pre-K teachers in the district. As Julie Babb, Director of Pre-K Programs for Charlotte-Mecklenburg Schools, explains, "We view coaching as the most effective way for teachers to receive on-the-spot learning opportunities."

Coaches spend different amounts of time with individual teachers, according to their level of need. A coach might take a teacher to visit a model preschool classroom, or invite a master teacher to model a lesson within the teacher's own classroom. Coaches may also facilitate learning opportunities for small groups of teachers with similar needs. In addition, coaches play a formal role in observing teachers and providing feedback on their professional learning goals, such as asking students higher level questions, or working on smooth transitions from one activity to the next. After meeting with the teacher for a pre-conference to collaboratively define a professional learning goal, the coach will return for a scheduled observation, and then meet with the teacher again for a debrief conference. During the debrief, the coach will prompt the teacher to reflect on what went well in the lesson, how engaged the children were, and the extent to which students met the objectives of the lesson. Babb notes, "The goal is to have teachers reflect more on their own lessons. We've learned that sometimes we have to tell them a little bit more than we'd like to, so they'll know the kinds of things we're looking for." This detailed guidance and feedback can help teachers effectively develop their instructional skills.

Coaching positions are full time, which enable the coaches to maximize the time they spend in classrooms. Yet each of the district's 17 coaches works with approximately 15 teachers—a heavy load that requires frequent transitions from one classroom and teacher to another.

However, it is unclear whether these promising reforms will be implemented. Any changes to the QRIS need to be approved by the state Child Care Commission, a politically appointed body dominated by private, for profit child-care providers who are reluctant to approve measures that would affect their bottom line. If the Department of Health and Human Services can move forward with updating the Star Rated License, North Carolina would once again assume its place as a leader in early education initiatives.

> ### IMPLEMENTING A LOCAL COACHING PROGRAM, CONTINUED
>
> Pre-K teachers also receive support from literacy facilitators who are housed at all Charlotte-Mecklenburg elementary school sites. These positions initially focused on grades K–5, until the district brought in a pre-K expert to help expand the focus. Babb explains,
>
> > We like to work collaboratively with the school, but we want them to understand this is not "junior kindergarten" which is now like first grade. Real learning can happen through centers and play. We provide that expertise to every single school.
>
> This commitment to investing in a strong local coaching program has paid off in a system that effectively supports pre-K teachers districtwide.
>
> *Source:* Interview with Julie Babb, Director of Pre-K Programs for Charlotte-Mecklenburg Schools (2016, January 21).

Alignment with K–12

Thanks to Smart Start, North Carolina has relatively strong alignment between birth-to-age-3 services and preschool. However, the preschool-to-3rd grade connection is less evident, particularly in the aftermath of shifting NC Pre-K away from the Department of Public Instruction to the Department of Health and Human Services. As John Pruette of the Department of Public Instruction observes, "We need a deliberate conversation around governance, about how to align and strengthen a system not just across zero to 5, but through grade 3."

One potential source of misalignment is an increasing focus on test scores that has even reached preschool. The federal No Child Left Behind law, coupled with a 2011 North Carolina law requiring children to repeat 3rd grade if they do not pass an end-of-year reading test, ushered in an era of high-stakes testing in elementary schools.[80] This accountability regime has placed pressure on preschool teachers, particularly at public school sites, to stop "playing" with their students and instead focus on traditional academic preparation, such as phonics drills. As one administrator in a public school system noted, "It's always about what teachers are doing wrong, not what kindergarten or pre-K is doing right."

Local NC Pre-K providers and administrators agree that the early elementary grades have become increasingly academic and focused on test preparation in recent years, creating discontinuity with the hands-on instruction taking place in NC Pre-K classrooms. A local administrator observes:

I think [schools] are really expecting kindergarten students to do more of "sit down to yourself, work on your sheet." And our kids aren't really accustomed to that, that's not how they spend their day [in NC Pre-K]. So when you transition to that kind of environment, it's stifling.

Another local administrator notes:

Suddenly you go from a fairly open pre-k environment with [learning] centers to sitting in a classroom. That's a big transition. You know, sitting all day, it's just an unnatural lifestyle. . . . Schools have got to understand the importance of developmental appropriateness. If [instruction] is not developmentally appropriate, the learning is not going to happen.

A new K–3 observational assessment introduced by the Department of Public Instruction may help to address the discontinuity between state-funded preschool and kindergarten, as it supports an instructional approach tailored to each child's development.[81] This groundbreaking work is part of the state's Race to the Top–Early Learning Challenge grant, and North Carolina is the leader of a 10-state consortium that also includes three research partners.[82] Rather than taking a one-time snapshot of children's readiness as they enter kindergarten, teachers spend the first two months of school collecting work samples and observations to document each child's academic, physical, and social-emotional development. This evidence goes into an electronic platform, generating an individual profile for each student that is maintained on a rolling basis through 3rd grade. By embedding the kindergarten entry assessment in a larger K–3 observational assessment process, teachers can home in on each student's strengths and needs, transforming teaching and learning in the early elementary grades.

Kindergarten teachers are collecting student evidence with the same electronic platform (Teaching Strategies GOLD) used to document child outcomes in many NC Pre-K classrooms. The kindergarten entry assessment is also aligned to both the K–12 content standards and the *Foundations for Early Learning and Development,* which are used in all NC Pre-K classrooms. However, state-funded preschool providers are not formally linked to the K–3 assessment process. Whether the K–3 assessment will maximize its potential to help achieve greater alignment by allowing NC Pre-K teachers to contribute observational data to student profiles, for example, remains to be seen.

BUILDING BRIDGES FROM PRE-K TO ELEMENTARY SCHOOL

A number of counties have made progress aligning pre-K and K-12 education in North Carolina. In Hoke County Schools, for example, staff development is a key area for promoting these pre-K and K-12 connections. Pre-K teachers have been invited to join an ongoing staff professional development program focused on literacy comprehension that includes teachers across the elementary grades. Elizabeth Mitchell, the district's Pre-K Director, reported that this is the norm in Hoke County: For district-run professional learning opportunities, administrators typically invite all NC Pre-K teachers, teaching assistants, and directors to participate, regardless of whether they work at a private or district pre-K site. Further, this exchange of knowledge is not one-sided; Mitchell reports that kindergarten teachers in the district are expected to be familiar with the state's pre-K learning standards, which help them effectively implement the state's kindergarten entry assessment. Pre-K is also included in the district's administrative structure— Hoke County Schools' Assistant Superintendent for Curriculum and Instruction oversees pre-K through grade 5—ensuring pre-K is considered in local decisionmaking.

Durham County has likewise made significant strides aligning state pre-K with local K-12 schools in recent years. Durham Public Schools created an office to oversee early education and established a clear point person that has developed a strong relationship with the local Smart Start partnership. Further, the district recently worked with the Durham Partnership for Children to revamp its transition to kindergarten program, enhancing linkages between families with young children and local schools. The updated program features dedicated transition teams at elementary schools, a series of events for families based on evidence of best practice, and a targeted kindergarten registration week to encourage families to register for school on time. The district's kindergarten transition activities also include more attention to the needs of Spanish-speaking families, an expanding demographic in the area. These connections have helped build bridges between local NC pre-K and elementary school classrooms.

Source: Interview with Elizabeth Mitchell, Pre-K Director, Hoke County Schools (2016, January 14); Interview with Laura Benson, Executive Director, Durham Partnership for Children (2016, January 29)

A Compensation Crisis for Child Care

Despite the progress that North Carolina has made in educating its early childhood workforce, in 2015, 64% of lead child-care teachers did not have an AA or BA degree in early childhood education; 38% did not have any AA or BA degree. With a $10.67 median hourly wage for a child-care teacher with an AA degree in early childhood education, and a $14.85 median hourly wage for a teacher with a MA degree in early childhood education, it is easy to see why a teacher might not choose to pursue additional education, or why a highly educated professional might choose to work in a public school setting with better pay rather than work in a child-care setting.[83] A local NC Pre-K provider identifies her greatest challenge as recruiting teachers, saying, "I feel like I run a boot camp, training up teachers who then escape to the [public] school system for health and retirement benefits.... Teachers leaving has been a monster." Anna Carter, President of the Child Care Services Association, agrees:

> We believe that we were helped with turnover by the economic downturn, because there weren't a lot of other jobs. When you have high unemployment, that helps. But now that the economy has had some improvement, this is what we were concerned we were going to see—more turnover. It will be interesting to see three or four years from now how that looks. We know if we don't do something for compensation—I mean, it's ridiculous to think about what we expect these teachers to do, and the impact they have on kids. And what they can get if they go work in the public school system. To go from $10 an hour to the school system, where you can more than double that and get benefits. It's unfortunate.

Because NC Pre-K is delivered through a mixed delivery system, problems in the child-care sector affect state-funded preschool as well. Advocates such as the Child Care Services Association and the North Carolina Child Care Coalition would like to see teacher qualification requirements for child care raised to the BA level that is required of NC Pre-K teachers, coupled with a suitable increase in pay. Statewide work groups were formed recently to address these intertwined issues of teacher compensation, training, and qualifications, as well as ongoing workforce support. Many key players are involved in this work, from state agency administrators to university experts and nonprofit leaders.[84] The goal is to ensure that infants, babies, and toddlers have access to caretakers with a level of preparation similar to that of teachers in preschool and kindergarten classrooms.

This work is a natural extension of the Child Care WAGE$ Project, an initiative of the Child Care Services Association that began in response to research showing that child-care quality is lowered by inadequate teacher education and high turnover rates. WAGE$ provides education-based salary supplements to low-paid child-care teachers (and directors) working with children between the ages of birth and 5 years at centers and in family child-care homes. The range of the supplemented salary is generally $13 to $17 per hour. The hope is that supplementing teachers' low pay will entice them to stay in the field and induce them to pursue additional education. If that happens, preschool children will have more experienced and better prepared teachers.

WAGE$ is offered throughout North Carolina as a funding collaboration between local Smart Start partnerships and the Division of Child Development and Early Education at the Department of Health and Human Services. A little over half of the state's 100 counties participate, but counties are now opting out as local Smart Start partnerships have been required to use more of their financial resources for child-care subsidies. The WAGE$ budget has been halved in the past 6 years.

Low reimbursement rates for child-care providers who offer state-subsidized care exacerbates the problem of poor compensation for teachers. The legislature has not significantly changed the assessed market rate for child-care subsidy reimbursement in almost a decade, despite an increasing cost of living and heightened expectations for the quality of care.[85] In 2014, North Carolina's monthly reimbursement rate for a 4-year-old child receiving care in Mecklenburg County was $670, 29% below the federally recommended 75th percentile of current market rates for this type of care. Similarly, the monthly reimbursement rate for a 1-year-old child receiving care in Mecklenburg County was $737, 31% below the 75th percentile of current market rates.[86] Stephanie Fanjul, former President of the North Carolina Partnership for Children, observes:

> We haven't been keeping up with costs, and so the rates we pay for the [child-care] vouchers are terribly unfair. The providers—nonprofit and for profit alike—have a point. You know, "You're not going to pay me fair rates, and then you want me to pay the teachers a fair salary?" The legislature controls the rates and it comes out of tax funds. They're in a really bad place. It may be one of those threads that could undo everything. If rates don't get fixed soon, the potential for there to be lots of erosion of the system is very, very real. Even Smart Start—especially Smart Start.

North Carolina's closely intertwined early childhood system means that financial problems in the private sector pose a broad threat to public programs like NC Pre-K.

Adjusting to a New Political Reality

Political attacks on Smart Start and NC Pre-K funding have receded in the face of pushback from a wide array of supporters. Governor Mc-Crory has been publicly supportive of preschool, and funding for NC Pre-K has been partially restored.[87] Members of the business community recently established a new organization called Business for Education Success and Transformation North Carolina (BEST NC), intended to focus attention on these issues. BEST NC members include Jim Goodmon and Walter McDowell, key supporters of Smart Start during Governor Hunt's administration.[88]

But efforts to rethink the early education system are viewed as a veiled threat in some quarters. Two committees are currently engaged in reimagining North Carolina's early education services. The Early Childhood Advisory Council, an appointed body, was started by Governor Perdue and continued by Governor McCrory, who shifted the composition of the committee almost entirely from Democrats to Republicans when he took office. The group is engaged in a systematic review of the costs, services, and outcomes of all early childhood initiatives in the state, and some advocates are concerned that the result could be additional program cuts.[89]

The second committee, a subcommittee of the joint legislative Health and Human Services Oversight Committee, recently released a report on subsidized child care, NC Pre-K, and Smart Start.[90] Some early education advocates feared that the committee would recommend downsizing or combining the programs, but the results instead focused on strengthening the existing early childhood system. Committee Co-Chair Representative Josh Dobson (Republican, 2013–present) notes:

> I'm pretty proud of our oversight committee, because it wasn't like the General Assembly imposing our views on the early childhood community. I feel like we needed to take a different approach, and bring in those who are actually at the ground level every day in early childhood.... I wanted to know how we could improve early childhood. Instead of imposing our views, you tell us how we can help.

Recommendations included increasing the coordination of state level governance of early childhood programs, updating NC Pre-K reimbursement rates, and improving the delivery of child-care subsidy services. Legislators have already introduced a bill directing the Department of Health and Human Services Division of Child Development and Early Education to conduct a cost study of NC Pre-K that fully accounts for administrative and local costs in public school, private child care, and Head Start facilities.[91] Another bill aims to increase alignment between the Department of Health and Human Services and the Department of Public Instruction through a collaborative planning process.[92] While the current 2016–2017 budget proposal offers an increase in child-care subsidy funding and a decrease in the required Smart Start local match rate, legislators do not appear to be considering a substantial investment to bring Smart Start and NC Pre-K funding back to pre-recession levels.[93]

KEY TAKEAWAYS

NC Pre-K, initially dubbed More at Four, is a state-funded, targeted preschool program for 4-year-old children who have factors that place them at risk of educational failure. North Carolina serves 22% of its 4-year-olds through this program in public and private settings across the state. Smart Start is a network of 75 nonprofit agencies offering "one-stop shop" service coordination for families and children birth to age 5 in each of North Carolina's 100 counties, with statewide coordination and support from the North Carolina Partnership for Children. A body of research conducted by the University of North Carolina at Chapel Hill's Frank Porter Graham Child Development Institute and Duke University has found positive effects associated with participation in both NC Pre-K and Smart Start. These effects include significant improvements in language, literacy, math, and behavior skills that exceed expected benchmarks for developmental growth for NC Pre-K students, with dual-language learners and low-income students deriving the greatest benefits. Counties participating in Smart Start experienced improvements in child-care classroom quality over time, and researchers found a reduction in 3rd grade special education placement rates associated with investment in Smart Start and NC Pre-K. Key takeaways from North Carolina include the following:

Although political champions can provide powerful support for early edu-cation, the downside is that early education programs may become political targets. Democratic governors have been key supporters of early educa-tion in North Carolina—Governor Hunt created Smart Start, and Gover-nor Easley started More at Four (now NC Pre-K). In doing so, they brought public attention to the importance of early education, engaged the state's business and religious leaders, and directed funding to both Smart Start and state preschool. Consequently, these programs came to be associat-ed with the Democratic party. When Republicans gained control of the General Assembly and governorship, both early education programs were targeted for funding cuts, and state-funded preschool was administratively restructured.

A purposeful balance between state oversight and local control can lead to widespread support for a program, serving as a protective factor when polit-ical priorities change. While a statewide nonprofit agency oversees Smart Start in North Carolina, county-level nonprofit agencies direct funds to meet local needs. This approach has been popular with citizens through-out the state, leading to grassroots lobbying in support of Smart Start when the General Assembly prioritized cutting taxes over funding early education.

North Carolina's complex early childhood system offers a rich array of birth-to-age-5 services, but can be challenging to effectively communicate and efficiently administer if not given careful attention. By layering NC Pre-K with Smart Start, North Carolina makes it possible for families with children birth to age 5 to access a wide array of services ranging from free books to parenting classes, in addition to high-quality state preschool services. However, it can be hard to effectively communicate the unique role that each program plays, particularly to policymakers who lack ex-perience with the system. In addition, duplication or inefficient delivery of services may occur if careful coordination is lacking at the local level.

At the local level, strong leadership comes from different settings, and is essential in offering high-quality programming. In North Carolina, state preschool can be administered at the county level by Smart Start or the school system. Strong local leaders originate from both sources, and play a key role in mobilizing community support and delivering high-quality services. Because Smart Start is a public–private partnership, local leaders must seek donations to supplement state funds, an activity that has be-come more urgent due to recent state-level funding cuts.

Integrating child-care licensing with a quality rating and improvement system (QRIS), and tying financial incentives to the results, can help improve program quality. North Carolina has established the Star Rated License system that combines child-care licensing with quality improvement efforts, and is one of the oldest QRIS systems in the country. All licensed early education providers in the state, including state-funded preschool and Head Start, participate. NC Pre-K providers and child-care providers must maintain a minimum quality rating to receive state funds, and tiered child-care subsidy reimbursement compensates better rated providers at a higher rate. Currently, 73% of children in the state receive four- or five-star child-care.

Building a strong early childhood workforce is a key piece of program quality. To make the financial incentive targets in the Star Rated License system feasible, North Carolina state administrators have focused on increasing the supply of well-prepared early educators. Their strategy has been to gradually raise teacher education requirements for child care and state preschool, while investing in scholarship and wage subsidy programs to support and incentivize teachers. While teacher education rates have improved and annual turnover has decreased, low compensation rates for child-care teachers and below-market subsidy reimbursement rates for child-care providers still pose a challenge in the state.

Though North Carolina's early education system remains a work in progress, it offers a comprehensive set of services for children birth to age 5. The state's work to revise its quality rating and improvement system and align early childhood instruction from birth through 3rd grade could help North Carolina to retain its status as a national leader in early education.

NOTES

1. Education Commission of the States. (2005, June). *Full-day kindergarten: A study of state policies in the United States*. Retrieved from www.fcd-us.org/assets/2016/04/FullDayKindergarten.pdf; *NC leads in offering full-day kindergarten*. Retrieved from buildthefoundation.org/2014/02/nc-leads-in-offering-full-day-kindergarten/

2. United Way of America Success by 6 (2005, July). *Stair steps to quality: A guide for states and communities developing quality rating systems for early care and education*. Retrieved from www.earlychildhoodfinance.org/downloads/2005/MitchStairSteps_2005.pdf

3. *Race to the Top–Early Learning Challenge Revised Final Results.* (2012, April). Retrieved from www2.ed.gov/programs/racetothetop-earlylearningchallenge/applications/chart-of-scores.pdf

4. Ponder, K.W. (2011). *The smart start story.* Unpublished manuscript.

5. North Carolina Partnership for Children (2015). *Fiscal year 2014–2015 report to the North Carolina General Assembly.* Retrieved from www.smartstart. org/ about-smart-start/2014-15-annual-report/

6. Unpublished data from the North Carolina Department of Health and Human Services, Division of Child Development and Early Education (personal communication, November 6, 2015).

7. Title I data from Pruette, J. (2016, February 25). *North Carolina early education system: Sustaining impact.* Presented to the Early Education and Family Support Subcommittee of the Joint Legislative Oversight Committee on Health and Human Services, 2015-16; Unpublished Head Start data from the North Carolina Department of Public Instruction, Office of Early Learning (personal communication, May 10, 2016); Special education data calculated by author using data from The National Institute for Early Education Research. (2016). *The State of Preschool 2015: State Preschool Yearbook.* Retrieved from http://nieer.org/ wp-content/uploads/2016/05/Yearbook_2015_rev1.pdf

8. Calculation by author using data from note 7.

9. North Carolina Partnership for Children (2015).

10. North Carolina Department of Health and Human Services Division of Child Development and Early Education. (2016, March 9). *North Carolina pre-kindergarten program (NC Pre-K) requirements and guidance effective SFY 2015-16.* Retrieved from www.wakesmartstart.org/wp-content/uploads/2015/10/NCPre-K_Program_Requirements_Guidance.pdf

11. Reynolds, A. J., Richardson, B. A., Hayakawa, M., et al. (2014). Association of a full-day vs part-day preschool intervention with school readiness, attendance, and parent involvement. *The Journal of the American Medical Association, 312*(20), 2126–2134. doi:10.1001/jama.2014.15376

12. Funding levels have been adjusted to 2015 dollars. *Current Operations Appropriations Act of 1993,* ch. 321, sec. 254, § 143B-168.12, 1993-321 N.C. Sess. Laws 1, 226-29; Ponder, K.W. (2011).

13. North Carolina Early Childhood Foundation (2015, April). *Early childhood budget trends in North Carolina.* Retrieved from buildthefoundation.org/ wp-content/uploads/2015/04/Early-Learning-Budget-History-April-2015.pdf

14. Funding levels have been adjusted to 2015 dollars.

15. Only three of 91 local NC Pre-K contracting agencies currently use the classroom model. Unpublished data from the North Carolina Department of Health and Human Services, Division of Child Development and Early Education (personal communication, May 15, 2016).

16. Funding levels have been adjusted to 2015 dollars.

17. The National Institute for Early Education Research (2016).

18. Department of Health and Human Services, Division of Child Development

and Early Education. (2015, August). *NC Pre-K payment rates by site type and guidance*. Retrieved from ncchild care.dhhs.state.nc.us/PDF_forms/NCPre-K_PaymentRatesGuidancebySiteType.pdf

19. See www2.ed.gov/programs/racetothetop-earlylearningchallenge/wards. html for a detailed description of North Carolina's Race to the Top–Early Learning Challenge award.

20. See earlylearningchallenge.nc.gov/ for a detailed description of North Carolina's Race to the Top–Early Learning Challenge activities.

21. Interview with Governor James Hunt (2015, November 3).

22. North Carolina Partnership for Children (2015).

23. Ponder (2011).

24. Ponder (2011).

25. Ponder (2011).

26. Ponder (2011).

27. Interview with Richard Clifford, Senior Scientist Emeritus at the Frank Porter Graham Child Development Institute (2015, November 3).

28. Ponder (2011).

29. Interview with Matt Gross, North Carolina Partnership for Children Policy Director (2015, November 2).

30. *Leandro v. State*, 488 S.E.2d 249 (N.C. 1997); *Hoke Cnty. Bd. of Educ. v. State* (Leandro II), 599 S.E.2d 365 (N.C. 2004).

31. Ponder, K. (2010, March). *Early childhood education and North Carolina's Smart Start Initiative*. Retrieved from iei.ncsu.edu/wp-content/uploads/2013/02/Ponder-Early-Childhood-Ed-and-Smart-Start.pdf

32. *Republican party takes control over NC General Assembly* (2010, November 3). Retrieved from www.wect.com/Global/story.asp?S=13434773

33. North Carolina General Assembly, Fiscal Research Division (2011, February 23). *House and Senate Subcommittees on Education and Health and Human Services: Spending targets and general guidelines*.

34. The National Institute for Early Education Research (2012). *The state of preschool 2012: State preschool yearbook*. Retrieved, from nieer.org/wp-content/uploads/2016/08/yearbook2012.pdf; Leslie, L. (2011, May 26). *Smart Start supporters protest cuts*. Retrieved from www.wral.com/news/state/nccapitol/blogpost/9650654/

35. *Hoke Cnty. Bd. of Educ. v. State*, No. 95 CVS 1158 (N.C. Super. Ct. 2011),

36. Sahadi, J. (2013, August 8). *North Carolina's republican tax experiment*. Retrieved from money.cnn.com/2013/08/08/pf/taxes/tax-reform-north-carolina/

37. Ponder (2011).

38. North Carolina Partnership for Children (2011, March 21). *McDowell County Partnership for Children & Families, child-care professionals and parents travel to Raleigh to ask McDowell County legislators to maintain investments in early childhood programs* [Press Release]. Retrieved from www.mcdowellpartnership-smartstart.org/Raleigh%202011%20Press%20Release.doc

39. See first2000days.org/about/ for a detailed description of the First 2000 Days campaign.

40. At the time of initial publication, the fiscal year 2017 adjustment to the 2015–2017 North Carolina biennial budget was still under negotiation.

41. See https://ballotpedia.org/June_Atkinson for a detailed description of June Atkinson's tenure at the Department of Public Instruction.

42. The National Institute for Early Education Research (2006). *The state of preschool 2006: State preschool yearbook.* Retrieved from nieer.org/wp-content/uploads/2016/10/2006yearbook.pdf

43. Interview with Ellen Peisner-Feinberg, Senior Scientist at the Frank Porter Graham Child Development Institute (2015, November 3).

44. Interview with John Pruette, Director of the Office of Early Learning at the Department of Public Instruction (2015, November 2).

45. Interview with Cindy Watkins, President of the North Carolina Partnership for Children (2015, November 5).

46. See fpg.unc.edu/node/4609 for an overview of Frank Porter Graham's Smart Start evaluation history; Bryant, D., & Ponder, K. (2004). North Carolina's Smart Start initiative: A decade of evaluation lessons. *The Evaluation Exchange, 10*(2), 7–8.

47. Frank Porter Graham Child Development Institute, Smart Start Evaluation Team (2002, September). *Demonstrating effective child-care quality improvement.* Retrieved from fpg.unc.edu/sites/fpg.unc.edu/files/resources/reports-and-policy-briefs/FPG_SmartStart_Demonstrating-Effective-CC-Quality-Improvement-September2002.pdf; Bernier, K., Boggs, V., Bordeaux, B., Scoville, S., Sotolongo, J., & Taylor, K. (2002, February). *North Carolina Smart Start evaluation notebook.* Retrieved from fpg.unc.edu/sites/fpg.unc.edu/files/resources/other-resources/FPG_SmartStart_ Evaluation-Notebook-February2002.pdf

48. Frank Porter Graham Child Development Institute, Smart Start Evaluation Team (2003, March). *Smart Start and preschool child-care quality in NC: Change over time and relation to children's readiness.* Retrieved from fpg.unc.edu/sites/fpg.unc.edu/files/resources/reports-and-policy-briefs/FPG_Smart-Start_SS-and-Preschool-Child-Care-Quality-in-NC-March2003.pdf

49. Peisner-Feinberg, E. S. (2014, May). *North Carolina Pre-Kindergarten program evaluation: Summary of research (2002–2013).* Retrieved from fpg.unc.edu/sites/fpg.unc.edu/files/resources/reports-and-policy-briefs/Summary%20of%20NC%20Pre-K%20Evaluation%20Findings%20 5-2014.pdf

50. North Carolina Department of Public Instruction, Office of Early Learning (2011). *Evaluation of More at Four state pre-kindergarten: The first ten years.* Retrieved from www.ncleg. net/documentsites/committees/JLEOC/Reports%20Received/Archives/2011%20Reports%20Received/ More%20At%20Four-January/More%20At%20Four%20-%2010%20Year%20Summary.pdf

51. Peisner-Feinberg, E. S., & Schaaf, J. M. (2010, October). *Long-term effects of the North Carolina More at Four Pre-Kindergarten Program: Children's read-*

ing and math skills at third grade. Retrieved from fpg.unc.edu/sites/fpg.unc.
edu/files/resources/reports-and-policy-briefs/MAF_EOG_full_report.pdf.

52. Muschkin, C. G., Ladd, H. F., & Dodge, K. A. (2015). Impact of North
Carolina's early childhood initiatives on special education placements in third
educational evaluation and policy analysis. *Educational Evaluation and Policy
Analysis, 37*(4), 478–500. doi:10.3102/0162373714559096

53. Johnson-Staub, C. (2011, September 14). *The relationship between licensing and QRIS: Challenges and opportunities.* Retrieved from www.clasp.
org/resources-and-publications/files/ QRISandlicensing-NARA-091411-final.pdf

54. See ncchild care.nc.gov/providers/pv_sn2_hpae.asp for a detailed expla-
nation of how points are earned for the Star Rated License.

55. See ers.fpg.unc.edu/c-overview-subscales-and-items-ecers-r for an overview of the subscales and items of the ECERS-R rating scale, and www.nj.gov/
education/ece/checkups/checklist.pdf for a more detailed ECERS-R classroom
quality checklist.

56. Tout, K., Starr, R., Soli, M., Moodie, S., Kirby, G., & Boller, K. (2010).
Compendium of quality rating systems and evaluations (Prepared by Math-
ematica Policy Research and Child Trends for U.S. Department of Health and
Human Services, Administration for Children and Families, Office of Planning
Research, and Evaluation), ES 1-2. Retrieved from www.acf.hhs.gov/programs/
opre/cc/child care_quality/compendium_qrs/qrs_compendium_final.pdf

57. Frank Porter Graham Child Development Institute, Smart Start Evaluation Team (2001, February). *Validating North Carolina's 5-star child-
care licensing system.* Retrieved from fpg.unc.edu/sites/fpg.unc.edu/files/
resources/reports-and-policy-briefs/FPG_SmartStart_Validating-NC-CC-Licensing-
System-February2001.pdf

58. All licensed programs must still meet health and safety standards. See nc-
childcare.nc.gov/providers/pv_sn2_ov_sr.asp for an overview of the Star Rated
License history.

59. Interview with Michele Rivest, Executive Director of the North Carolina
Child Care Coalition (2015, November 2).

60. North Carolina Department of Health and Human Services, Division of
Child Care and Early Education (2016, January 1). *Subsidized child care market rates for child-care centers.* Retrieved from ncchild care.nc.gov/pdf_forms/
center_market_rate_table_effective_01012016.pdf

61. North Carolina Department of Health and Human Services, Division of
Child Care and Early Education (n.d.). *Resource quality packet.* Retrieved from
ncchild care.nc.gov/PDF_forms/prelicworkshop_ResourceQualityPacket.pdf

62. North Carolina Department of Health and Human Services, Division of
Child Development and Early Education (2016).

63. Personal email with Karen Ponder, former president of the North Carolina
Partnership for Children (2016, May 18).

64. Child Care Services Association (2003). *Working in child care in North*

Carolina: The North Carolina child-care workforce survey 2003. Retrieved from www.childcareservices.org/_downloads/NC2003wfreport. pdf; Child Care Services Association. (2015). *Working in early care and education in North Carolina: 2015 workforce study.* Retrieved from www.childcareservices.org/ wp-content/uploads/2016/01/2015- Workforce-Report-FNL.pdf

65. Howse, R. B., Trivette, C. M., Shindelar, L., Dunst, C. J., & The North Carolina Partnership for Children (2013). *The Smart Start resource guide of evidence-based and evidence-informed programs and practices: A summary of research evidence.* Retrieved from www.smartstart.org/wpcontent/ uploads/2015/05/SmartStartEBEI_Guide_052615.pdf

66. The National Institute for Early Education Research (2016).

67. North Carolina Department of Health and Human Services, Division of Child Development and Early Education (2016, March 9).

68. Scott-Little, C., Brown, G., & Collins, E. (2013). *North Carolina foundations for early learning and development.* Retrieved from ncchild care.nc.gov/ pdf_forms/NC_foundations.pdf

69. Unpublished data from the North Carolina Department of Health and Human Services, Division of Child Development and Early Education (personal communication, November 6, 2015).

70. See www.child careservices.org/ps/teach-nc/ for a detailed discussion of the T.E.A.C.H. scholarship program.

71. See the "What is the history of the T.E.A.C.H. Early Childhood Project?" FAQ at www. childcareservices.org/ps/teach-nc/ for an overview of T.E.A.C.H. program history.

72. Interview with Anna Carter, President of the Child Care Services Association (2015, November 6).

73. Carter interview (2015, November 6).

74. NC Pre-K teachers with an existing teaching license may earn a Preschool Add On certification in lieu of a birth-through-kindergarten license. See ncchild care.nc.gov/pdf_forms/NCPre-K_75. TrackstoLicensure.pdf for detailed discussion of the different pathways to birth-through-kindergarten licensure.

75. Teachers must hold a BA or BS degree in early childhood education, child development, or a related field (human development/family studies or child psychology) with an overall grade point average of at least 2.5. Teachers with a BA or BS in a nonrelated field must take at least 24 semester hours of coursework in child development or early childhood education prior to pursuing a birth-through-kindergarten teaching license. Participating teachers may be eligible for scholarship assistance through the T.E.A.C.H. Early Childhood Project. See ncchild care.nc.gov/pdf_forms/NCPre-K_FAQ Teach EducLic.pdf for a detailed discussion of birth-through-kindergarten licensure.

76. Interview with Cynthia Wheeler, Senior Manager at the Department of Health and Human Services, Division of Child Development and Early Education (2015, November 4).

77. Interview with Tamara Barnes, Regulatory Services Chief and former Interim Director of the Department of Health and Human Services, Division of Child Development and Early Education (2015, November 4).

78. Interview with Jennifer Johnson, Assistant Director for Education and Quality at the Department of Health and Human Services, Division of Child Development and Early Education (2015, November 4).

79. See www.researchconnections.org/files/meetings/ccprc/2015/B-5-Cassidy.pdf for a detailed discussion of EQuIPS.

80. Current Operations and Capital Improvements Appropriations Act of 2012, Part VII-A, sec. 7.A.1.(b), § 115C-83.1A-115C-105.41, 2012-142 N.C. Sess. Laws 1, 38–45.

81. See earlylearningchallenge.nc.gov/k-3-formative-assessment for more information on the K–3 Formative Assessment in North Carolina.

82. K–3 Formative Assessment Consortium (n.d.). *Overview of a groundbreaking new early learning project.* Retrieved from www.buildinitiative.org/Portals/0/Uploads/Documents/BUILD%20-%20K-3%20Consortium-AZ.pdf

83. Child Care Services Association (2015).

84. Carter interview (2015, November 6).

85. Gross interview (2015, November 2).

86. National Women's Law Center (2014, December). State child-care assistance policies: North Carolina. Retrieved from www.nwlc.org/sites/default/files/pdfs/ccsubsidy2014/north_carolina-child care- subsidy2014.pdf

87. Rose, T. (2015, September 27). *Governor's visit highlights early childhood development, business and education.* Retrieved from hmountainx.com/news/governors-visit-highlights-early-childhood-development-business-and-education.

88. See http://best-nc.org/best-nc-members/ for an overview of BEST NC.

89. Clifford interview (2015, November 3).

90. North Carolina General Assembly, Joint Legislative Oversight Committee on Health and Human Services, Subcommittee on Statewide Early Education and Family Support Programs (2016, April). *Final report to the full committee.* Retrieved from www.ncleg.net/documentsites/committees/JLOCHHS/Final%20Reports%20to%20the%20NCGA%20from%20Oversight%20Committee/2016%20Joint%20Legislative%20Oversight%20Committee%20on%20HHS%20Report.pdf

91. Study Costs Associated with N.C. Pre-K Slots, H.R. 1040, 2015 Gen. Assemb., Reg. Sess. (N.C. 2016).

92. Collaboration of State Agencies/Early Educ., S.R. DRS45436-LUz-115C, 2015 Gen. Assemb., Reg. Sess. (N.C. 2016).

93. Office of State Budget and Management, Office of the Governor (2016). *Governor Pat McCrory's 2016–17 recommended budget adjustments.* Retrieved from ncosbm.s3.amazonaws.com/s3fs-public/documents/files/BudgetBook_2016-17_2.pdf

CHAPTER 6

Building High-Quality Programs
Lessons From the States

What does it take to create high-quality early childhood programs? That's what these case studies set out to determine. The most important lesson is that there is no one answer.

Washington, Michigan, North Carolina, and West Virginia: These states vary substantially in size, demographics, and political makeup. Further, they have taken distinctive approaches to their early education strategies and they have followed different paths, each marked by decisions, lessons learned, and corrections made. They began their journeys at different points—Michigan with a small pilot program for 4-year-olds, North Carolina with a comprehensive program for infants and toddlers. They developed in different ways—Washington serving only the neediest children, reaching fewer than a quarter of its preschoolers, West Virginia opening its doors to all. Regardless of where a state started and how far it has gone, each path taken was a path to success. Each state has confronted a host of choices about how best to design, manage, and pay for these initiatives. And while each is a work in progress, and each has experienced challenges and setbacks, each one has been able to expand and improve its early childhood programs.

The importance of those choices cannot be overstated. The decisions a state makes will have a major impact on whether early education is good enough to realize its promise—in the short run, to better prepare children for kindergarten; in the longer run, to reduce special education assignments and grade retentions, and raise high school graduation rates; and, eventually, to boost income, and reduce reliance on welfare and incarceration.

Until now, policymakers have not had much guidance on how best to address nuts-and-bolts issues, such as how to design programs with quality in mind, how to fund programs given tight state budgets, or how to build political will to invest funds in early education. Nor has there been much direction for administrators on how to manage program administration, how to support the professionals working with children on a day-to-day basis, or how to blend and braid funding streams to offer children full-day programs that meet the needs of working parents. These case studies fill that gap by analyzing how four states have built high-quality early education systems.

While there is not a one-size-fits-all response to the question of how to expand access to, and embed quality in, early education, there are common elements in these states' efforts to make good early education a reality. This chapter flags these themes and offers insights for policymakers and program administrators nationwide.

PRIORITIZE QUALITY AND CONTINUOUS IMPROVEMENT

The significant body of rigorous research showing both short- and long-term benefits of early education focuses on high-quality programs. Though most states aspire to offer top-flight early education to all children, the reality of resource limitations obliges them to balance access and quality. Many states are challenged by trying to implement a high-quality program while simultaneously struggling with funding, workforce and space constraints, the divergent requirements of other programs serving young children, and variations in local needs and capacity. Recognizing the critical role of program quality to positive child outcomes, each of the states has invested in strategies to improve its early education program.

At the foundation of quality efforts, the states define and use state quality standards that incorporate assessments of adult–child interactions, as well as structural factors, such as adult–child ratios and facility requirements. The commitment to quality is reflected in their early learning standards and quality metrics. At the inception of its preschool program 30 years ago, Michigan specified program design standards, and although the standards have been revised and updated since then, the emphasis on quality remains the bedrock. North Carolina established preschool metrics that are both rigorous and evidence-based. West Virginia's program is guided by robust state standards that draw on the professional standards set by two highly-regarded national organizations, the National Institute for Early Education Research and the National Association for the Education of Young Children. Washington's preschool performance standards include expectations for family engagement, as well as physical, nutritional, and mental health support.

What matters most are the interactions between children and teachers. Washington uses CLASS (the Classroom Assessment Scoring System) to collect observational data on teaching practices and guide professional development. CLASS is also being used in a growing number of West Virginia counties. Michigan uses the Program Quality Assessment developed by HighScope.

The states have developed quality rating and improvement systems to support continuous improvement, reinforce program quality, and provide a basis for program accountability. The standards in each state serve a dual purpose: supporting providers' efforts to improve the program, while also assuring that providers meet at least minimal quality standards. Michigan, North Carolina, and Washington have made significant investments in developing state quality rating and improvement systems (QRIS) that convey statewide, coherent visions for quality and a common approach for improvement. But ensuring program quality does not have to be a state responsibility. In West Virginia, local administrators are responsible for developing and administering systems to foster quality, with its county-led continuous quality improvement process. Here, local administrators set objectives for quality improvement efforts; develop plans to collect and analyze fiscal, program, child outcome, and classroom observation data; and inform decisions related to program improvement.

To give teeth to the quality rating and improvement systems, the states link funding to the QRIS. Michigan, North Carolina, and Washington have tied the per-child funding a program receives to its QRIS rating. In these states, providers must achieve a minimum rating on the state quality rating and improvement system to participate in the pre-K program. Washington also recognizes the importance of investing to enhance quality, and thus provides a range of grants and tuition subsidies designed to help providers boost their quality rating.

State agencies cannot effectively operate or support quality improvements on their own. Local administrators make sure that what is designed in the state capitols makes sense for their communities. Diverse community needs can best be met with a strong local infrastructure. Michigan has turned to intermediate school districts, regional government agencies generally organized around county lines, to administer preschool at the local level, monitor quality, and deliver support tailored to individual districts' needs. In North Carolina and West Virginia, counties have substantial managerial responsibility. County-level teams in West Virginia assess local needs and help identify priorities, create improvement plans, deliver professional development, and target resources appropriately.

Having strong local infrastructure not only increases the capacity to deliver high-quality preschool statewide, but is also the most effective way of addressing regional needs or concerns. Washington is the exception, giving state grants directly to community partners. Although a centrally administered program may be efficient, it can be challenging to meet the needs of communities with very different local contexts.

INVEST IN TRAINING AND COACHING

The interaction between teachers and children is critical to a program's success, and strong programs ensure that staff know how to create learning opportunities that are language-rich and hands-on, that address the whole child, and that are developmentally appropriate. These four states place heavy emphasis on boosting the quality of preschool teachers, focusing both on their credentials and on their interactions with students.

They invest in strengthening teacher quality by providing specialized training. Community and 4-year colleges are critical partners here. The strongest programs are those that include significant clinical training linked to useful coursework and that emphasize teaching and learning as well as child development. All four states require their lead teachers to have a degree with an emphasis in early childhood education, child development, or a related field. Michigan, West Virginia, and North Carolina require that lead teachers have at least a bachelor's degree. As these states phased in this standard, they gave teachers several years to meet the degree requirement.

In early childhood education, turnover is a serious problem, and so these states encourage teacher advancement and retention through scholarships and salary supplements to teachers who have returned to school for additional training. North Carolina, West Virginia, and Michigan have adopted a nationally-recognized program, Teacher Education and Compensation Helps (T.E.A.C.H.), which awards scholarships for additional teacher education. North Carolina also has created WAGE$, another nationally recognized program that subsidizes preschool teachers' salaries based on their education.

But training has to be available where the teachers are. That's where the local community partners play an important role, by offering training programs that are accessible to providers. This can be done by offering courses regionally in community colleges, county offices of education, or districts. In West Virginia's apprenticeship program, child-care workers and pre-K assistant teachers remain employed and receive mentoring while taking classes at West Virginia's community and technical colleges. West

Virginia and Washington offer online courses to make opportunities accessible in rural areas.

The most direct support for teachers comes in the form of classroom-based coaching to improve program quality. And, when the coaching is tied to adult–child interactions, teaching and learning can really be strengthened. Michigan employs county-based Early Childhood Specialists who offer onsite improvement support based on results of the Program Quality Assessment to all pre-K teaching teams throughout the year. Washington offers onsite support to both state preschool and child-care providers through its quality rating and improvement system. In North Carolina, all preschool teachers receive coaching during their first three years in the classroom. Although West Virginia does not have a statewide coaching program, many districts have their own coaching and mentoring initiatives.

COORDINATE THE ADMINISTRATION OF
BIRTH-THROUGH-GRADE-3 PROGRAMS

Early education is a complex system encompassing multiple programs, including state-funded preschool (both publicly and privately operated), Head Start and Early Head Start, and child-care subsidies, each of which is structured differently. While the K–12 system concentrates on classroom teaching, early education often integrates social services and health services. States must determine how to administer this array of offerings efficiently and equitably, providing the leadership and resources that support good classroom practice. And while pre-K historically has been kept entirely separate from K–12, these four states are seeking to create a seamless educational experience for youngsters, aligning what is taught and how it is taught from preschool through elementary school.

States have fostered coordination by housing all children's services under one umbrella or creating a children's cabinet that works across agencies. This coordination among the agencies that administer early education programs is essential. Washington created a cabinet-level department; Michigan and North Carolina created a single agency housed in the Department of Education and Department of Health and Human Services, respectively. West Virginia did not create a single agency; rather, it promoted coordination through formal cross-organizational structures.

Where early learning programs sit in the state's organizational chart is more than a bureaucratic matter. The priorities of educators, health officials, and social service administrators may well differ, and those differences can affect the shape of early education. Placing early education programs in the Department of Education, as Michigan and West Virginia have done, fosters alignment with the K–12 system, while locating them in the Department of Social Services, as North Carolina did, strengthens ties with child-care and health programs. Interagency collaboration is essential, even when many of the early education programs are housed in a single agency. Washington consolidated many programs in a cabinet-level department, but it also maintains a joint task force designed to foster coordination among the several child-serving departments.

Coordination within local communities is equally important. West Virginia created interagency teams responsible for overseeing local implementation of the state pre-K program. With representatives from public education, preschool special needs, child care, and Head Start, as well as parents and providers, these collaborative teams ensure local needs are met by determining recruitment and enrollment practices and curriculum, and focusing on continuous improvement processes. They also determine where to establish pre-K classrooms to make sure families have access to programs in the locations that work best for them, near their homes or their work. North Carolina's Smart Start likewise provides the local administrative oversight and strategic planning that brings coherence to a complex system. In Michigan, the intermediate school districts and their designated early childhood contacts develop the local vision for early childhood education, provide oversight, and ensure support for early childhood teachers.

At both the state and local levels, program administrators improve coordination across programs and systems by sharing data and aligning curriculum and assessments. Recognizing that robust data systems are an important tool for maintaining high-quality programs, these states are expanding their data systems to incorporate information that spans the birth to school-age spectrum. Creating such systems has posed significant technical problems, but these states' experiences show that, with effort and will, those difficulties can be overcome. West Virginia's data system includes a pre-K component that holds individual child assessment, health, and attendance data, as well as program assessment information. This rich database helps in designing programs and provides teachers with relevant information, easing children's transition from pre-K to kindergarten. Washington employs the same child assessment tool for both state pre-K and full-day kindergarten classrooms.

STRATEGICALLY COMBINE MULTIPLE FUNDING SOURCES TO INCREASE ACCESS AND IMPROVE QUALITY

Because a single source of funding is rarely adequate to provide a quality education, these states rely on myriad sources of revenue; unfortunately, those funding sources are prone to the vagaries of politics and budget processes. For example, when state funds for early education were cut in North Carolina, its programs had to rely more heavily on federal and local dollars. In Michigan, financial support for preschool increased under both Democratic and Republican governors. However, year-to-year budget fluctuations make planning at the local level difficult. In West Virginia, by contrast, pre-K is mainly funded through the state's school aid formula. This policy makes the budget more predictable because funding for pre-K cannot be cut without affecting the entire state school aid formula.

States fund early education programs with dedicated state dollars combined, or braided, with funding from Head Start and other federal programs, such as Early Head Start and Temporary Assistance for Needy Families (TANF), to make the most efficient use of available resources and to expand access and quality. By combining Head Start and other federal programs with state money, the states have been able to deliver pre-K to more children—universally as in West Virginia, or targeted as in Washington, Michigan, and North Carolina. In West Virginia, state funds make up about two-thirds of prekindergarten funds, while community partners raise the balance through Head Start, TANF, Title I of the Elementary and Secondary Education Act, and the Child Care Development Fund. In Michigan, community partners combine state and Head Start dollars to fund full-day programs. However, because each federal and state program has its own eligibility and reporting requirements, managing such complex funding streams can be difficult for many local providers. As a result, some providers have left federal dollars on the table. In Washington, for example, many providers have opted not to braid child-care and preschool funds because it is burdensome to do so, even though the revenue would make it possible to expand the school day.

To meet their local needs, many localities secure funding from local sources as well. In North Carolina, Smart Start directors at the county level apply for grant opportunities and seek financial and in-kind donations from local community members. In Michigan and other states, some school districts allocate funds for preschool classrooms, dedicate administrative resources for the programs, and provide professional development designed specifically to advance the knowledge and skills of preschool teachers.

States also pay for early education by leveraging short-term funds and public–private partnerships. North Carolina requires Smart Start agencies to raise 15% of their budget, a portion of which supports pre-K providers, from private sources. In Michigan, Washington, and North Carolina, federal Race to the Top–Early Learning Challenge grants underwrote investments in quality rating and improvement systems and assessments. Washington leveraged an investment from the Gates Foundation to pilot and study coaching supports and also to pilot the state's quality rating and improvement system. It then leveraged its Race to the Top funds to expand the system.

CREATE BROAD-BASED COALITIONS AND SUPPORT

Political will drives these state efforts. Launching a high-quality early education initiative, and expanding and improving the program over time, is hard work. Policymakers must contend with a patchwork of federal, state, and local programs, each serving a particular group of children, and each with its own goals, regulations, and administrative systems. Further, in many states the money required to deliver good early education is perennially in short supply. Overcoming those challenges requires substantial political adroitness and broad support.

State and local administrators bring together advocates, politicians, philanthropists, practitioners, business leaders, and policymakers, to promote high-quality, accessible early education. Michigan's business leaders became early childhood supporters after reviewing brain development research alongside the positive results from an evaluation of the state's preschool program that recognized the substantial return on investing in the program. In North Carolina, evidence of long-run gains in crime reduction led prosecutors and police officers to back early education. A broad-based coalition can promote increases in early childhood investments by sustaining momentum for the program. When Washington legislators proposed an increased investment in child care and state preschool, coupled with heightened quality standards, the Early Learning Action Alliance helped to broker a unified response among its member organizations. In North Carolina, political support for Smart Start, a long-time program offering coordination of birth-to-age-5 services, waned when conservative politicians took control of the legislature and governor's office. But local communities, conservative and liberal alike, successfully lobbied for the program's survival.

Use of public–private partnerships is one tool that can catalyze broad-based coalitions. In Washington, the business community and philanthropic partners have come together in partnership with the state to support early education. Another tool to catalyze support is research carried out within the state. Advocates have made good use of the fact that studies carried out by highly regarded research organizations—the HighScope Educational Research Foundation in Michigan, the Washington State Institute of Public Policy, and the Frank Porter Graham Child Development Institute in North Carolina—have shown that each respective state's preschool program has generated positive results.

Political will is further advanced by offering parents a choice of providers. Incorporating private, as well as public, early education providers in state programs has helped to win over parents and caretakers, who can choose the setting they believe best meets the needs of their children. Such partnerships operate in all these states. Michigan, for example, requires that community partners receive 30% of the state's preschool slots and West Virginia mandates that at least half of all preschool classrooms be run either jointly with Head Start or with private providers. In North Carolina, concerns voiced by the religious right that state-funded early education would intrude on parents' rights were allayed by the assurance that families could select from private providers that met the state's quality standards.

A political champion is key to launching a major early education initiative and garnering support for greater investments as a program grows. In three of the states we reviewed, governors led the charge. During the 1980s, Booth Gardner advocated for pre-K in Washington, and 20 years later, Christine Gregoire led the drive to expand the program. In Michigan, Jennifer Granholm established a public–private partnership to support investments in early education, and her successor, Rick Snyder, led the push for expanding the preschool program. In North Carolina, James Hunt launched a program for infants and toddlers, and his successor, Michael Easley, made prekindergarten a signature initiative. In West Virginia, legislators such as Senator Lloyd Jackson and Senator Robert Plymale championed the creation and implementation of a universal preschool model, receiving important support from governors and other political leaders.

CONCLUSION: REALIZING THE POTENTIAL OF EARLY EDUCATION

These states, committed to public early education, are striving to make preschool better, understanding that quality is essential to realize preschool's potential. They have addressed critical challenges that reach from the statehouse to the classroom. A fundamental lesson is: *There is no single roadmap to delivering excellent early childhood education.* Nonetheless, each of the states we studied relied on similar overarching strategies. By supporting continuous program improvement efforts, focusing on teacher training, coordinating the administration of early education programs, creatively combining funding sources, and building a broad-based coalition of support, Washington, Michigan, West Virginia, and North Carolina are advancing high-quality early education opportunities for their youngest citizens.

Delivering top-quality early education is a complex undertaking and none of these states is ready to declare, "Mission accomplished!" It will take time and effort—as well as public investment—before the goal of delivering seamless, high-quality support for young children can be fully realized. But these states are heading in that direction. Their experience should offer useful lessons to state and local policymakers across the country who are committed to providing high-quality preschool for all.

Index

About the Authors

Marjorie E. Wechsler is principal research manager at the Learning Policy Institute (founded by Linda Darling-Hammond) and co-leads the organization's Early Childhood Learning team.

David L. Kirp is a professor of the Graduate School at the University of California, Berkeley, a senior scholar at the Learning Policy Institute, and a contributing writer at *The New York Times*.

Titilayo Tinubu Ali, Madelyn Gardner, Anna Maier, Hanna Melnick, and *Patrick M. Shields* are all with the Learning Policy Institute.